THROUGH

A

BOY'S

EYES

THROUGH

A

BOY'S

EYES

The Turbulent Years
1926–1945

Louis Posner

SEVEN LOCKS PRESS

Santa Ana, California
Minneapolis, Minnesota
Washington, D.C.

Seven Locks Press
P.O. Box 25689
Santa Ana, CA 92799
(800) 354-5348

Printed in the United States of America

Individual Sales. This book is available through most bookstores or can be ordered directly from Seven Locks Press at the address above.

Quantity Sales. Special discounts are available on quantity purchases by corporations, associations, and others. For details, contact the "Special Sales Department" at the address above.

Library of Congress Cataloging-in-Publication Data
  [Is available from the publisher]

ISBN 0-969765-74-5

Cover & Interior Design: Sparrow Advertising & Design
Photographs: Louis Posner
Editorial Services: PeopleSpeak

Dedication

To my son, Robert,
and all the future generations

Acknowledgments

To Margret for her patience and Robbie for believing;
To Tanya for all the talk and counsel;
To Robin for the confidence and Pam for trying so hard;
To Brad for trying so hard and Howard for his help;
To Pauline for the rewrite;
To Professor Harran for the first edit and her counsel;
To my publisher for believing that my story should be published, PeopleSpeak for the terrific editing work and to Sparrow Advertising & Design for the choice of the cover;
To my pal Charley, who encouraged me to write my story;
To all of you and everybody else who was involved,
Many, many grateful thanks.

Foreword

Recent years have seen the publication of many Holocaust memoirs, but Louis Posner's remarkable *Through a Boy's Eyes* will be a significant addition to that growing list. It is remarkable for many reasons, not the least of which are the author's adventurous spirit and his optimism in the face of enormous danger. It is also remarkable for the variety of experiences it so honestly recounts. Posner sees Hitler with his own eyes, watches as the Nazis take over Berlin, and faces challenges and dangers that test his spirit and his physical stamina to their limits.

As with many survivors, for Posner it would be years before he could bring himself to write his story. Yet the decades seem to have sharpened, not dulled, his memories of his Holocaust experiences. It is a story of a "tough little guy" who vowed never to be beaten into submission and who was prepared to do almost anything to survive. It is a story of grit, of determination, and of sheer audacity in the face of overwhelming odds. It is the story of one boy, on his own, unwilling to be consumed by the Nazi death machine.

The following memoir is filled with many events and encounters. Focusing as it does on action, it would be easy to miss the underlying questions present in the work, perhaps best summarized in the following statement: "Sometime during the early morning hours, I realized what had happened to me. What pleasure did those animals get from beating a boy half to death just for walking slowly? Did this make them superior? I had seen men viciously and cruelly beaten. I had seen heads bashed in and eyes closed forever. Day in and day out,

I saw men become weaker and thinner and finally carted off to the gas chambers and the ovens. I had often wondered why cruelty was inflicted on other inmates, but now that it had happened to me, I comprehended it even less. If there was a God, how could he let all this happen?"

Louis Posner's book challenges us to ponder those questions, even as it engages us in the remarkable saga of his survival.

Marilyn J. Harran
Professor of Religious Studies and History
Chapman University
Orange, California

Introduction

Do not fear your enemies
The worst they can do is kill you.
Do not fear your friends
The worst they can do is betray you.
Be afraid of the indifferent ones
For they will neither kill nor betray you.
But only with their silence and quiet consent
Do murder, betrayal, and injustice exist in this world.
                                        —Anonymous

The years from the 1870s through the end of the Second World War constitute one of the most fascinating and most devastating periods in the history of humankind. The Industrial Revolution entered society with such momentum that the ordinary person had little time to comprehend it and even less time to absorb its effects. Only a few had the time or perspective to write about it. In contrast, after the Great War, many people wrote about the horror and sufferings that those four years induced. Many also hinted at the futility of war, a lesson that few learned, especially in Germany. In the years following the Second World War, a great many people recorded their experiences during that time, and many scholars since then have reflected upon those experiences and struggled to survey and interpret the panorama of events.

As a result, a vast amount of material is available through books, archives, and films. These works offer many opinions about what occurred and do so in very different forms, from historical narrative to autobiography. Yet what unites many of these writers is their desire to learn from the past and to prevent the agony of those years from

ever being repeated. Many of these works, especially those that are auto-
biographical, reflect the very personal experiences and perspectives of
those who lived through the events of the time. My personal history is
unique, however, in that it is written with young people in mind so that
they will learn the lessons their parents may have already forgotten.

This book is based on research, but it rests upon the foundation of
memory. I used the sources listed in the bibliography only to verify
what I remember or perhaps to check a name or a date. All names in
this book have been changed except those of well-known people.

Do I intend this work to be an accusation and a warning? Yes, I do.
I challenge readers to ask themselves, Have we truly learned from the
events of Nazi Germany? Do we continue to be self-centered, con-
trolled by our greed? Are we so blind that we do not see what is
unfolding around us? Writing of the last days of the Weimar Republic,
Hannah Arendt, the philosopher and author of books such as
Eichmann in Jerusalem and *The Origins of Totalitarianism*, wrote,
"We young students did not read the newspapers in those days."[1] And
Hannah Arendt was Jewish.

Have we learned the lessons of the Holocaust and do we stay
actively informed, or do we too continue to be lulled and bored by the
politicians and preachers into a deadly complacency? Are we too so
afraid of our own fear that it does not let us recognize the danger signs
to society? How could a democratic nation allow the Nazis to come
to power? How could a land of such great culture, the land of Bach
and Beethoven, of Goethe and Schiller, become the home to cultural
conformity, to an equation of race culture and Aryanism?

Throughout history, ever since the dispersion of the Jewish people,
Jews have been regarded as an ideal scapegoat. It is one thing to
assault, but then it is another to preach in church on Sunday "Love
your fellow man and your neighbor as yourself"—only to look the
other way when that neighbor is taken from his or her home, beaten,
and sent to a death camp. How could the church, which preaches love,
let these events happen? How could the world, when it learned of

---

1. Cited in Peter Gay, *Weimar Culture: The Outsider as Insider* (New York:
Harper & Row, 1968), 70.

what was happening, remain silent and disbelieving? Was it simply easier to say "What can I do? I am only one"? And how could the Jews allow themselves to believe that each stage of persecution, of loss of rights, was the last? The victims were the innocent and the helpless. At least in that time, the guilty were protected, and when at last the day of judgment came, no one was guilty. No one knew anything; no one had done anything; each one blamed the other.

Hitler understood an individual's need to feel important and to feel a part of something larger than oneself, especially during a time of social crisis. To give a man importance is to gain his right hand; to convince him that he is part of the most important events of his time is to gain his left hand; to give him the power to further that event through blind obedience is to own his soul. The German people were told that the Jews did not matter—worse, that they were an infestation upon society and that eradicating them contributed to the well-being of society. People were given the power to kill without guilt or punishment and were even rewarded. The hatred that the Nazis created enveloped not only their own land but those lands they occupied as well. The Nazis found not only sympathizers but active participants for their killing machine. And if anything went wrong, who would possibly believe acts so brutal and inhuman could ever have occurred?

I am often asked if it is not time to forget, to put these terrible events into the silent vaults of memory. But we *must* not forget that power and greed, and above all, apathy and silence, allowed these events to occur.

I wish young people to understand that because of that apathy and inaction, millions—from the old and distinguished to babies in their mothers' arms—were gassed and burned, and by those acts, the Nazis hoped to extinguish a people and their memory. It is our duty to remember and to never allow those events to be extinguished from our minds and hearts. As long as that flame of memory burns within us, these events will not be repeated, and inhumanity will not again conquer our souls.

Chapter 1

I awoke with a start. "Papa, Papa, what was that noise?"

"I think it was a piece of shrapnel. Go have a look."

I climbed over Papa's body and out of our bed, put the chair under the window, and stood on it. Our tiny room, called a mansard, was located just under the roof. After pushing the pane toward the roof and hoisting myself into the window frame, I could just reach the piece of metal lying nearby. I grabbed it and slowly worked my way back down into the room.

I held the metal out in front of me for Papa to look at. He confirmed that it indeed was shrapnel, probably from a large artillery projectile. Curious as to what had happened, Papa sent me to get a newspaper.

I flew down the five flights of stairs, ran to the corner to buy a newspaper, and while walking back read the headline:

GERMANY DECLARES WAR ON THE BENELUX
COUNTRIES AND FRANCE

There was a call for general mobilization of the army and a citizens' call to arms.

Back in our room, I breathlessly said to Papa, "It's war. Look at the big headlines!" Catching my breath, I sat down and translated from French into German the headlines and two articles about mobilization. Papa listened carefully while he smoked a cigarette.

When I finished reading, Papa said that Hitler wouldn't give up until he conquered all of Europe. Then he told me to get dressed because the Belgian authorities would be there shortly to pick us up.

I was puzzled. "Why, Papa? We didn't start the war."

Papa explained that although we didn't do anything wrong, we were foreigners and Germans besides. We were stateless. It didn't matter that he volunteered for the army, wanting to repay the Belgians for giving us asylum. With the declaration of war, we weren't refugees any longer—we were the enemy. In a country at war, foreigners were often interned for the duration so they couldn't become spies.

We were dressed in ten minutes and immediately heard a knock on the door. A voice ordered, "Open up, this is the police!"

At the door stood two Belgian policemen in uniform. They told Papa to pack whatever items we needed for one night and to go with them.

They led us down the stairs, out the front door, and into the street. The landlady stood in front of the house and gave us a look of understanding. All around us we saw other police with men—only men—who lived in the neighborhood. Everyone was scurrying. Papa and I walked in front of the policemen on the short trip to the city hall/police station. I wondered if this was happening to my friends, too.

In the station, everyone was talking at once. After an hour, it was our turn to approach the desk where several officers were asking questions and filling out papers. Papa responded to their questions, and then the officer looked at me. "Is this boy with you?"

"Yes, he's my son."

The man left the desk and returned with a captain, who addressed Papa and asked how old I was. When Papa responded that I had just turned fourteen, the captain informed Papa that I could neither stay there nor go with Papa. I was too young to be interned and would have to go back home. The captain said dismissively, "I don't have time to discuss this with you, but your son can stay with his mother. He can see you in the morning—I might have a better answer by that time."

Papa tried to explain our situation. "My wife is not in Belgium. There isn't anybody else he can stay with."

"That's not my problem," the captain said and walked away.

Papa told me to wait while he talked more with the captain. I stood in the corner, my stomach feeling like a big knot and my heart pounding wildly. Papa's face was red and he was waving his arms as he talked, but the captain walked away again. As Papa came back toward me, he shook his head.

He instructed me on what to do. "Here's your school paper identifying you as a student. Go home, straight home. Pack our suitcase with the *most important* items and put what is left over in a sheet in the corner of the room. Then, tomorrow morning, take the suitcase to the Caserne du petit Chateau. That's where they're taking us I was told. Ask to see your papa. I hope I can make some arrangements for you by then. Here is another paper that proves you live at our address and are registered at the city hall in the community of Molenbeek St. Jean. That should be enough to identify you."

I tried to be brave as I said farewell. As I left, I turned back and looked at Papa one more time. He had tears in his eyes. I ran back and hugged him and then raced from the building.

I felt bewildered and alone as I walked back to the mansard. The room was very empty without Papa. It was late in the day—I was hungry, tired, and very depressed. Papa had left me ten francs, but none of the shops were open, so I would have to wait to eat.

Within an hour I had gathered everything into the suitcase as Papa had instructed. I fell into bed and was immediately asleep.

When I awoke early the next morning, I remembered what had happened. I quickly put the room in order and then, taking the heavy suitcase, went downstairs. I was very quiet, but no one was in the house to hear me; all the tenants and the landlord had left. No public transportation vehicles were running, but the streets were crowded with people in private cars and carts, pedestrians, and bicyclists, all fleeing the city with what few possessions they could take. They must be headed for the French border, I thought.

Constantly changing the heavy suitcase from one hand to the other, I walked more than a half hour to reach the caserne. I asked the guard outside the gate if I could enter to visit my papa.

"There is no one here but soldiers. Is he stationed here?"

"No, no. He came here last night from the police department in Molenbeek."

"Oh, the foreigners. All of them went to Schaarbeck early this morning."

"Schaarbeck? It will take me over two hours to get there!"

The suitcase felt twice as heavy as I trudged toward Schaarbeck. Finally I arrived at a huge park where thousands of men had gathered to locate family members. Whenever I asked if anyone knew Papa or anything about him, I was usually ignored. Some men shook their heads. Others gave me dirty looks and snarled comments. After three hours, I was exhausted and discouraged. I had walked all day and not found Papa. I hadn't even eaten breakfast yet. I sat down and smoked the cigarette half I'd saved, not caring if Papa saw what I was doing.

But no one cared whether I smoked or not. I realized I was on my own and that thought brought me to tears.

"Lutz? Lutz Posener? Is that you?"

I swung around toward the familiar voice. "Oh, Mr. Kohn, maybe you can help me. Do you know where my papa is?"

"He left early this morning with the first contingent of 150 men. No one knows where they are being taken, and even the authorities don't seem to know much. You might as well return home and do the best you can under the circumstances. If you see my wife, please tell her I am all right and will let her know where I am as soon as I can. If I see your papa, I will tell him I talked with you and that you are waiting to hear from him."

Thanking him, I picked up the suitcase, looked around once more, and started toward home. I felt helpless and drained. Tears rolled down my cheeks. I arrived at the mansard not knowing how I got there and completely exhausted. The little room was so pathetic looking. I unpacked the suitcase, and with our belongings again in place, the room was somewhat more inviting. Hunger gnawed fiercely at my insides, but I fell onto the bed and slept soundly.

Chapter 2

How did I come to be alone in a foreign country at the age of four-teen? My story begins in Posen, Poland, where my parents met and where my father's ancestors had lived for many generations before they migrated to Germany. My story nearly ended forever in Poland as well—at Auschwitz.

My mother was born in Poland and spoke only Polish and Yiddish—the two languages I heard in my first seven years. She was brought to Germany by my papa.

A soldier in the First World War, Papa was inducted in 1914 when the war started. His two brothers were called, too. I was told that Grandpapa collapsed and died of a heart attack when he heard that his oldest son was shot on his first day at the front. Papa's other brother was a commercial artist and spent the war drawing war maps far away from the front. Papa spent all four years of the war at the front: two years in Poland and two in Belgium and France. He received an Iron Cross, first and second class; a Cross of Honor; and a Purple Heart.

He met my mother while he was in Poland. His patrol was resting in a suburb of Lodz on a Friday afternoon. All Jewish soldiers carry a tallis (prayer shawl) with them, usually around their knapsacks. From a nearby hut, Papa's future papa-in-law, a *rebbe*, was scrutinizing the soldiers and their gear. He recognized my Papa's tallis and told his daughter, "Lea, it is the Sabbath evening, and no Jewish man should be out alone, German soldier or not. Go out and bid him to come and share the beginning of the Sabbath with us."

When Papa entered the *rebbe*'s home, the Sabbath candles were lit and Lea added another setting at the table. The *rebbe* started the rit-ual with the *Kiddush*, the benediction over the wine. He broke off a piece of challah, dipped it in salt, and again said the benediction.

Top: Lea, Kurt, and Lutz Posener (age 2), March 4, 1928; *bottom:* Kurt Friedrich Posener in German uniform, July 10, 1917

Everyone followed his example. The dinner was eaten in silence and ended with a short prayer.

Papa liked what he saw of Lea—she was strongly built, not bad looking, maybe in her twenties—but her face was taut with anger. Papa thanked the family and said good night. Lea joined him outside and lit a cigarette. To see a woman smoking surprised him. In no time, their conversation became a heated argument about politics. Lea's father came out to calm them down. That made them laugh, finally breaking the ice.

Papa saw Lea every moment he could, and after five days he proposed. She said yes right away and her father gave his blessing. Papa's commanding officer gave him a two-week furlough to get married and settle his bride in Berlin, Germany. Lea's father performed the ceremony, then they went to Berlin, where they married again in city hall. They got a small place in the northern part of the city where Papa had worked and lived before the war. He introduced Lea to Felicitas, his younger sister who lived in Berlin, and sent announcements to his mother and two sisters in Breslau, Germany. With Aunt Felka (Felicitas's nickname) in Berlin, Papa felt Lea had someone to turn to for support while he was gone.

* * * * *

I was born on April 9, 1926, at Number 12 Auguststrasse in the northern part of Berlin, and my first seven years were spent in that same area. My earliest memories are of my mother's heavy asthmatic breathing and the domestic turmoil in our home.

Although Papa was born in Berlin and became an apprentice bookkeeper at AEG (Allgemeine Electrische Gesellschaft, an electric company), he grew up in Breslau. He was a mathematical genius who knew the answers to problems posed by his teachers almost before they were written on the blackboard. He worked as a bookkeeper while attending the University of Berlin. In two years, he was sworn in as a chartered accountant and in 1914 received degrees in taxation and accounting. After the war, companies weren't hiring accountants, so Papa opened his own office. His first clients were wartime friends; later, word-of-mouth advertising brought him additional business.

In 1923, inflation hit the country and times were hard, but by the time the economy had settled down, Papa had important business-people as clients. He soon learned that they would pay enormous sums to avoid paying even more in taxes. Papa juggled figures and represented his clients in court. He once told me that he was the biggest honest thief there was.

Mama, on the other hand, abhorred moneymaking. She was basi-cally a Bolshevist (extreme left-winger) and kept a kosher household for the sake of tradition. Her interests were chiefly in politics. (In fact, she worked with Communist groups that tried to gain power in post-war Germany. She not only sympathized with German Socialists Karl Liebknecht and Rosa Luxemburg but also admired Russian revolu-tionary Leon Trotsky.)

Even when I was very young I had nothing but mischief in my head. I got away with a lot because of Mama's absorption with political matters, which consisted mostly of raving and protesting in the streets.

Our fourth-floor Fransecky Strasse apartment consisted of a kitchen, living room, and bedroom, which contained a large bed and an iron crib. The toilet was located between two floors, and we bathed at a public bathhouse. Because Papa and Mama smoked heavily, the place always stank of tobacco. (Mama smoked fifty cigarettes a day.)

In my fifth year, our family life soured. Papa came home for dinner only on Friday nights; on the other nights he worked.

I loved Fridays. Mama cleaned the house thoroughly and put clean sheets on the beds and a fresh tablecloth on the table. Then we went to the Jewish markets to buy kosher chicken and carp to make gefilte fish. When the house and the food were ready, Mama and I went to the public bathhouse and bathed together.

When we came home, the house was flooded with the wonderful smells of chicken, onions, freshly baked challah, and floor polish. I felt tremendously secure and loved. Dressed in clean clothing, I had a newborn feeling. I still feel that way today when I see a woman *bentshn di likhter* (blessing the candles). Papa came home to dinner already bathed and in clean clothing.

Before dinner, Papa and I went to *shul* (temple), a large room with an altar and an armoire for the holy scrolls. In the middle of the room was a podium with a table and two benches where the reading of the Torah took place. Other benches were available for the men of the congregation; women were seated upstairs, behind a curtain. Mama never went to *shul*. Papa had reserved seats for himself and me.

One year at Chanukah (the Festival of Lights), Mama decided that the boys of the congregation should form a human menorah (candelabra). Each boy had a sheet draped over his shoulders and a simulated flame of cardboard tied to his head. Of course, I was one of the boys. Eight were dark haired; then there was me—blond and blue eyed. Papa watched with pleasure. Seated next to him was a traveling salesman, not a member of our congregation. During the tableau, the salesman turned to Papa.

"Excuse me. Is this a regular *shul*?

"Yes, of course," replied Papa.

"So, what is this little goy [Gentile] doing in this *shul*?"

Papa was so insulted that he almost left. When he related this incident to Mama, she laughed until she cried.

The only times I remember Mama being at peace were when Papa came home from work early and agreed to play the piano. While I sat on Mama's lap, he played mostly children's songs.

* * * * *

On April 9, 1932, I turned six, and on the 18th of that month I entered school. Dressed up, with a satchel on my back and a small lunch bag hanging from my shoulder, I carried a cone-shaped cardboard container filled with candies to school that day.

My parents walked me to Danziger Strasse, where there was a *weltliche Schule* (progressive school). After all the parents left, the teacher explained to us that we would be learning about the world, its continents, and its citizens: colors, creeds, brotherly love, understanding, and tolerance. Later, Papa explained that the school was supported by the Communist Party. I actually didn't care for the teacher and disliked the school system, but I proved to be a good pupil, bright and quick. The teacher liked me. Much later, I found out he really liked Mama more than anyone else.

Lutz (age 6) on his first day of school, Berlin, April 1932

We learned about the world of Communism and heard lots of stories about Russia and its revolution. I was thoroughly questioned at home on what I had learned.

I didn't really understand what was happening in the adult world. I often saw men marching in groups and shouting slogans. Walking home from school, I occasionally saw street fights between groups of men. They used sticks, rubber hoses, and even long knives, and usually there were wounded on the ground to be carried away by their comrades afterward. Frightened but fascinated, I'd watch from a safe distance, then run home and tell Mama. Sometimes as I returned from school, I saw Mama standing on our balcony, shouting at men who were marching in the street: "Long live Marx. Long live Lenin. Down with the Nazis. Kill those rotten Brown Shirts." She'd be so excited she would run into the streets and follow the marchers, still shouting, never aware that I was watching.

Exhausted, she'd return and then become aware of me. She'd be so enraged she'd beat me black and blue. When her rage subsided, she'd look at me uncomprehendingly, breathing heavily and coughing. At night Papa would see my bruises and the two of them would get into a shouting match. When that was over, they'd looked at me accusingly as if to say, "It was all your fault; you started this." I'd cry myself to sleep. This happened time after time.

As punishment for misbehaving, Mama would threaten to lock me in the closet where a dark man would take me away. I became so paranoid that I thought every closet had a dark man, and I would not go anywhere dark. Where we lived, a push button on the ground floor lit up the stairway for three minutes and then shut itself off unless the button was pushed again. I would push the button and dash up the stairs. The light always went out when I was midway up the fourth flight, no matter how fast I charged upstairs. I would scream as I rushed up the rest of the way and then pound on our door. Mama would drag me in and beat me, all the while screaming obscenities.

I was so afraid of being left alone that when my parents went out in the evening, I would lie in bed shaking and crying. One evening when they had been gone a long time, I opened the window to the courtyard and yelled for Mama. I didn't know it, but they had only gone to a neighbor's home for a drink. Hearing me yell, they came home, pulled me away from the window, and put me in bed. Amazingly, that time there was no beating.

Street gangs began to form. The boys in one gang wore brown shirts and short black pants. Five or six of us Jewish boys banded together and were joined by a few non-Jewish boys whose parents were not Nazi sympathizers. After school, brawls between the groups took place. Our weapons were tree branches, rubber hoses, and whatever else we could find. I often arrived home with black eyes, loose teeth, bumps on the head, and sore knees, elbows, and back. Each time Mama would patch me together again, her eyes shining if I told her we'd won. I became a good street fighter.

I wasn't at all spoiled. If I didn't eat my spinach at lunch, it was served to me in the evening and again in the morning until, very hungry, I ate it. In this way, I learned that food was precious and everything tastes good to someone who is hungry.

My teacher talked to me about the different political parties, especially the Communist Party. My love of history and geography stems from his talks and from conversations with Papa in Belgium when we were together. I was taught that Germany could not accept the loss of the Great War as a military failure. In a 1920 speech, Paul von Hindenburg blamed the politicians; this theme was repeated so often by the military that finally the people accepted it. Germans had always liked the military and its pomp, and the red faction (Communists) had a difficult time overcoming this feeling.

After so many years of monarchy, it was difficult for Germany to accept democracy. Unemployment was high and war reparations were a heavy burden. When the market crashed in the United States in 1929, it affected the whole world. Germans became very disenchanted with their weak government and poor living conditions and didn't believe that conditions would improve. Most people were unaware of what a major change was taking place politically in Germany. My mother was convinced that Communism and the liberation of workers would solve everyone's problems.

Her heavy smoking, asthma, and emotional agitation caused a sharp decline in her health. On Monday, February 6, 1933, she was rushed to Moses Mendelsohn Hospital with nicotine poisoning. She had been coughing heavily for a month, which caused ruptures in her lungs. Nicotine had seeped into these openings and poisoned her. She would have to remain in the hospital to rest, so it was agreed I would stay with the Alpers, clients and very good friends of Papa's.

The Alpers had the whole floor of their building, a large portion of which housed their men's and boys' garment manufacturing business. Seventeen seamstresses and three cutters were employed there. I loved to sit on the cutting table and watch the huge shears cut the wadding. The area not used in the business was living space for the family.

Mama developed pneumonia the Wednesday after she entered the hospital and then on Friday had a heart attack. On Saturday morning after *shul*, Papa took me to the hospital to see her. I was told to behave myself and not talk too much. The smell of ether and disinfectant unsettled my stomach. As my parents talked, I stared at Mama, trying to decide why she was sick—she didn't look it. She squeezed my hand and kept her eyes on Papa.

She whispered to him, "Kurt, take the boy and leave Germany. Bad times are coming for all Jews, regardless of nationality. Remember my words: the Jews of this country will be unwelcome."

He listened but discounted what she said. "What could happen to me? I am a German citizen and a former soldier. Everything will be all right."

Mama gave my hand one more squeeze and then she lay back in the bed and closed her eyes. When I kissed her cheek, she opened her eyes and smiled at me. Papa led me out of the hospital and back to the Alpers' place.

That night I had nightmares about Mama walking around in her nightshirt, yelling at everyone to leave the country and to kill every Nazi on the way out. I woke up sweating and frightened.

Chapter 3

I didn't want to play the next day and waited inside for Papa to come for me. Shortly before noon, he arrived and took me into the kitchen. He stroked my hair and with an unsteady voice said, "Lutz, you must be brave. Mama passed away at one o'clock this morning."

I stared at him, dumbfounded. I knew it couldn't be true. We walked to the hospital and all the while I was thinking that she would be better when we got there and she'd come home with us.

She lay in bed, her face a peculiar white but very peaceful. When I touched her hands I found they were stiff and cold.

Only when we were back at the Alpers' did I start to cry. Papa told me later that I was inconsolable until Mama's funeral service three days later. We rode to the Weissensee Cemetery in a taxi and entered a plain room with white walls. Mama's body was wrapped in a white sheet. Two long white candles were burning near her head. A rabbi came in and led me by the hand to the office, where I waited. From the window, I could see only flower beds and a cobblestone road. I fell asleep, waking when Papa finally returned.

I was told that an Orthodox Jew's body is wrapped only in a sheet, without clothing or jewelry; that a coffin is not used, only four boards held together with a rope but no nails; and that when the body has been lowered into the grave, the rope is pulled out.

Aunt Felka and several other people were waiting for us when we arrived home. Everyone sat on low stools. As I later learned, they were sitting shivah—sitting on low stools for eight days as a sign of mourning.

The next day in school, the teacher inquired about my mother's health. "She's dead. We buried her yesterday," I told him.

He turned white, sat down, and stared at me. I became uncomfortable and kept to myself for the rest of the day.

On Friday, Papa picked me up at the Alpers' and we went to the Rykestrasse Synagogue. It was very large and quite beautiful, and it had an annex that housed a school. The rabbi was a friend of Papa's. During the service, Papa led me from the rear to the middle of the room, where we were met by the rabbi and the cantor, who recited a prayer. Papa and I said the *Kaddish* (prayer for the dead) and then sat down in the front row. The rabbi spoke about the dead and dying in his sermon. The whole ceremony made a tremendous impact on me. To this day, I am moved when I hear the "Lekho Daudi" (the song for that occasion).

I was pleased when Papa stayed at the Alpers' for dinner. Having lost my mother, I guess my feelings turned toward him at that time. But he left a few hours later and I went back to school the next day—mad at Mama for leaving me, at Papa for making me stay at the Alpers', and at the teacher, too!

When the Alpers left their little girl and me in the care of the house-keeper on Sunday, I took shears from the garment room and cut off as much of my hair as I could reach. The Alpers' housekeeper put me to bed. When I awoke, Papa was there.

"Lutz, we've had our anger and tears," he said sadly. "I can't leave you here forever, but I don't have the time to take care of you. A housekeeper won't do. I think the only solution is for me to get married again. It won't happen right away. In the meantime, you must stay here and behave."

I promised him, unhappy but resigned. Actually, I was busy completing my first year of school with excellent grades. The school was closed soon afterward because of its political leaning, and I later learned that my teacher was sent to prison. I never saw him again. I went to a public school on Grosse Weinberger Strasse. The teacher was pro-Nazi and harassed me from the beginning.

"Well, look here—a Jew-boy," he sneered. "The Commie school couldn't make it so they closed down and sent you to a good German school. Here you'll learn something if your Jewish brain can comprehend it. No playing hooky or skipping classes. You'll learn discipline and order."

On and on he went, but his words went in one ear and out the other. The less attention I paid, however, the more abusive he became.

After school in my third week there, four boys jumped me, pushing me from one to another. Still angry at the recent loss of my mother, I struck out at anything within reach. When my nose was bloody, one eye was swollen half closed, and my ribs and stomach hurt, one of the boys decided that I'd had enough.

"What a pair of fists!" he said. "You're one of us now. We always meet on the corner of Franzecky and Weinberger before going over to Danziger Strasse to teach the gang there a lesson."

We all shook hands. As I walked home, I was confused. The teacher hated me because I was a Jew, but the boys liked me because I could hit hard, Jew or not. I didn't understand it.

Two days later, I met the gang leader. He looked me up and down.

"You look okay, not like a Jew, and I hear you don't fight like a Jew. We'll see. We need good fighters to get rid of those red bandits."

I smiled vaguely, with no idea what he was talking about. He divided us into four groups of six boys each, giving each one a thick tree branch, a rubber hose, and instructions.

We marched along until we saw a group of boys approach. Our leader gave the signal and we began hitting them. A half hour later, the other gang retreated and a shout of victory went up from our gang.

On the way home, I met a boy from the gang we had just beaten. "Hey, Lutz, remember me? Why were you fighting against us? Don't you know what this is all about? Don't you read the signs on the street? Your mother was one of us."

I couldn't read well yet and didn't know what he was talking about.

"The Nazis are trying to seize power and kill all the Communists. There are signs all over the city about voting and getting rid of Jews and other foreigners."

I was skeptical and asked how he knew this.

"My papa told me. Besides, I hear the yelling and shouting on the streets."

The next day, the boy, Heinrich, took me down Weinberger Strasse to Schonhauser Allee to show me what was happening. We stopped at the *Littfassauellen* (tall, round advertising posts) and read the political parties' flyers. I remembered Mama screaming at marchers from the balcony and her fights with Papa over political matters. We approached a huge rally in Bulowstrasse. A man was standing on a podium, yelling into a microphone. He spoke about Communism and the workers of Germany and said that the military wanted to take over the country, which would mean its end. While Heinrich and I stood at a distance, a group of men wearing brown shirts, black riding pants, and black boots approached. Each wore a big swastika on the left shirt sleeve and a belt diagonally over the shoulder. The group surged into the crowd, wielding clubs. Frightened, we ran away from the square.

When we were at a safe distance, Heinrich reminded me that the Reichstag was burned in February and that his papa told him the situation would only get worse. When Hitler has power, his group will persecute Communists and Socialists and attack Jews. I remembered what Mama told Papa just before she died.

We walked slowly along the Grenadier and Dragoner Strassen, inhabited only by Jews, most originally from Poland. Many were Orthodox with long beards and long, black coats. Almost all spoke Yiddish.

"I hope you've seen enough today, Lutz, to stop fighting us," said Heinrich.

Back at the Alpers', Gustav, the head pattern cutter, listened to what had happened to me. Lighting a cigarette, he confirmed what I had heard. "Lutz, there's no question that Hitler and his kind will take over Germany, and I know what will happen to Jews. You'll have to decide which side you're on."

As time went by, I made only a pretense of fighting. When it became evident that I was faking, I was beaten and tossed out of the gang. Afterward, the gang members kept their distance because they knew I'd fight back. In school, my grades suffered and I was beaten for the slightest reason. The teacher seemed especially displeased that none of this fazed me.

On May 10, one hundred days after Hitler became chancellor, "Das Horst Wessel Lied," the official hymn of the Nazi Party, was sung everywhere. Joseph Goebbels, the minister of propaganda, organized a spectacular event called Book Burning Night. Any book thought to denigrate the Nazis or Germany and its people was burned. Many National Socialists were poorly educated and knew nothing about the fabulous authors and their books, so they burned everything without thought. Papa told me later that 20,000 volumes were burned in Berlin that night amidst inflammatory speeches by Goebbels and other leaders.

The following day, Heinrich and I went back to the square. Many of the Jewish-owned shops had signs posted on the windows saying "Germans, fight back; don't buy from Jews." Brown Shirts stood guard at each of these shops. As we walked the streets where Jews lived, we saw no one. And on Brunnenstrasse near Alexanderplatz, Jews were being herded together and marched off by the SA—Sturmabteilung (Storm Detachment).

As we watched, a number of SA troopers marched by, and some smiled at us. One even spoke to us: "Isn't it wonderful that we're finally getting at the throats of the Jew rabble?" We just smiled and nodded. When I returned to the Alpers', Papa was there, and I knew from his face that he had found out about my poor schoolwork and brawls. After a lecture on mending my ways, he said we might be together soon. In the meantime, I was to be sent to a couple in Potsdam, Germany, who took in boys and girls in the summertime.

* * * * *

In June, Papa and I took the metro to Zehlendorf and then a taxi to the outskirts of Potsdam. While the taxi waited, Papa carried my suitcase and we entered a huge house, where we were met by a smiling woman.

"How do you do. I am Mrs. Kapellner."

Papa gave his card to her, told me to behave myself and write to him, and quickly departed in the taxi. Mrs. Kapellner took me upstairs to a large room with five beds on each side. I was assigned a bed and cupboard for my clothes and told that someone would come for me when it was lunchtime. I unpacked and looked around. Everything was clean and neat. Through a window I could see tall pine trees surrounding a wide lawn, swings, and sandboxes. Some boys were playing soccer and handball. Girls were playing catchball (a game like soccer but played using one's hands instead of one's feet) and hopscotch.

I was led outside and introduced to a tall, curly-haired redhead nicknamed Theo, although his name was Joachim. Theo introduced me to many of the children and described the daily routine. I also met Nora and Inge, the Kapellners' children. It was almost impossible not to love Inge, the younger of the two, who was three years older than me. Theo and I became close friends, nicknamed by the others "Pat and Patachon," (like "Mutt and Jeff"), who were a comic team in the movies.

Chapter 4

Four weeks flew by. Before all the children were to leave, the Kapellners had a wonderful party. When the departure day arrived, Inge kissed me wetly on the lips and ran back to the house. I licked my lips with delight.

Long after all the other children departed, Mrs. Kapellner came out to tell me Papa couldn't pick me up because of urgent business. I was given money for transportation and emergencies and put into a taxi with instructions on how to return home. As Inge waved from an upstairs window, I was driven away.

When I got off the metro, Papa was waiting in a great hustle and bustle of people. He hailed a taxi to take us to the Alpers', where I spent the rest of the day getting reacquainted with everyone, and especially the Alpers' daughter. When I told her about Inge, she reminded me that I had promised to marry her.

Papa and I dined at Aschinger Restaurant on Alexanderplatz. We had the house specialty: pigs' feet, puree of peas, sauerkraut, and unlimited rolls. Papa had *Bock* beer; I had nonalcoholic malt beer, which was very popular with young people. Before we finished, Papa revealed some shocking news: he was to be married in September. It was an arranged, contract marriage to a woman from a well-to-do Polish family originally from Kempen, Posen, and now living in Breslau. She had never been married, and raising a young boy would be a new experience for her. Papa felt that we needed a woman in the house. I promised to get along with her and not cause trouble outside the house. This last part was very important, Papa said, because times were becoming difficult. Jewish professors and professionals were being dismissed and restricted, and he thought that more problems for Jews were sure to come.

His news wasn't all bad. We were to live near the Oranienburger Strasse Synagogue, which meant I could go to a different school.

I wanted to think about what had been said and told Papa I'd like to walk home. On the way, my thoughts centered on whether or not I would like my new mama.

* * * * *

For the wedding, I was outfitted with a navy officer's suit with long pants, an officer's cap, patent leather shoes, and white gloves. I also had a small dagger to be worn at my side just for that special occasion.

When the ceremony began, Papa waited inside the synagogue for my future mama, who entered through the front door. Her face was covered by a veil and she wore a long white dress. Fascinated by the ritual and the rabbi's words, I was surprised when it ended as Papa kissed her. In the vestibule, while everyone talked and embraced, Papa introduced me to my new mama. She kissed my cheek; her skin was as smooth as a peeled peach. Shorter than Papa, she was on the chubby side.

Afterward, there was a party at Aunt Felka's with many people and all kinds of food. Many of Papa's friends and business colleagues were there. Aunt Felka played the piano, and Uncle Eddie sang songs until the dancing began. Mutti, my new mama, had three guests. Among them was her cousin Dora, seven years old, whom Papa called Mickey Mouse. Dora, or Doerchen as her mother called her, and I were fed special treats in the kitchen and taken to another room, where we both fell asleep. I didn't remember Papa taking me to the Alpers' place, where I awoke the next morning.

I was excited when Papa arrived to take me to our new home at 28 Oranienburger Strasse, where Mutti was waiting for us.

While Papa took my belongings to another room, I wandered through a big living room, a dining room, and a special room for Papa's piano. Papa and Mutti's bedroom and mine shared an adjoining bathroom and a toilet. There was a kitchen and another toilet and across the hall was Papa's office. All of the ceilings were high, like a museum's, and each room had floor-to-ceiling tiled heaters.

In my room were a dresser, an armoire, and a shelving system for my books and toys—although toys didn't last long with me; I enjoyed taking them apart to see what was inside.

Before dinner, with Mutti at his side, Papa told me the household rules: We would always eat in the dining room; hands must always be washed before eating; Mutti's kosher (clean, pure) kitchen could be entered only with her permission; Papa's office would also be off limits to me; I must not try to open the locked baby grand piano; Sabbaths and holidays would be observed; everyone would be seated at the table at the same time; prayer and breaking of bread would start the meal; benediction and Papa's finishing a cigarette would end the meal. Eight o'clock would be my bedtime. Mutti would inspect my clothing and cleanliness. I was to be punctual, orderly, clean, and obedient. All these rules were tall orders for me.

On the other hand, Papa and Mutti would entertain once a month; they would listen to or play music. I might go to movies on Sundays and perhaps concerts, circuses, and other entertainment.

Papa took me to the Koppell Platz Schule to be registered. I would be going to the *Kinderhort* (day care center) for three hours after regular school.

At first it was difficult making new friends and doing new school work. Bernhard, a distant relative of Mutti's, and I skipped kindergarten and made up excuses. He wasn't too bright, but we got along and together got into fights with other kids.

At home, life was not good. Mutti was very nervous and lashed out at me, verbally and physically, for any reason. I misbehaved even more because I knew she didn't like me. If she saw I'd been fighting, she beat me. Papa was too busy to see me much, and he always took her side.

We moved again in the spring, three days before my eighth birthday. Our new home was on the second floor of a five-floor building on Veteranenstrasse at the bottom of a hill. It was as big as the one on Oranienburger Strasse. The area was very interesting. There were many fine stores, a movie house, an ice cream parlor, a bakery, and a cabinetmaker's shop. In the basement of the house next door were a rag collector and a coal supplier. Up the street in a huge tenement complex was a dairy with cows. Next to it was a large arched arcade where fruits and vegetables were sold.

Kleine Hamburger Strasse School was a public school that both Bernhard and I now attended. I had to make new friends all over again, and all the students but one were Gentiles. I met a boy named Gruft when I helped him fend off four big bullies. After an awful fight, during which one of the bullies was badly hurt, our teacher appeared from nowhere.

"What's going on here?" he demanded. Before I could answer, he continued, "You Jews don't tell the truth anyway. You hurt a German boy. How dare you even touch him!"

At home, before I could explain, Mutti beat me for being late and fighting. When Papa arrived, I had to tell him what happened. He believed most of it and praised me for defending the boy and myself. But he also insisted I try harder to please Mutti. As I started to leave, he told me that I would be sent to Aunt Martha's in Breslau for a summer vacation. That was wonderful news.

* * * * *

When summer arrived, I said goodbye to Mutti. At the train station, my suitcase was put in my compartment and Papa handed me a bag of toffees. The locomotive whistled and emitted blasts of steam; a green light flicked on and the train moved out.

I slept most of the night. About seven o'clock the next morning, we pulled into Breslau Station, where Aunt Martha and her daughter, Ruth, waited to hug and kiss me. The streetcar took us to the corner of Moritz Strasse, where they lived in a fourth-floor apartment. For the first time in my life, I met Papa's mother, a thin figure with white hair and a warm smile. My cousin Ruth and I shared a room but had separate beds. I'd never slept in a room with anyone before, except in the dormitory, and never in a girl's bedroom.

Many photographs were displayed in the living room: the oldest son, Walter, and his wife, Klara, who had moved to a kibbutz in Palestine near the Negev Desert in 1926; the second oldest, Heinz, and his wife, who moved to England in 1929; and Lutz, who left for London in 1931 to be joined soon by his wife, Stephy. There were pictures of Grandpa and Grandma with their children: Uncles Eugen and Siegfried, Papa, and Aunts Martha, Alice, and Felka. There was a photograph of Aunt Martha's husband, who had died sometime in the past. There was one of Papa, Mama, and me as a tot and one showing Papa as a soldier.

Left to right: Aunt Martha, Ruth, Stephy's mother, Lutz (age 8), Stephy,
July 1934

Aunt Martha thanked me for the gifts Papa had told me to give the family. After I answered many questions, I was told I could do as I pleased while I was there; I could even go into the streets to play with some other boys. And there would be picnic trips outside the city.

One night, Ruth and I were in our beds, whispering about all kinds of things. Before long we were giggling and discussing boy-girl matters, not realizing Aunt Martha had entered! After a lecture, I was moved to another room. Otherwise, I was having a great summer!

On August 2, 1934, President von Hindenburg died and the country mourned. At his burial in Tannenberg, East Prussia, his son asked the German people to honor his papa's request that Adolf Hitler succeed him as head of state. On the 19th of August, Hitler was elected by a large majority. Papa wrote me saying everything was fine and he hoped I was having a good time, but he wrote to Aunt Martha that there was a certain amount of tension throughout Berlin and I should stay in Breslau as long as possible. When it couldn't be put off any longer, Grandma and I left for Berlin.

Friedrichstrasse Station was filled with SA men and many, many black-uniformed men with "SS" (which stood for Schutzstaffel [protection squad]) on their lapels. Papa shook my hand, kissed Grandma, and told me I looked as though I'd had a fine summer.

Mutti awaited us at the door. Surprisingly, I got a big hug and kiss.

Grandma and I went out daily for two weeks, roaming through the city. We visited department stores, pastry and coffee houses, four circuses, and a fair. Too soon it was time for her to return to Breslau. I gave her a teary goodbye. A week later, Papa received a telegram saying Grandma had passed away in her sleep. I walked to the park and tried to understand why such a good person had to die.

Chapter 5

Once I was back in Berlin, I was so busy with new friends I stayed out of trouble for the most part. Guenther, who lived in an apartment building across the street, couldn't come to my home because he was Lutheran, but I often went to his apartment. His parents were always very nice to me.

Many evenings Papa, Mutti, and I went to the opera, concerts, or first-run movies. On my birthday, Aunt Felka gave me a wonderful surprise gift—a Zeppelin ride around Berlin.

At Christmastime, Guenther's parents invited me to their home and gave me a lot of chocolate and a present. When I arrived home, however, Mutti's reception was cold. She accused Guenther's family of trying to poison my mind with their Christian ideas. Papa tried to calm her to no avail.

After she stomped out, I apologized to Papa. He said not to worry too much about it.

* * * * *

At Passover and Easter, Mutti was quiet, but she knew I sneaked nonkosher Easter eggs; that made me a "goy" (non-Jew) and therefore unacceptable to her. Papa didn't help matters either. He won a ham at a Masons' meeting and brought it home! When Mutti saw it, she became outraged, opened the window, and threw it out! Luckily no one was walking beneath the window just then.

At my school, I was the only Jewish student left. Nearly all Jewish parents had put their children in private Jewish schools. One morning instead of the usual prayers before lessons, everyone was told to stand, salute, and say a poem of adoration of the Fuehrer. I stood but did not salute or say anything. When the teacher saw this, he stopped the poem. "Posener, Jew boys do not stand. Sit down." Afterward, I had to write on the blackboard ten times "Jew boys do not stand" and received five lashes on my backside with a bamboo stick.

Many Jews had left Berlin. Most of the German children were in uniform; the little ones belonged to Kueken Gruppe (Small Boys' Group), Jungvolk (Peoples' Boys), or Hitler Jugend (Hitler Youth). Most girls were members of Bund Deutscher Maedchen (Association of German Girls). They talked to me only when they were not in uniform.

* * * * *

At Pentecost, Papa and Aunt Felka decided to have a big meeting of our friends to discuss the rumors that restrictive laws were to be instituted by the Nazis. It didn't sound exciting to me, so I decided to spend the time with Guenther and Bernhard.

We roamed around the north end, where we lived, walking up and down streets and boulevards. We didn't have any money, so while Bernhard distracted the owners of several outdoor markets, Guenther and I stole some fruit. And we got free milk by helping to unload milk from delivery wagons and carry it into stores. We had a great time.

During our roaming, we saw signs on benches saying "No Jews allowed to sit—for Aryans only." On store windows there were other signs: "Same business with new German owner" or "This establishment had changed owners. Former proprietor passed away." It was the same in the south end. And in the east end we were stopped by two *Schupos* (policemen) who asked many questions and then told us to go back to where we came from.

When Guenther left the city with his parents for a few days, Bernhard and I toured the west end. Past Alexanderplatz and walking on to Friedrichstrasse, we saw museum buildings and statues in the parks. At the Unknown Soldiers' Memorial, people had assembled for services. At the Sports Stadium, buildings were being readied for the Olympic Games to be held the following year. On the Kuh-Damm or Kurfuersten Damm (literally, Prince Elector Dam), there were elegant restaurants and nightclubs and the KA DE WE, or Kaufhaus des Westens (Shopping House of the West).

One day, Bernhard took me to the roof of a building and down some stairs to a small storage room. Cautioning me to be silent, he opened a door slightly, which gave us a view of a stage. Before long, music started and a woman in an evening gown appeared on stage. Dancing to the music, she began to slowly remove her clothing. Soon she had only a small piece of cloth in front of her and two small covers on her breasts. And then with a twirl, she had nothing on! I stopped breathing. When we were able to move, we left quietly.

I was two hours late coming home, and Mutti met me with a stick in her hand. After telling Papa two different stories that he didn't believe, I was forced to tell him where we really had been.

"Did you like what you saw?" he asked. "Was she good looking?" When I admitted I liked it, he sent me to bed without a lecture.

Bernhard and I continued our explorations until the final day of Pentecost, a Saturday. That evening, Papa, Mutti, and I taxied to Aunt Felka's place, where many people were already seated. Papa spoke first.

"We need to decide how to protect ourselves because the Nazis are here to stay. Many businesses have been sold involuntarily; learned people are refused teaching, working, and research positions; authors cannot publish; attorneys and doctors are restricted in their practices.

"Many have left the country. Our children are badly treated in public schools. Parks and other public places are off limits to us. Goebbels and his propaganda machine are slowly influencing the German people. And Julius Streicher's hate paper, the *Stuermer,* is being read more and more. The situation won't get any better. The questions are, What can we do about it, what are our rights, and is it already too late to do anything?

"I've talked to rabbis, some Zionists, some liberals, and some extremists. They don't have any answers. Most of the wealthy have sold their properties and left or are planning to leave. But where does one go? I have relatives in Palestine, but I'm not sure I want to go there. How can we leave everything here and just go?"

I would have liked to have heard the responses, but I fell asleep and woke up in bed at home in the morning.

* * * * *

During class one day, my mind wandered and I couldn't answer a question the teacher asked, which upset him. Later at recess, two boys in Jungvolk uniforms approached me and two of my friends.

"Hey, you guys," they said to my friends, "don't you know you're not supposed to be friends with Jews?" Then they turned to me. "You, Jew-boy, better scram or else."

I didn't back down and soon we were fighting. I had one of them on the ground, ready to punch him, when the teacher pulled me off of him.

"How dare you hit a uniform—a German uniform! How dare you dirty this uniform with your dirty Jew hands! Into the classroom! Recess is over."

In the classroom, I explained what happened. Although two boys sided with me, the teacher made me bend over a bench, and he hit me until I screamed. Hearing the noise, the principal entered, took the teacher outside, and told me to go home. He said not to tell anyone what had happened and to come back to see him the next day.

At home, Mutti drew me a bath and caught a glimpse of my backside. That night, Papa examined the marks on my back under a strong light. "Who would do this to a child? I'll go with you tomorrow and get you into another school."

* * * * *

In the morning, Papa and I went to the principal's office, where Papa refused to accept the principal's explanation that my beating was only an accident. After a tongue-lashing by Papa, the principal gave him my transfer papers. On the way to Oranienburger Strasse to enter a temporary private school, Papa said it was all for the best and he hoped I'd do better in the new surroundings.

My new teacher was Miss Heilbronn. The class was mixed—boys and girls. While the other children were at recess, she brought me books and papers and asked many questions. At noon I was talking to several boys in the schoolyard when I saw Miss Heilbronn eating something raw. One of the boys, Otto, indicated she never ate anything cooked. This was weird, but Otto said she was a fair teacher and that I would like the school and no one would call us dirty names. For a while, everything went well.

At that time, we belonged to the congregation at the Rykestrasse Synagogue, which was smaller than the Oranienburger Strasse Synagogue but just as nice. I liked the chief rabbi, Rabbi Weill, and every Saturday I attended services until he saw me and nodded his head. Then I would slip outside to play soccer and return just before the service ended. Once when the rabbi visited our home and Mutti asked if I had been at the service, he assured her that he had seen me. That made her feel better and I was out of trouble.

On Saturday evenings, Papa usually invited two colleagues and their wives to come over for supper. We would have smelly cheese and beef tartare and I'd have my favorite malt beer. The men would play cards and drink beer and slivowitz, a potent drink that made my eyes tear when I caught a whiff of it. The women drank coffee and ate cookies and chatted. At eight o'clock, Papa would say good night to me, and no amount of begging on my part would delay bedtime.

* * * * *

In mid-October 1935, there was a second meeting at Aunt Felka's. Again, Papa was the first to speak.

"They finally did it. On September 15, the Nuremberg Laws were formulated. They form a pseudobasis for German Jews' loss of their rights as citizens. Jews will be forced to take Jewish surnames. Passports and other documents will be marked as belonging to a Jew. A Jew can be judged and condemned for *Rassenschande,* 'sexual intimacies with a German thereby damaging the Aryan race.' These restrictions are published under the heading of the 'Law for the Protection of the German Blood and the German Honor.' German philosophers, scientists, theologians, and the doctors not only condone all this, but they defend this fascist concept of race culture and purity of the German Reich. Those who have already left should be congratulated for their foresight. We who remain are stuck in a hostile world.

"The newspaper *Rundschau* has issued a declaration for unity, Jewish pride, severe self-restraint and a great willingness to sacrifice. An election is to be held determining representation of all German Jews.

"I am sure the Nazis will hold big rallies everywhere. It is advisable to remain inside as much as possible. Many have been arrested as so-called unwanted elements—just as happened in 1933—and taken to various camps. I will have to give up all my non-Jewish clients, and there will be other restrictions on my business."

Although I didn't understand all of this, I was sure it wasn't good.

* * * * *

Despite the hostile climate, we celebrated New Year's Eve in style. The house was full of people. Mutti prepared lots of food and Papa poured the red wine for our midnight *Gluehwein* toast. I was permitted to set off firecrackers in the street while Papa watched from the window. The streets were filled with people celebrating for what might be the last time.

* * * * *

When Rykestrasse School had made room for all the Jewish students who wanted to attend, my temporary school was dissolved, and I advanced to a higher class at Rykestrasse School. Miss Heilbronn was still my teacher, but we also had a second teacher for Hebrew and music classes. Physical education was intensified, reflecting the approach of the Olympics Games in August.

Papa had tickets for the entire two weeks of the games, and I was given an album with spaces to insert pictures of the gold medal winners. The city prepared for the event by removing all anti-Jewish signs, and two German Jews were allowed to compete in the games to mask what was really taking place in Berlin and the rest of Germany. Papa and I had very good seats for the opening ceremonies in the crowded stadium. Schools were closed and everyone was very excited. I busied myself obtaining many of the winners' autographs for my album. The most notable athlete at the games was Jesse Owens, a black man from the United States. When I asked for his autograph, he patted my head, then nodded and smiled at me. The whole event was quite exhilarating for a young boy.

* * * * *

As soon as the games were over and school recommenced, everything was even more restricted. I could tell Papa was very concerned, and one day he asked me if I would like to live in a kibbutz in Palestine as my Uncle Siegfried's son was doing. After some thought I decided to stay with Papa. Papa's income had declined and we had to take in a renter to help with expenses. I was told not to ask questions about anything or talk to anybody about what was happening.

*****

In the first part of 1937, I frequently arrived home with black eyes, bruises, loose teeth, bloody noses, and sore knuckles. Mutti would be so enraged she'd beat me, but by then I knew how to protect myself. Bernhard and two other rowdies were my only friends since Guenther had moved to another city.

In school, I found a way to work out my aggressions in physical education class. The coach, Rudi Sonnenfeld, liked me; I was his star athlete, having become skilled at gymnastics—the horizontal and parallel bars, the side horse, the rings, and floor exercises. One time, Papa asked Mr. Sonnenfeld how I could be so good in class and so difficult outside. Dodging the issue, coach said I had power, strength, and agility and that I was very limber. In his classes, I was very willing and obedient!

In the spring of 1937, a big athletic meet was held and since I was enrolled in the Maccabee-Hacoah Athletic Club, I represented both the school and the club. Papa was pleased. When I wanted to join a boxing team, Mutti protested, but Papa thought it would be good for me, so three days a week I worked out—wrestling, a little jujitsu, punching bags, rope skipping, and shadow boxing. Although I got knocked down in the ring, I enjoyed the sport and all other athletics. Mutti constantly complained that my schoolwork suffered.

All that physical activity toughened me, and my reputation as a roughneck grew. I was constantly challenged, and most non-Jewish boys stayed away from me. When I arrived home showing signs of having been in fights, I always told Papa that I wouldn't put up with being called "filthy Jew pig" and that I just did what he'd told me to do in the past—I fought back when hit. Although Papa was proud, he planned to resume my chess lessons, so I would develop my mental skills, not just fighting skills.

Toward the end of July, I saw a Jungvolk boy hit and kick a nice little girl in my class. I grabbed his uniform shoulder strap, pulled him away, and beat him until some adults separated us. That night the boy's mother came to our place and discussed the incident with Papa. After the woman left, Papa told me he'd have to appease her by paying a sum to cover the boy's medical expenses. This event resulted in a family meeting where I was told that I was a danger to everybody, so I would be staying with the Kapellners in Zehlendorf for a while and would commute to school by subway.

Chapter 6

The next day I said goodbye to my friends. Mutti helped me pack and when Papa arrived home, I received instructions and was given money to buy a book of student stamps; one stamp allowed subway rides for a month. My commute would take an hour each way. Every Monday, instead of going directly back to the Kapellners', I was to bring my laundry home.

Before I left for the Kapellners', Mutti's cousin Doerchen and her mother joined us for dinner. While the adults visited in Papa's office after we had eaten, Doerchen and I promised each other we would always be friends. To seal the deal, she kissed me. Doerchen's mother announced that her daughter would also go to the Kapellners' soon. As I drifted off to sleep, I felt happy about that news.

* * * * *

Papa and I boarded the subway. After forty minutes, the train emerged into daylight and continued to the end of the line. We walked the four blocks to the Kapellners' and were met at the gate by Nora, who remembered me from four years before.

Mrs. Kapellner greeted us at the door of the large house and showed us out back, where there were swings and other playthings. There was scaffolding for installation of a horizontal bar. Further on into the forest, called Grunewald, there was a pond where a small boat could be used in the summer and skating was possible in the winter. Nearby was Krumme Lanke lake, where there was swimming in the summer. Mr. Jacobson came from Neukoeln each morning to teach swimming and act as our private tutor. Staying with the Kapellners at that time were six boys, including me, and two girls.

When it was time for Papa to go, I walked him to the gate and waved until he was out of sight. I felt empty.

The dorm room had fourteen beds; mine had a view of the back-yard and pond. I quickly stored my belongings and left the room to avoid loneliness. Downstairs, a very grown-up Inge greeted me; she was now twelve years old and in two more years, she informed me, she would be able to join her older sister, Nora, at the lycée (high school) in Zehlendorf.

The other children began to arrive. Heinz was to be enrolled in a Jewish trade school, while his brother, Jochem, would continue in public school in Zehlendorf. Jacob, quite tall, looked like a "schlemiel" (nincompoop). Tiny eight-year-old Ernst immediately asked me to be his friend. Peter, age thirteen, entered with Mr. Jacobson and stood nearby while he recited the house rules to me. Mr. Jacobson was quite large; I knew I'd better avoid trouble with him. After answering a barrage of questions, it appeared I was accepted by the group.

Dinner was preceded and followed by Mr. Kapellner's prayer book recitations of benediction and thanks. That first night, as I ate a meal of noodles with cinnamon and sugar, two slices of rye bread, and milk, Inge smiled meaningfully at me.

After dinner I wandered around, inspecting the nice library. I also played chess with Heinz, winning easily because he wasn't too skilled. When I mentioned that my papa was my chess teacher, Mr. Jacobson, who had been watching us play, told me he was aware my papa had been written about when he entered chess tournaments and that perhaps we could have some tournaments of our own at the Kapellners'.

Upstairs for the night as we got ready for bed, there was much talk and "boasting" among the boys in our room. Of course, the stories were made up for the most part.

The next day I awoke at 6:30—my last day before school started. Everyone else had already made his bed and was getting dressed. I rushed to catch up in the noisy scramble to get ready for breakfast. Little Ernst came to me to tie his shoes and I agreed to teach him how later. In the dining room, Mrs. Kapellner and I talked, deciding that I must leave the house by 6:15 each morning to make the connections for my trip to school. Frieda, the cook, would give me sandwiches for lunch, and when I returned I would have milk and do homework before I could go out to play. I was told that Mr. Jacobson was in charge and had Papa's permission to punish me if necessary. There was to be no brawling. As one of the children at the Kapellners' on a permanent basis, I was expected to help those who came only for short vacations.

After breakfast, I left to find my way to the station so I would be able to get there rapidly the next day. That matter settled, I returned to the Kapellners' and wandered down the hill to the pond. Frogs croaked. I sat down and let my mind wander.

Suddenly, I was pushed from behind; Inge wanted me to walk to the woods with her. There she confided that although I was younger than she was, I was now her boyfriend. On the way back we met little Ilse and took her into the house; left alone, she sometimes wandered away. While Inge helped in the kitchen, Jochem and I worked out on the horizontal bar outside. Mr. Jacobson had been the apparatus champion of Germany for two years and we knew we'd learn a lot from him.

I liked it at the Kapellners', but I decided that when possible, I would stay in the city after school was over for the day to roam around with Bernhard. (As time went on, I would spend quite a bit of time trying to come up with good excuses for being late.)

* * * * *

Early the next morning, I jumped out of bed and hurried to get ready, had breakfast, and left for the station. Mrs. Kapellner warned me not to dawdle or I'd miss the subway. Arriving in good time, I chose a seat near the conductor. The doors closed and he hit the window to signal we were ready to leave. As I watched the beautiful landscape roll by, I noticed only a few other people were on the subway. At each stop, more and more got on until many people were standing. At my stop, I got off and walked toward school, arriving at 7:50. Snickers and whispers greeted my arrival. A boy next to me explained that everyone knew I had to live in Zehlendorf because I'd beaten up a boy and was considered too dangerous.

When Mrs. Radchewsky entered the classroom, she was not pleased to see me. "Ah, Posener. You have a lot of catching up to do. I don't think you'll make it. Anyway, all you can do is beat up little boys. What do you have to say for yourself?"

Insolent as ever, I responded, "Mrs. Radchewsky, I don't owe you an explanation. I don't care what you think of me and don't need your approval. Call my papa if you need any information."

The school day finally ended. Mr. Jacobson was waiting to supervise my homework when I arrived at 3:15. I rushed to finish so I could change my clothes and play outside.

Outside, Peter questioned me about my athletic skills. I told him my best sports were soccer and handball or catchball; I was pretty good at bar work and okay in track and field. When the short-term boarders arrived there would be contests and a boxing tournament. Peter's papa had gotten him into the Maccabees and he had two cousins who were fighters. Bubi, the Kapellners' nephew, was in the Maccabees, too, and he would be taking part in the tournament. Peter chuckled as he related that Mr. Jacobson always tried to best him in boxing bouts but reacted very badly when he lost.

"Mr. Jacobson is not bad in most sports." Peter explained, "and used to be very good when he was younger. Now he is hotheaded and has a big ego."

When all the boys arrived home, we played ball. Mr. Jacobson had to drop out early—he became easily winded because he was a smoker.

After the game everyone went into the playroom, where Mr. Jacobson outlined upcoming events. "In two weeks, sixteen boys and girls will arrive for four weeks. Everyone is to help, play, and be good companions; no hanky-panky. We'll have outings and competition games, and names will be drawn to make up the teams."

* * * * *

The rest of the week passed very rapidly. I began to get used to the Kapellners' place and my trips to and from school.

On the following Monday, I walked home and rang the bell. Mutti wasn't too upset that I had forgotten my laundry. I told her about all the activities at the Kapellners' and at school. She fed me a wonderful meal and loaded me down with a bag of cookies, cake, and other treats to take back and share with the others. I arrived at the Kapellners' quite late, but Frieda had saved me some supper. The sweets from Mutti were soon eaten by the other children.

The next Monday, I didn't forget to take my laundry to school with me, but the package got me into trouble. After school, the boy I had beaten up identified me to two of his chums. They were quite big and stared at me as I walked by.

"You going anyplace, Jew-boy? How would you like to take on someone your own size? Or maybe you don't have time now because you have a package ready to send to Jerusalem where all the dirty Jews belong." One of them kicked the package out of my hand.

Before they could say any more, I kicked one in the groin. But another one grabbed me and held my arms behind me while the little guy kicked me. While I rolled on the ground, I saw my friend Avram beating up the largest one.

After they left, Avram helped me up, handed me my package, and walked with me a little way. I was afraid that Mutti would be upset if she noticed I'd been fighting. But I was lucky; she didn't notice.

*****

The vacationers and the permanent boys and girls had a great time during the next four weeks. I was finally able to meet with Bernhard, whose family lived very modestly in a bad section of the city, as did many other families. We decided to visit the Acker Halle (Central Market), where all kinds of meats, fish, vegetables, fruits, breads, and delicacies of many countries were sold. We wandered around until Bernhard became tired, and then we shared an ice cream. Realizing that it was getting late, we rushed to his place to retrieve my school books and dashed to the subway station. When I arrived at the Kapellners', Mr. Jacobson didn't ask any questions. With a sigh of relief, I knew I could meet Bernhard again to explore the city.

That summer I learned to swim a little and became an expert on the horizontal bar. My soccer and catchball skills were outstanding. Jochem, Peter, and I became great friends. Bubi, the nephew, knew some people I knew from the Maccabees, and gave me lessons in defending myself. I took long walks with Inge and we talked about girls and boys, which added to my education in the facts of life.

On Mondays, when I took my laundry to Mutti, Papa was never there. No explanation was ever given.

In mid-August, school started again. In the city, I saw uniforms everywhere: black and brown on both young children and older people. When I met Guenther, he informed me that non-Jewish students were being instructed not to associate with Jews and told we were the scum of the earth and someday Germany would get rid of us all. But he went on to say that his papa did not believe in the Nazis' cause and would not join the Nazi Party.

In September, Papa informed the Kapellners I was to stay with Mutti for two weeks while he was away. I was not to ask questions. I'd be going back to the Kapellners' when he returned, but in the meantime I was to behave.

At school, Coach Sonnenfeld approached me at lunch recess. Competition between the schools would be starting soon, and he wanted me to be one of the students representing our school. He said I'd have to get permission from Mutti because it meant I'd be late arriving home. Mutti approved my practicing for the school competition but reminded me that I shouldn't plan on competing next year because I'd be too busy studying for my bar mitzvah. My deadline for arriving at home was set at five o'clock.

One day, Bernhard was waiting for me after school. I admired him; he had such a fiendish mind! He was delighted to hear that I'd be able to chum around with him for a couple of weeks. We decided to visit Dragoner and Grenadier Strassen, where many Polish Jews lived. Nazis were constantly hovering about there. Crossing Rosenthaler Platz, we neared Buelow Platz where big rallies had been held. Now it was being used for Hitler Youth gatherings and other big Nazi functions. Bernhard thought it was going to be renamed the Horst Wessel Platz.

We wandered into a bakery where the smells were so good we wanted to stay forever. At a nearby butcher shop where Mutti bought chicken, the shop people looked quite different with their *peyes* (earlocks) and long beards. They spoke only Yiddish and didn't look at us with favor. Some of the stores sold books and other *shul* items: prayer shawls and tefillin, candelabras for Sabbath and Chanukah, and silver ornaments for holidays. I loved to browse and see everything on display. In one of the shops I was called the "educated *sheygets*" (non-Jew). We looked around but didn't touch anything. Bernhard said the proprietors were not clean and not German. I felt differently and reminded him that they were still Jews and the same as us.

We decided to wander over to Mulack Strasse, aptly nicknamed the "street of prostitutes." One or two sat in each window, tapping their fingernails on the glass when they heard anyone come by. They wore heavy makeup and evening gowns. Most of them looked pretty awful. When I was younger, they scared me, but now that I was older, we enjoyed teasing them.

We were having so much fun that I didn't arrive home until nearly seven o'clock. Mutti met me at the door, crying. I asked her what was wrong.

"You were almost two hours late and I was worried sick. In these times, who knows what can happen. Go eat your dinner and then off to bed."

I wondered why she didn't hit me. At least I'd have felt better if she had. After dinner, I lay awake in bed, thinking of all the places Bernhard and I had been that day.

* * * * *

Papa returned from his trip. He had been in Breslau visiting family members who hadn't left Germany yet. He told me all the family news. Aunt Martha and Ruth had gone to Palestine, and Lutz's wife had joined Lutz and Heinz in England. He reminded me that I had refused to go with the *aliyah* (the immigration to the Jewish homeland) to join Uncle Siegfried's boy, who had immigrated to Palestine in 1936. Aunt Alice was still struggling to raise her three children. Uncle Siegfried was in Prague, Czechoslovakia, and Uncle Karl was probably in Hawaii again. I liked Uncle Karl, who used to tell me stories about the Hawaiian Islands and his native woman and their two children.

* * * * *

In school, my grades continued to be poor except for the first hour in Mr. Schreiber's class. I liked his teaching methods and received praise often. He sent notes home to Papa and Mutti about how well I was doing. Mrs. Radchewsky and I were still feuding; I gave her a bad time whenever I could, which was quite often because I was in class with her three hours a day.

One day I placed tiny glass bulbs containing foul-smelling liquid under each of her chair legs. When she sat down the bulbs broke. Within two minutes the room stank. When she found the smashed bulbs near the chair's legs, she immediately knew I was involved. Another student confirmed she had seen me do it. "Thank you, Bertha," said Mrs. Radchewsky. "Posener, out of the class! Sit in the hallway the rest of the hour."

At recess, two boys and I cornered Bertha and I told her what would happen if she tattled on me again.

After school, an ice slide was created by a group of boys. We had a lot of fun running and sliding along its length. Before I realized it, I'd missed my subway and I arrived back at the Kapellners' over two hours late. Mr. Jacobson believed my story, but I made the mistake of telling Jochem what really made me late. Overhearing the truth, Mr. Jacobson boxed both my ears several times. "That will teach you to tell funny stories." From then on, I was very careful not to let him catch me at anything.

* * * * *

On the Monday before Christmas, Papa was already home when I arrived. "Lutz, how would you like to go with me to Werhtheim and browse around?"

"Would I!" I cleaned up a bit and put on my winter clothes.

As we walked to the store, people rushed by us in the cold, bundled in heavy clothing. Inside the store, a wave of warm air carried the scent of perfumes, which I love. The store was crowded and there were many displays of Christmas goods. Papa warned me not to touch anything and to be very careful. The top floor had displays of crystal and porcelain, but more important to me, the toy department was on that floor. Four toy trains sped along a network of tracks, hissing and blowing whistles, stopping at their own red and green traffic signals. Along with the other children there, I was fascinated.

Papa took me past the china department. Somehow, my coat sleeve became hooked on the corner of a tablecloth. I didn't realize it and kept walking until I heard crystal and china falling on the hardwood floor. Papa stared in horror and then propelled me into a nearby elevator.

Luckily, no one recognized us. If Papa had had to pay for all those broken pieces, it would have cost a fortune.

* * * * *

The Christmas and New Year holidays passed and 1938 began. It was time to remember the past and to try to see the future. In April I would advance one class and be 12 years old. I would begin to study for my bar mitzvah. I'd been attending a *kheyder* (Talmud Torah school) twice a week after school.

I was also trying hard to stay out of trouble. Boys who were Hitler supporters often waited for me outside school and yelled insults at me. I boiled inside but remembered Papa's instructions and just walked away.

* * * * *

Passover in 1938 fell on my birthday and I stayed at home for the week. On Friday morning, Mutti sent me out early one morning so she could get the Seder meal ready.

Four couples joined us for the two Seder nights. The good talk and good food were very enjoyable. Papa looked like a biblical patriarch in his special clothes.

* * * * *

A few days later, Bernhard picked me up and we walked to Mulack Strasse. Lighting a half cigar he had pulled from his coat, Bernhard took a few puffs and handed the evil smelling thing to me. I was reluctant to try it, but he kept urging me. We both puffed away. I was feeling pretty bad by the time I arrived home. I told Mutti, who looked at me suspiciously, that I was going to bed. When Papa arrived home, I heard him and Mutti talking. I was lying as still as I could so I wouldn't throw up.

Papa came close to my bed and took a whiff. "Mutti said you don't feel well. I think I can help that. Come into my office."

"Oh, I'm all right, Papa. You don't have to."

"Nonsense. That's what I am here for. Come."

He sat down at his desk and took a box of cigars out of a drawer. He cut off the tip of one cigar and handed it to me. While I puffed one end, Papa held a match to the other. With his urging, I puffed away until it was finished. By then I was really feeling awful.

"Now I hope you've learned a lesson. I don't ever want to see you smoke. Understood? Off to bed with you."

Off to bed? I rushed to the toilet and vomited so hard I could hardly make it back to bed. I spent most of the next day in bed, too.

My next report card was not bad, except for Mrs. Radchewsky's comments that I was rotten, foul, loud-mouthed, and lazy; if I didn't improve the following year, she said, she would flunk me. I was not too upset by her threat because I was busy training hard for the upcoming gymnastics competition. Papa would be there.

The big day arrived and Papa was in the front row. I performed extremely well, individually and as a team member. Coach Sonnenfeld praised me profusely and said I was among the best of the competitors he'd trained. On the way home, Papa beamed at me. "Well done, Lutz. Well done! I am proud of you, son." That I'd pleased him made me feel wonderful.

I hadn't realized that Mr. Jacobson was at the competition. But when he saw me later, he shook my hand and said, "You were very, very good, Lutz. At least I taught you something." But his comment couldn't spoil my pleasure at having done so well.

* * * * *

The next week we began preparing for the boxing event to be held the Sunday before vacation started. Prizes would be awarded and there would be races, fun games, gym exercises, and a soccer game between us and children from another home.

The other big event was Dora's arrival to live at the Kapellners'. She had grown up a lot and I was tickled to be with her. Her mother wanted me to look after her, which I certainly didn't mind doing.

* * * * *

The children assembled early on the morning of the competition and received their assignments from Mr. Jacobson. Nora and Mrs. Kapellner supervised the races while Mr. Jacobson and another man were in charge of the eight boxing matches. By the time my turn came, six matches had already been completed. Jochem won his; Heinz and Peter lost theirs. That left only Bubi and me to compete. I won my match, emerging with a bloody nose, a closed eye, and a sore wrist; Bubi won, too.

Before the soccer match began, Dora put ice on my rapidly swelling eye and I was ready. The field looked like a colorful carnival because we were wearing whatever colored clothing we could find. Hotly contested, the game ended in a tie. I won two prizes, which Inge handed out. When she gave me mine, she whispered, "See you next Saturday."

Chapter 7

When I returned home, Papa said he would be away for two days and I must stay with Mutti while he was gone.

At school the next day, Mr. Schreiber had shocking news: "The Nazis are having parades for the next few days and I've heard that Brown Shirts and Black Shirts will attack Jewish establishments. So you all should stay home." I wondered if that's why Papa went out of town.

While Papa was away, Guenther and I decided we wanted to watch the parade on Unter den Linden. In the past, Mutti had insisted that Guenther ask her if I could go out with him. I think she liked him. This time she said yes. Of course, he didn't tell her where we were *really* going! I'd been to parades like this before with Guenther, and no one had ever asked me if I was Jewish. When we arrived where the parade was to be held, there were masses of people. We shoved our way toward the main platform and climbed a lamppost for a better view. The boulevard had been cleared and we could see cars approaching from a distance.

The crowd roared. The first three Mercedes automobiles filled with dignitaries drove up. Then a fourth auto arrived bearing Goebbels and Rudolf Hess and a fifth one with Heinrich Himmler and some others in uniform. The last vehicle to arrive carried Hitler, who was standing and saluting the crowd. The fat one, Hermann Goering, was with him. Hitler's vehicle stopped in front of the platform, and Hitler and Goering joined the other officials already in place on the reviewing stand. The crowd continued to cheer wildly.

As Hitler saluted each unit and flag, many large tanks, guns, and soldiers marching in goose step passed in review and planes roared overhead. We were so close I could see Hitler's lips move as he talked. When the parade had passed, Hitler started his speech. At first he commended the military and praised the fatherland and the National Socialist Party. Then he began condemning the Jews. Guenther and I looked at each other but didn't dare move. The crowd cheered every third sentence Hitler spoke. Finally the speech was over and we could leave.

We hurried toward our homes. Because it was after five o'clock, Mutti would probably be very upset. On the way past Alexanderplatz, we saw SA and SS men who were making some women polish their boots and some men brush their uniforms. A sign on display said "The Jews can do this work best. They are not capable of doing anything else." I felt physically ill.

Guenther grabbed my arm and we walked away in silence. At first we didn't realize we were being followed by two Hitler Youth members. When they caught up to us, they stood in front of us. "It looks like the event at the Alex didn't please you. Either you are Jews or you are against our Fuehrer. We will have to see which it is." We looked around to see if there were more of them. Seeing no one, I nodded to Guenther and we kicked them in the groin; Then while they were doubled over, we kicked them in the face. As they lay on the ground screaming, we ran toward my place. We agreed not to tell anyone about our afternoon. We hoped we wouldn't meet and be recognized by these Hitler Youth later.

After a beating by Mutti for being so late, I was ready for bed, feeling good inside that we had defeated those two thugs.

Father returned from his trip on schedule. I said goodbye to Guenther and Bernhard and returned to the Kapellners' with clean laundry and Mutti's cookies. School was over and we had six weeks of vacation. We were kept busy with various kinds of games in perfect weather. At the lake I learned to swim a little more. And Inge and Doerchen each taught me a bit more about kissing.

* * * * *

When vacation ended and I rode into town to attend school again, I noticed more changes in the city. Guenther and his mother had moved away—no one knew where—after his father was detained. Papa cautioned me to be very careful about what I said and not to ask any questions. He said that many men had been picked up and put in camps and some had been deported to Poland if they were originally from there. He looked very worried, and Mutti always looked as though she had been crying.

I saw some boys I knew well, but they turned away. When I grabbed one and asked him what was the matter, he said, "We can't talk to you anymore. You're a Jew and an enemy of our fatherland. The sooner you leave, the better."

When we questioned our teacher in bar mitzvah class, he told us that the German Reich wanted to get rid of every Jew. He said that suddenly Jews didn't have any friends. Anybody who helped or sympathized with Jews was considered an enemy and dealt with accordingly. He went on to say that he thought everything would get worse, citing some ugly incidents. When I asked him why they were happening, he told me that I should ask my parents. But asking Papa and Mutti was like asking a wall. They just said they'd talked about it "later."

I thought maybe Bernhard could give me some answers, but when I went to his apartment it was empty and a man was whitewashing the apartment walls. The manager looked scared when I asked him where the Tennenbaums were. After looking around to be sure we were alone and no one could hear him, he whispered, "They were all deported to Poland last week. The poor woman, she constantly cried, and the little guy didn't say anything. The Gestapo hauled them out of their beds at night. They were not allowed to take anything. My Ilse hurriedly put a coat around Mrs. Tennenbaum's shoulders. What a disgrace."

I walked away with my head down. Papa was in his office and knew what was bothering me.

"Sit down, Lutz. I know you found out about the Tennenbaums. This is what is going on: Hitler and his followers want to get rid of the Jews in Germany and possibly throughout Europe—maybe even the world. Most businesses have changed hands, some have changed names. As you've seen, Teitz had to sell his department store. It is called Union now. Many more leading Jews have left, and more are trying to leave. Polish Jews are being deported. Restrictions are heavy. I have been able to keep books only for friends since 1936. I was approached by a high SS man to fix his books so he wouldn't have to pay any taxes, but I refused. So you see what has been going on, but I don't know what to do about it.

"One more thing—and Mutti doesn't know about this. Doerchen's mother and Doerchen will probably have to leave for Poland."

"Why? Doerchen isn't Polish!"

"Well, Doerchen's mother has told everybody that Doerchen's father is a traveling salesman and that's why he's never home. But actually, Doerchen hasn't got a father. Her mother was never married and since she was born in a region that is now Poland, both of them are considered Polish. That's why Doerchen's mother is scared. You must not tell anyone what I've told you. Now go take the subway to the Kapellners'."

On the way to the subway, I thought over what Papa had said. Suddenly I felt strange. Were people staring at me? Every time someone in a Nazi uniform walked by, I felt weird. When I arrived at the Kapellners', I tried to be very nonchalant with Dora.

* * * * *

Two weeks went by without incident. Then, on the first Sunday in September, I got into a stupid argument with Peter. I tried to hit him, but he ducked and my fist went through the thin wall! This made me even madder, so I punched Peter in the stomach. He doubled up on the floor. An ambulance was called.

Three hours later, Papa arrived. As we walked in the woods, he asked, "How could you do that to a friend?"

"We had an argument, and I got angry."

"Never, ever get angry. They had to put quite a number of stitches in Peter, and this will cost me a fortune. You injured a human being and a friend. Please avoid fighting."

I promised and he left. For the rest of the day, everyone reminded me how wrong I'd been.

In three days, Peter was released from the hospital and we walked into the woods to talk. He raised his shirt to show me his wound. "See, it doesn't look so bad. I told my parents and your father that it was as much my fault as yours. Let's continue to be friends and promise not to argue about anything in the future." We shook hands, grinning. I was very relieved!

* * * * *

The following Monday, I went to visit Papa's friends on Christinenstrasse. When the door opened, I saw the mother crying. One of the boys said they had been ordered to leave for Poland with only two small suitcases. Their father was Polish, which by Nazi rules meant they and their mother were, too. They were to report to Buelow Platz at noon on Wednesday. Sadly, I said goodbye to the boys and kissed the mother on her cheek.

When Wednesday came, I told Miss Heilbronn I had to leave school at eleven o'clock because my father wanted me for something at home. No one questioned me, so I rushed to Buelow Platz, where a crowd of people was surrounded by SS men. The SS was trying to herd the people onto seven trucks, but the process was very slow. The SS started to shout and beat people while onlookers cheered them on. An SS man standing next to me elbowed me in the ribs, grinning. "Man, these pig Jews, these filthy Polacks. It's about time that they all get thrown out. They deserve nothing better. We don't need such Jew scum." I just listened. Turning around, I saw my friends already on the truck but didn't dare wave at them. The mother nodded slightly, and I nodded back at her and the boys. When trucks were filled to the brim, they slowly moved out. The SS and all the people who had been watching left, so I had a chance to yell goodbye and wave to my friends. In a minute they were gone and I was standing alone, dumbfounded at what had happened.

When I arrived back in Zehlendorf, Mr. Jacobson told me that two men came to take Dora away and that Peter would be leaving the next day. His parents were emigrating to Johannesburg, South Africa, on Saturday. Two other children, the Holzes, would leave next weekend to join their parents in London. In the dorm, we all watched Peter pack. He gave me his soccer ball.

When everyone was in bed and the lights were out, I thought of Dora and how I would miss her. Tears rolled down my cheeks. Peter came over and we sat on my bed for a long time, not saying anything. In the morning, I said goodbye quickly and left for school.

After school, I went home and saw Papa briefly. Mutti was in a state of shock and not able to talk because of what had happened to Dora and so many others. I wandered the streets and took the subway to the west end. Walking around, I saw many signs and placards

announcing that a place was Aryan or had changed into Aryan hands.
Big signs said "Juden *Verboten*" (Jews prohibited) or "Juden *Nicht
Erlaubt*" (Jews not allowed).

* * * * *

The Holzes left on the weekend. Afterward no one wanted to do
anything; we just moped around. When I couldn't stand the silence
any longer, I went out in the cold to walk and think about everything
that had happened. Many children were no longer in school; all my
good friends were gone. Most of the teachers seemed very absent-
minded, although Mr. Schreiber was the same as always. My *kheyder*
teaching had stopped some time before because many *rebbe*s had left
the country. My cousins Kurt and Roeschen had left for a kibbutz in
Palestine after staying at our home for three days.

In the city, the air felt charged with electricity. SA, SS, and many other
uniformed people were everywhere. The *Schupos* (regular police) were
beginning to add swastika insignias on their uniforms. Nazi flags flew.
All the non-Jews who used to be my friends turned away when they saw
me. Their parents just looked at me and said nothing. In stores and
shops, the clerks were uneasy—no more joking or laughing.

The worst were the rallies and meetings where there was much
shouting and many speeches, always on the same theme: "These dirty
Jews are to blame for all the trouble in our fatherland." It wasn't just
people in the lower social classes who believed this rhetoric. Many
upper class and society people shouted and cheered with the crowd. A
tremendous hatred radiated from these gatherings, and it was increasing at an alarming rate.

* * * * *

For the next several days, I didn't return to the Kapellners' right
after school. Instead, I walked around the city, observing everything.
Sometimes I gave the Hitler salute to avoid any trouble. I began to
think I should have left with the *aliyah* when my cousin Lutz went to
Palestine two years ago.

One morning on the subway, the man next to me was reading a newspaper, *Der Voelkische Beobachter* (the People's Observer). He looked at

me. "Can you imagine that, little one? A Polack Jew-boy fired two shots at the Legation Counsel Ernst von Rath and mortally injured him."

I nodded. "How do they know it's a Pole?"

He replied, "That is absolutely clear. This guy is seventeen years old, his name is Herschel Grynspan, and the French say he is a Pole. It happened in Paris, you see."

He kept reading. "I wonder what ruckus this will cause. When Frankfurter shot the Nazi Gustloff in February 1936, it caused anti-Jewish action."

Coach Sonnenfeld was waiting for me at the school entrance. "Posener, go to your classroom right away. I don't know if we'll keep the school open today." Only six or seven students had arrived. In a few minutes, the principal entered, whispered to the teachers, and walked out. Mrs. Radchewsky turned to the class. "All right, pupils, there will be no school today. I expect everybody to be here tomorrow morning. Please go straight home; don't linger in the streets."

When I arrived home, Mutti opened the door. "Lutz, I don't think you should be here. Your father is gone—I don't know where. Our renter was picked up by her niece for the day. Here, I'll give you something to eat for the trip."

I returned to the Kapellners'.

* * * * *

Classes were held the next day, even though some children didn't attend. On the way back on the subway, I read a newspaper article stating that the young Pole who shot the German was arrested and made a statement that he did it because he felt bitter toward Germany. A few days earlier, his parents, a sister and a brother, and 17,000 other Jews had been deported to Poland. (It had been decided that because they took up space in Germany, the Poles must leave the country. But in October 1938, Poland stopped accepting many deported Poles, leaving them nowhere to go.)

The article hinted that retaliations would be made against all Jews. Goebbels was quoted as saying that it was intolerable for Germany to have thousands upon thousands of Jews controlling entertainment, collecting rent, and owning property that legally belonged to

Germans; that German citizens were being shot outside Germany; and that the problem had to stop and would be dealt with accordingly. Reading all this, I began to understand the situation and be scared.

When I arrived at the Kapellners', I gave the newspaper to Mrs. Kapellner. Her husband wasn't home and neither was Mr. Jacobson. Later, while we were having dinner, a neighbor came in. "I think you should know that the German diplomat shot in Paris has died," he said. "You should lock all the doors." He left hurriedly.

The night passed without incident at the Kapellners'. But on the subway in the morning, many people were talking about the burning of synagogues and looting of stores. I heard one man say, "It's only fair. A Polish Jew killed our man, so we must take revenge."

I got off at the next stop and walked along the street. Mobs were watching hoodlums throw stones into Jewish store windows. Then the merchandise was dragged into the street and torn apart. Wherever I looked, small bands were destroying property and looting. Bystanders cheered whenever a window was broken.

As I approached the Fasanenstrasse Synagogue, I saw firemen standing and watching as flames spewed forth from the building. A huge crowd also watched. Farther down the street, groups of men in rows of five, surrounded by SA and SS men with rifles, were being marched toward the train station. Edging close to one of the groups, I asked what was going on. "Shhh. We've been arrested and are being taken into custody somewhere."

A voice yelled at me. "You, peewee, get away from the Jews. Leave that rabble alone." I walked away, and when I'd gone three blocks further, I smelled smoke and saw flames shooting up into the sky. It must be the Oranienburger Strasse Synagogue, I thought.

Before I could reach the school, I passed by Dragoner and Grenadier Strassen. Furniture was being thrown out of windows and houses burned. The Jewish residents were huddled in one spot, looking very frightened. From the windows of a little *shul* that was also a butcher shop, flames were shooting in the air. Two SA men carried four or five holy scrolls from the shop and threw them on the ground. The scrolls were stomped on and then set afire. I couldn't believe what I was seeing.

An SA man nearby grinned at me. "Look how nice this all burns. Here, take this match and light the other end."

"No, no, you do this much better than I could."

He laughed as the Torahs were burning. I felt sick to my stomach and left, glad he didn't realize I was a Jew.

A block away from the school I saw SA men throwing furniture and books out the windows. I didn't go any closer but continued to Mutti's. She was horrified when she saw me. "What are you doing in town? These hordes have been at it since last night. Everyone is insane and you walk the streets?"

"But, Mutti, I only found out on my way to school. Where is Papa?"

"Papa is hiding someplace. Go back to the Kapellners' right away and stay there until someone calls and tells you the school is open again."

When I reached Zehlendorf, only Jochem, Jacob, and the three Kapellner women were left there. All the other children had been taken home by their parents. I did not attend school for the next two weeks. At the end of the second week, I returned to school, but the teacher sent me back to Papa and Mutti's. We prepared to leave Germany.

Chapter 8

On my last day of school in Berlin, I got off the subway at 7:30 as usual. Throwing my bag of books over a shoulder, I showed my pass to the Friedrichstrasse exit guard. It was still dark outside and very cold. I walked up Alexanderplatz and Prenzlauer Allee. A classmate joined me.

We talked about who would be missing from school today and how our friends Mia's and Herbert's parents had been picked up Sunday night. No one knew where they had been taken.

"I'm in real trouble," I told him. "Jochem, one of the guys where I was staying, asked me two weeks ago if his brother Heinz could borrow my two suitcases because he had to move. He promised to return them in four days, so I let him take them. But Jochem told me that Heinz lost them. Now my mother wants to know where they are. I told her I forgot them and would bring them back next week. Maybe I can come up with a good story by then."

"Lutz, you always seem to find trouble!"

As we opened the door to the classroom, tiny Miss Reich, the principal, was very disturbed. Inside the classroom, only a third of the class had arrived.

Miss Heilbronn, our teacher, saw us. "Don't sit down, Lutz. Your mother wants you to come home immediately, and you are not to stop anywhere."

I rushed home, through the big portal doors, and up two flights of stairs. Mutti peered through the peephole when I rang the bell.

"Lutz, you don't have your suitcases."

"I didn't know that I would be coming back so early today."

"I don't think you even have them anymore. Your Papa is home and wants you in his office."

I went into his office, shook Papa's hand and sat down.

"Lutz, we are going shopping and I don't want any smart remarks while we do. We are being forced to leave Germany. Probably just the two of us will go tonight. For now, trust me. I will explain later."

I was puzzled, but the thought of a shopping spree with Papa (who was usually very generous) excited me. People we met on our previous outings always greeted Papa with respect.

Papa then turned to Mutti. "Cilla, you had all day to decide what you want to do—come with us or stay here."

"I can't leave my belongings—yours too—my money in the bank, all our valuables."

"I haven't worked in a year and half. My money has been eaten up. Even if we sell what we have, that money won't last long. What will we live on if we stay here?"

"Can't we use my money?"

"Cilla, Cilla, your bank account has been closed for over a year. Surely the Nazis won't reopen it. And who would buy what we have, knowing it belongs to Jews? One of these days, I'll be picked up and put in a camp to be forgotten. Haven't you heard what is being said: 'Jews are our calamity'? I must leave this city and this country. I was born here and have fought for my country, but I am not wanted here anymore. I would only choke slowly to death. Your decision will not prevent my leaving."

"What about the boy, Kurt?"

"Of course, he'll come with me." You will have to decide for yourself. We'll be back about four o'clock. We have to leave at five o'clock sharp, so if you are coming, be packed and ready by half past four."

I said goodbye to Mutti and we left.

First we went to the Salamander shoe store. After trying on quite a few shoes, we finally found the right ones. Papa paid with a check made out for a somewhat larger amount than the cost of the shoes.

We went on to Herti, the underwear store, where we bought two sets of undergarments for each of us. Again, Papa overpaid by check and received quite a bit of paper money in change.

At noon we took a taxi to Aschinger Restaurant. The waiter greeted Papa and showed us to a corner table. We ordered the house specialty—

pigs' feet in gelatin with sauerkraut and puree of peas, and fresh rolls.
I had a nonalcoholic malt beer and Papa had a regular beer. After this
wonderful meal, Papa relaxed with a cigarette and the waiter brought
the bill.

We were soon off to Wertheim, a very large department store. I
loved the store's aromas of perfumes and colognes and the fine
leathers and clothing. The toy section was fantastic, and the escalators
were so exciting. I was fitted for a new suit, two shirts, and a sweater.
After the tailor adjusted the trouser cuffs, Papa told me to put on the
new suit and the new underwear and socks, too. I put all my old
clothes in a bag and sat down to wait for Papa's return.

Over an hour later, he came back with two new suitcases. I put the
rest of my new clothes in one suitcase. We left the store through the
back door. In the alley, Papa threw our bags of old clothing into a
garbage bin, looking around to make sure we weren't seen. We arrived
back home by taxi.

Mutti opened the door. Her face was swollen and her eyes were red.
"Kurt, I can't leave all my things, and I don't feel well. I am not strong
enough. Maybe Lutz can stay with me until you get settled and send
for us."

"Send for you! What do you think we are doing? This isn't a picnic or luxury boat ride. We are leaving Germany, where all the Jewish
people have been persecuted since these maniacs rose to power.

"Lea was right when she said on her deathbed 'Kurt, take the boy
and leave Germany. Bad times are coming.' I am just sorry I didn't listen to her then, but better late than never. Of course, the boy is coming with me! I won't leave him at the mercy of these murderers. Who
knows what they'll come up with next?"

"Kurt, don't shout. Someone might hear you."

"I don't care. For the last time, are you coming?"

Sobbing, she said, "I can't. I just can't."

"Okay. Lutz, say goodbye and let's go."

Tearfully, I said goodbye to Mutti, who was crying uncontrollably.
Papa pulled my arm. " Go downstairs and wait. I'll be right there."

I heard him tell Cilla goodbye and that he'd let her know where we
were. He came slowly down the stairs. We went out to the corner to
wait for the streetcar that would take us to Potsdamer Bahnhof (the

train station). I turned to look at the windows of our apartment and saw Mutti at the window, holding a handkerchief. On the streetcar, I turned around again to see Mutti one more time, still standing at the window. The streetcar rounded the corner. Papa was silent.

At the train station, I watched the suitcases while Papa bought the tickets. At the gate, our tickets were taken as a man in civilian clothing scrutinized us. "Going to Cologne, are you?"

"Yes, my son and I, to visit my sister who is quite ill."

"How old are you, boy?"

"Twelve and a half, sir."

The ticket taker indicated that the train would leave at 6:14 from platform five. We walked to the platform and had seventeen minutes until departure. I told Papa that I didn't like being questioned at the gate and he felt the same way. We entered the puffing, hissing train and found our way to a compartment.

Suddenly, a group of eight men walked toward our car. Papa grasped my shoulder so hard it hurt me. The men appeared to be civilians. They were accompanied by two other civilians who seemed to be Gestapo (secret state police), easily recognizable by their clothing. The eight civilians boarded our car and knocked on the door of our compartment, asking if the seats next to us were empty. When my father replied yes, they entered and sat among us, keeping their hats on, which in Germany was not polite.

The whistle blew and the train moved out while the men sat stiffly and stared into space. I tried to read but felt very intimidated. The conductor came by to take tickets from us and paper slips from the men. When the conductor left, one of the men asked Papa if he was going to Cologne. Papa replied that he and I were indeed going to Cologne and that I was his son.

The man relaxed noticeably. "Thank God. We did not dare speak because we thought your son might have been a Hitler Youth. He doesn't look like you."

"You can rest easy. We are going to Cologne, away from all this—as far as possible."

With a collective sigh, they all took their hats off. To my shocked amazement, they had no hair!

Their spokesman said they had just been released from Buchenwald. He pointed at his head. "This is one thing they do. We aren't supposed to talk about all they did to us in the camp. We were told the Gestapo has very long arms, that we're free now and should forget about what happened. We are worn out, physically and emotionally. We just want to get home to our families."

I listened with my mouth open, not understanding all of it. I was suddenly very sleepy.

We arrived in Cologne in the morning and said goodbye to our compartment mates. We saw some of them greeted with joy and tears by wives and children. Papa and I walked to a boarding house just a few blocks from the station.

The door was opened by a chubby middle-aged woman who said, "Come in, please. I am Mrs. Berg. Your room is ready. I'll show it to you and then you can have breakfast in the refectory."

The room was large and bright with one bed, a table with two chairs, an armoire, and a small dresser. A bathroom was down the hall, and a public bath two streets away. Papa explained that we would have to live very carefully and this might not be our final lodging. Downstairs, Mrs. Berg served us breakfast, and Papa smoked a cigarette as he told her about our trip and the men we met.

"Yes," she said. "There are still more in Buchenwald and Dachau and some in Oranienburg. Many people from Germany and Austria have been here for some time. It takes money for papers and a guide, and many have been cheated or misled. Some are stranded here. There are spies and also Gestapo and SS *Spitzels* (informers) everywhere."

We followed Mrs. Berg's directions to the Jewish Committee office, shivering because of the cold. As we approached the office, crowds of people were speaking many different dialects. Papa registered our names and we left to find some addresses where there might be people who could help us. As I waited for him outside one of the buildings, two men walked by and one said, "Welcome to the human refugee disaster area!" At the last address we visited, Papa found two people who might be able to help us later.

It was late afternoon when we wearily walked back to Mrs. Berg's home. After eating some of her delicious soup and fresh rye bread, we went to our room and were soon asleep.

* * * * *

The next day, Papa planned to show me the city, but first we had to check with the committee. We found nothing new there. We walked along many very old streets. The steeple of the Cologne Cathedral towered above the buildings. A tourist information pamphlet indicated the city dates back to 50 A.D. The cathedral was started in 1248 and finally finished in 1880. A tremendous architectural accomplishment, it was 443 feet long and 282 feet wide, and its spires rose 512 feet.

The large synagogue in a newer section of the city had been burned down on *Kristallnacht* (Night of Broken Glass), when looters and arsonists had free rein. As we wandered around the cathedral, Papa told me there was nothing wrong with visiting places of other faiths; it broadened one's mind and gave one a better understanding of fellow humans.

The Rhine River was crowded with barges loaded with coal, grain, steel, and other commercial products. Most of the Rhineland was politically left—Die Rote Front (The Red Front). Papa said he didn't know whether that faction was any better than the Nazi movement.

After an exciting day and dinner at Mrs. Berg's table, we were ready for a good night's sleep. I was getting used to Papa's very loud snoring!

In the morning, a number of new people, refugees like us, sat at the breakfast table. After breakfast, Papa checked in with the committee, which still had nothing for us, so we continued our sightseeing. We saw the Rathaus (city hall) and union guild buildings. In the Glockengasse, near the building where the famous 4711 Cologne is made, we ate lunch at a little restaurant.

* * * * *

The weekend passed rather quickly because Papa had bought a chess set and some reading material. Papa used to win all our games but after much practice and some children's tournaments, I was better competition for him.

During the week, I was free to wander around while Papa went about his business, but I was cautioned not to say anything important to anyone. I wandered into two toy stores and a department store, where I rode the escalator up and down and up and down. Naturally, I was told to leave! I walked on to the red lantern district. As in Berlin, prostitutes in evening gowns sat in windows. When men passed by, the girls tapped on the window and invited them in with smiles.

I saw many brown-shirted Nazis and men with floppy hats, obviously Gestapo, especially in areas where refugees were milling around. I reported this to Papa. He told me it was becoming uncomfortable for us here and we would leave soon for Aachen, Germany, where there was a place for us to stay. On Thursday evening, Papa talked with Mrs. Berg. He handed her some money, and I knew we would be leaving in the morning.

*****

It was cold the next morning at five o'clock when Papa woke me. "Come on, little man. It is time to move on."

Mrs. Berg served Papa coffee and me hot chocolate, and she had fixed a sack of sandwiches for us to eat on the train. In the cold and dark, we walked briskly to the station. The streets were almost deserted.

Few people were in the station, but those unpleasant men were everywhere. We boarded and went immediately to a compartment, sitting away from the window so we didn't attract attention. We ate the sandwiches as the train pulled out with a toot and a hiss. All along the way, we stopped at small towns to pick up people, arriving at Aachen in the late afternoon.

We were met outside the station by a man sent by Mr. Schnitzer, Papa's contact. His old Opel automobile coughed and sputtered as it plowed through the snow reluctantly. It took us past fields with heavy blankets of snow and stopped at a large two-story farmhouse. The front door opened and an elderly man motioned for us to come in.

He introduced himself as Yup Schnitzer and told us the house rules. "I can keep you here for only a week. My son will return in two days, and you can arrange your trip with him. Please don't wander around too much; keep out of sight. The Gestapo stops by sometimes and when they do, you will have to stay upstairs and be quiet. The Nazis are everywhere because we are close to the border. Now let me show you to your room."

The room was bright but quite small. What was I going to do all day? Papa went downstairs to give Mr. Schnitzer some money toward our stay. When he returned, he emphasized that I was to keep my complaints to myself. A modest lunch was brought up: dark bread with butter, some cold cuts, a small piece of cheese, milk, and coffee.

I stared at it ruefully.

"I know, Lutz, but we'll eat whatever there is. The Schnitzers will give us signals to tell us what's happening. One knock means food, two knocks means be quiet, three knocks means be very still, and four knocks means danger."

After lunch, Papa showed me the door at the end of the hall where we would go through a closet and up some stairs to hide if the need arose. We didn't unpack very much because we had to be ready to leave on a moment's notice.

The day passed and, somehow, the weekend. It was cold outside so we stayed in bed to keep warm. The food remained somewhat meager, even though Papa was paying quite a bit for our stay.

Monday afternoon a car drove up. We heard car doors slam, and through the window in our room we saw two young men approach the house. We heard voices and footfalls, the sound of people coming upstairs, silence, then a gentle knock.

Papa opened the door. "Heinz, Jochem, I am glad you've made it. We are still waiting for Roeschen, and Mr. Schnitzer's son will be here tomorrow. We'll be able to make plans then. You must be tired from your trip, so have a good night's rest and we'll talk tomorrow."

* * * * *

It was snowing in the morning. Before long, we heard a car stop outside. Apparently it was Mr. Schnitzer's son. Papa and the two visitors went downstairs. When Papa returned, he told me we would leave Thursday evening and not to ask any questions.

In the afternoon another car arrived. A pretty woman got out and walked toward the front door. Papa warned me against using last names, then went downstairs to help Roeschen get settled.

When he returned, he sat down and explained our situation. He said that the anti-Semitism had gotten so bad in Berlin we had to leave or we would be picked up, put in a ghetto or camp, or even killed. The Nazis wouldn't give us permission to legally leave the country. When Papa made arrangements to stay in Cologne, he had no idea Mutti would want to remain in Berlin.

He bought the items we needed for the trip on credit, and he made out checks for more than the purchase price to have money for our trip. Mutti would pay our debts with gold and silver. That way, we would be able to return if we wished.

He had to keep his plans a secret so as not to raise any suspicions. Although everything had gone well so far, we weren't safe yet.

Now that Heinz, Jochem, Roeschen, and we were all together, we would try to cross the border illegally into Belgium. Papa indicated that leaving the country was an expensive undertaking. In some way, Gestapo people also were helping us, and that made the cost even higher.

To cross the border we would have to walk a long way and be very careful. If the Belgian or German gendarmes caught us, we would be sent back to Berlin. I didn't want to think of what would happen to us then.

Looking at me thoughtfully, Papa continued. "For tonight, you will carry my silver pocket watch and silver cigarette case, which my papa gave me for my bar mitzvah. At your bar mitzvah I will give them to you to keep."

Papa carried his gold watch and cigarette case. We opened the backs of both watches and put a twenty-mark bill in each. We filled both cigarette cases and I carried some matches.

"Think about what I've told you tonight and ask any questions you must before we leave here. While we travel, I don't want any questions, and you must not start talking to anyone at any time."

Papa told me that our destination was Brussels and I was to learn French and Flemish in school there. This was disappointing news. I had thought there would be no more school.

* * * * *

The next morning, we ate a modest breakfast and then were joined by Roeschen, Heinz, and Jochem. We would begin our journey tonight with Papa leading, followed by me, Heinz, Roeschen, and finally Jochem. The snow was quite deep, and it would be very cold.

The day passed slowly. At six o'clock, we ate our last meal for a while. We thanked Mr. Schnitzer and piled into the car. We rode in utter silence. Mr. Schnitzer's son left us in front of a large house. We quickly entered and stood waiting in a large living room. A door at the far end opened and two men and a woman entered. One of the men looked like a member of the Gestapo. The woman took Roeschen into another room to search her. The Gestapo guy searched each of us in turn, and we took everything out of our pockets.

"Anybody have any extra money hidden? You can take only ten marks each." Naturally, we shook our heads no. He left.

Roeschen came back, very distressed. Another Gestapo man entered. "You will be here for about an hour. Sit down. You may smoke, and here are some magazines." He left, too.

Roeschen whispered to my Papa, "Would you believe it, Kurt? I had to take everything off, bend over, and spread my legs, so the woman could search me. I felt like a whore." Papa assured her it would pass.

The Gestapo entered the room again with a new person. "This is your guide. He knows the way and you can trust him. He does not speak any German. Good luck to you all!"

We followed the guide, and before long we were in a cold, dark forest where the snow was so deep it was difficult to walk. My feet were wet and I was miserable. Suddenly we stopped. We couldn't see the guide.

"Spread out!" Papa warned. "The guide has left. I think he saw gendarmes!"

Papa ran and I followed as fast as I could. We hid behind some trees, breathing heavily and shaking.

Fifteen minutes passed and the guide reappeared, motioning us to follow him. We left the cover of the trees and continued through the woods. After an interminable time, the guide stopped for us to rest. It was 3:45 in the morning and we still had more than two hours of walking to do. I wondered more than once if we would make it.

We were all dragging. I asked Papa every five minutes how much longer we had to go. He answered with patience, although he must have been as tired as I was.

Finally we saw a clearing ahead. The guide waved goodbye and left. We walked another hundred yards toward an embankment and crouched down. "Keep your heads down," said Papa. This is the border and patrols come by constantly."

"Kurt, it's six o'clock. Where is the car?" Roeschen asked.

"I don't know. We'll have to wait. Be quiet. Heads down. I hear voices."

Boots crunched in the snow and strange words rode on the air. Belgian gendarmes marched past without seeing us. After five minutes went by, we heard a car and saw its headlights. The car stopped nearby and the headlights went out. A flashlight blinked SOS in Morse code—our signal. We hurried toward it and got into a limousine. It glided silently away. After we'd driven fifty yards, the lights were turned on and we sped toward Brussels.

When I woke up, it was daylight. We passed a policeman wearing a funny oval-shaped hat; we were truly in Brussels! The limousine worked its way through the traffic and halted in front of a building. Motioning us to get out, the driver left without saying anything. Brussels was no warmer than Germany, I discovered. The streets were awash with melted snow.

Inside the building, which was the Jewish Committee headquarters, voices spoke German with what I thought was a heavy Austrian accent. I heard Yiddish, some French, and another language I could not understand. A woman came toward us and spoke in German: "Come with me. You need a warm drink, and you must be hungry. The boy looks dead."

Although cold and clammy, I was more relieved to be out of Germany and to be among friendly faces. While we sipped a hot drink, Papa explained to me that of the 500 marks he had paid for the two of us to cross the border, the Gestapo men, the farmhouse owner, and the guide each got a share. If the Belgian Border Patrol had caught us, and taken us back, those men would have gotten a share, too. Then we would have been sent back to Berlin and would have had to raise another 500 marks to escape again.

Chapter 9

That December day in Brussels at the committee headquarters, we had our first encounter with the Belgians. The hot chocolate we were given was really delicious. Everyone was waiting for living assignments. We left to find a place to stay, but first we went to buy some new clothes; what we had worn on our perilous flight from Germany was in tatters.

I had noticed several boys look at me and snicker. Papa explained that in Belgium, boys over twelve didn't wear short pants—they wore long pants or golf trousers or knickers.

At the store, Papa found a sweater and a pair of gray trousers with long, belled pant legs. I felt so good when I put them on; they fit perfectly. The old clothes were thrown away.

We found a pair of solid leather shoes that also fit well. "Do you want to keep them on?" said the clerk.

I didn't understand what he was saying, but I signaled that he could throw my old ones away. Walking in my newly laced shoes, I joined Papa who was also in new clothing.

Out on the street, Papa followed some directions on a piece of paper. In a large window of one building sat a very fat woman. We entered and Papa and the woman conversed in Yiddish. I gathered that she had one room with two beds, which we, Jochem, and Heinz could have for only two weeks. We returned to the committee office to receive the money for our two-week stay and then went to the city hall to register as foreigners and obtain a permit to stay in Belgium.

The city hall was a very drab building, not much different from the official buildings in Germany. With the paperwork finally completed and evening approaching, the four of us looked for a restaurant along streets that looked different in the light from the street lamps. Thanks to Papa's modest abilities in speaking French, we were able to get a large table and order from the menu: rabbit with potatoes and other vegetables, soup, salad, coffee, and dessert. All this for four people cost only six francs and fifty cents!

While we waited for the food, Papa outlined our plans. Tomorrow we would return to the committee office to get more information about living and working conditions in Brussels. He said that although the Belgian government allowed us to stay there, many people were opposed to the idea. They resented our taking up space in their country. Some Belgians were anti-Semites and anti-Germans whose hatred dated back to the war of 1914–18.

Having eaten hardly anything all day, we eagerly devoured everything, finishing off with pie and coffee, milk for me, and cigarettes for them. When we were full, we realized how tired we were and we left for our room.

When Papa opened the door to our room, there wasn't much to see—two beds separated by a table, two chairs, and a wardrobe. We had no heat, but we managed to sleep pretty well.

In the morning, Papa said we should take our packed suitcases with us to the committee house because he had a bad feeling about staying in that room. The woman who had helped us the day before gave Papa directions to where we might find a better place. Jochem and Heinz left before we did. All day Papa and I walked up and down streets without finding anything, but finally we arrived at a very crowded meeting place where everyone was speaking either Yiddish or German with wild hand movements. It was pretty comical and even Papa laughed.

Papa told me to stand near a counter while he moved around the room. Food, as well as writing pads and other helpful items, was available. The room was warm and my eyes drooped, even though there was no place to sit and fall asleep. My eyes flew open when I felt a hand on my head.

"Ah, look at all these curls. Such a pretty boy. Greetings, little one," said a large woman who looked Austrian.

A well-dressed man was with her. Just then, Papa returned and rescued me, and we sat down at a table with three men. I made sure my suitcase was between my legs because I felt there might be thieves in the room. Papa ordered vegetable soup, potatoes, a small piece of meat, green beans, and milk. When we finished, Papa smoked and talked with the men. One man, who'd been in Brussels for over a year, said there was no way to leave without money, connections, and a relative in another country who would be a sponsor. He felt refugees were unwelcome in Belgium, and he yearned to return to Germany.

Papa looked at him. "Going home is a dream! That madman and his cronies won't let you return to the fatherland. They want to conquer all of Europe, one country at a time. No one will raise a finger. Hitler blames us for everything that happens and has conned the church into thinking the same. Those who protest will be done away with. They'll build more camps, deport more people, and poison the minds of the rest of the world. We have to leave Europe because people in every European country are so aroused they will persecute us, too. Look at the refugees in Holland, Belgium, and France who can't go anyplace. And that's only the west. I hate to think of Poland and other eastern places.

"The best thing is to sit tight here and see what happens. My boy and I have to find a place to stay and then he is going back to school. And he must get ready for his bar mitzvah."

"Papa, you mean I have to go to school?"

"Of course. You have to stay in school at least until you are fourteen. Then maybe we can find you a place to apprentice so you can learn a profession."

This was not very welcome news for me!

When we arrived back at our room, Jochem and Heinz announced they'd found a place of their own and would move soon. Two days later, Papa also found a place for us to move to on December 29. The cost was twenty-five francs for a small room. The owners had a butcher shop in the back where they made sausages.

On Christmas Day, Papa was invited out for a drink and came home rather drunk. While Heinz and Jochem laughed at me, I tried to remove Papa's clothes as he lay on the bed. Twice he giggled and pulled the tablecloth off the table, throwing everything to the floor. I decided to leave the things on the floor and get some sleep.

Each day before we moved, Papa took a pillowcase and begged in stores for food, clothing, and bedding. Every day he came back with a full case—new clothing, two blankets, five sheets and pillowcases, and some good food. I loved the Belgian bread—white with raisins, it tasted like cake. It reminded me of Mutti's challah. I wondered how she was but didn't want to bother Papa by asking him.

* * * * *

Two days after Heinz and Jochem left, Papa and I moved, too. The day was very cold, and we had to stop many times as we walked to the new place, carrying all our belongings. When we arrived at the new place, a woman greeted us. "Good morning, Mr. Posener. And that is your son, naturally."

"Yes, good morning."

I nodded my head and we started up the stairs, stopping to rest on each floor. The mansard, as this little place was called, was located on the highest level of a five-floor apartment house. Papa opened the door to a small room that contained one bed close to the wall, a potbelly stove, a chair, a small table, an armoire, and a small nightstand. There was no electricity, and we would save our candles to be used only for emergencies. Whatever needed to be done would be done in daylight.

Papa was matter-of-fact. "I know it is small and cold, but it is the best I can do. This will be a hard teacher of life for you, but let's make the best of the situation. The better our outlook, the easier it will be to survive these bad times. The day after tomorrow we'll get you settled in school. You'll learn French and Flemish, which will be a great help to us."

Concerned that I would not understand what they were teaching if I didn't speak the language, Papa assured me that I'd learn the language in no time.

It was cold and I was very anxious about school. But the end of the year 1938 passed quietly.

* * * * *

Papa walked me the short distance to school. It was just like the one in Berlin but without a synagogue. After registering me with the

Apartment house in Brussels where Lutz and his father lived from
December 1938 to May 1940

principal, Papa left and I was taken to my classroom. The teacher greeted me in German. "Good morning. It is very nice to have you in my class." The teacher, a tall man about Papa's age, pointed to a bench for me to sit on. Speaking first to the class in French and then translating for me, he said the boys were to help me. At the first recess, I stayed by myself, just looking around, until a boy spoke to me. The teacher interpreted, "This is Paul and he'd like to be your friend. Go with him to the cafeteria and he'll show you around. Classes stop at 11:45 for lunch in the cafeteria, and then you go home. You will then come back for the afternoon session, 1:45 to 4:00."

Paul introduced me to many boys, and at lunchtime he led me to a building two blocks away. In the basement, benches and tables lined three walls. Tables with big pots and plates were along the fourth wall. Women served the food and seconds were allowed if anything was left over. However, nothing was left by the time I was ready for more. As we left after lunch, a giggling girl smiled and said goodbye to me. Paul winked at me. We then left for our homes; he lived a block away from me. I made him understand that I'd pick him up on the way back to school.

I ran the rest of the way home, pretty happy at how the situation had turned out. I told Papa everything as he cooked his meal on the potbelly stove. Before long, it was time to return to school, and Paul was waiting to walk back with me.

* * * * *

The first week went well. I was able to make simple requests and discovered the trick of eating fast and getting seconds before the food was all gone. When I arrived home, I would eat again. "A growing boy," said Papa. Papa found a Hebrew teacher who would instruct me for my bar mitzvah. By the end of March, I could speak and read French quite well, although writing was more difficult. I liked French and could converse with Paul, who was a tremendous help.

When I was not working with the Hebrew teacher, Papa took me to a café and I played chess. I was very good, but he wanted me to become even better so we could play in tournaments. He promised to teach me billiards later.

Newspaper articles indicated that conditions in Germany were not good. Mutti confirmed that in her letters. She sent a big package of bedding to us and wrote to an aunt in New York. The aunt agreed to prepare an affidavit to make it possible for the three of us to immigrate to the United States, as she had done for twelve other relatives. Papa had written to an uncle of Mutti's in Colorado, and he sent a ten dollar bill in one of his letters. That was a feast day for us.

* * * * *

Two weeks after my birthday in April 1939 was my big day. Papa had met the great rabbi of Brussels, and my bar mitzvah would take place in the big synagogue—quite an honor. I was so nervous, I constantly had to make trips to the bathroom. Papa had bought me a new navy blue suit for the occasion. His gifts to me were the silver cigarette holder and silver pocket watch his father had given him—the ones I had carried across the border.

We took the streetcar on that sunny, warm day. In the synagogue, I saw my Hebrew teacher and other people we knew. It was a Saturday and the place was filled. Papa and I sat in the front row. The reading of the Torah started and then I stood next to the rabbi and cantor, reciting texts I'd learned in the last year. My singing of the psalms wasn't too good because my voice was changing, but I managed to complete my part. The Rabbi spoke from the high pulpit as I stood in front of him, gazing upward. He spoke about brothers and their keepers and helping a fellow Jew. Then he congratulated me and Papa, gave the benediction, and handed me a prayer book, a tallis (prayer shawl), and a pair of phylacteries. I stuttered a thank-you.

After the service, Papa and I shook many hands and received many mazel tovs (best wishes). Papa and I and some friends went to a café where a big feast had been prepared for us. I received many presents and some money. I was so elated!

At home I read a letter from Mutti and one from relatives in Palestine. Father smiled at me. "Well, Lutz, I'll bet you're glad it's over. You did very well and I am proud of you, son. Now you have a year to decide what you want to learn when school is finished next year. Which reminds me—you never bring any homework home."

"I don't have any. I am not familiar with the language yet."

"For math, you need to be familiar? Those are figures; you're already familiar with figures!"

The next day when I was at recess, I saw Papa speaking with my teacher. When I arrived home at noon he said, "No homework? That was some fib you told me. You've been telling the teacher you don't understand, my little con artist. From now on there will be homework every day, and I will supervise it. Also, it is time you join a scout group, the Hanoar Hatzioni."

On Thursday, we walked to the group's meeting place in the middle of the city. As we entered, I heard boys and girls laughing and talking. Willie, a tall young man with horn-rimmed glasses, greeted us. He led a group and was also the director of the section. After some discussion it was decided that I would be placed in a group of refugees led by Karl, who was twenty-six years old. The group met twice a week and took trips on Sundays.

After Papa left, Willie introduced me and told everyone I could speak French and Flemish. Most of the section members were from Germany. Karl began to speak about Zionism, Palestine, and Hitler. It was very interesting as I hadn't heard anybody speaking about these subjects. When the hour-long meeting was over, everyone headed home in groups except me; no one lived near me, so I walked home alone.

*   *   *   *   *

Very early on Sunday, we gathered at the meeting place. Most of the boys were wearing khaki-colored shirts and shorts and what Karl described as scout hats. The shirts bore all sorts of insignias. A half hour later we started out, marching through the city in pairs or threesomes. After an hour and a half, we arrived at some huge playgrounds. Many groups sat together talking, singing or playing games. We stored our gear—mostly knapsacks—while the four group leaders conferred and made decisions on the day's program.

Various contests began and continued through the day, stopping only for noonday lunch—some of the boys shared their food with me. I had so much fun I hoped the day would never end.

*   *   *   *   *

Each day in school we sang for a whole hour, rehearsing the entire score of the "Blue Danube." I felt like an idiot and only mouthed the words.

In the scouts, I had been changed to Willie's group and had met his brother Eugen, a nice guy. I was learning a lot about Judaism, Zionism, and Palestine's history, as well as about kibbutzims, the Diaspora, the pioneering Hechaluz movement, and the *aliyah*. By vacation time, I was well versed in all of these subjects. Wearing the uniform Papa bought me, I looked like a real scout.

Only one new girl had joined the organization; she was from Vienna and she was gorgeous. Of course, I fell in love immediately, but she only liked me.

Willie announced a big two-week jamboree to be held in Dinant-Anhee in northern France. The cost was ninety francs. Papa said I could use the money I received at my bar mitzvah and suggested I could earn the rest. Through a friend of a friend of Papa's, I was hired as a page at the Grand Hotel for three weeks after school ended. The job paid twenty francs a week plus tips with a uniform provided. I was ecstatic!

Most of the scouts were going to the jamboree, so Papa suggested that I hitchhike with some of them. He said that motorists frequently give rides to scouts. So all concerns seemed to have been addressed.

Before I left, Papa took me to a big Belgian restaurant in another section of the city. Refugees didn't frequent the place, and no one knew us there. Seated in a corner away from the other diners, he talked very seriously to me. A letter from Mutti stated that the situation in Germany had gotten much worse. Papa reminded me of the synagogue burnings; the Nueremberg Laws, which had been extended to the annexed territories; and the exclusion of Jews from certain hotels and from dining and pullman cars on trains. Hitler, who had forcefully encouraged Jews to leave Germany, now said openly that Jews should be annihilated in the coming war. Church leaders had received letters blaming Christ's assassination on the Jews, and hatred was being promoted among Christians.

German economic policy required that Jews forfeit all precious metals and gemstones to the government. New taxes were directed toward Jews, and Jews were forbidden to live in houses with Aryans. Papa felt the Nazis wouldn't stop with annexing only Czechoslovakia; Hitler meant to conquer all of Europe, destroy the Jews, and rule the world.

England had halted Jewish immigration into Palestine because of Arab protests and because England needed Arab oil. Papa said there was a lot of anti-Semitism in most free countries—even America had anti-Jewish elements. If a war occurred, Jews would be blamed for everything everywhere.

Papa had more bad news. At the American consulate, he found out that Mutti could no longer leave Germany. And since she was named as the main person in the emigration affidavit, we couldn't use the affidavit to leave for the United States either. Papa informed me that there was a children's transport, so I could go to the United States alone, or I could go to Haifa and stay with relatives or on a kibbutz.

I assured him that I wanted to remain with him. I asked him why Jews were blamed for everything. It couldn't be because of Christ's death 2,000 years before—we weren't there! Why was I considered different? I didn't feel or look or act different.

Papa explained that people in the majority seemed to dislike minorities. Politicians and preachers could sway public opinion against minorities, blaming them for unpleasant events. Minorities couldn't defend themselves; they were fewer in number, lacked leadership, or were not allowed to protest because of their religious beliefs.

I indicated that I comprehended most of what Papa had said, then we began to talk about my new job at the hotel.

* * * * *

When the last day of school arrived, the class somehow managed to sing the score of the "Blue Danube" as it had been rehearsed so many times, and that was the signal to disperse for the summer.

The next day at the Grand Hotel, I dressed in my page's uniform for my first day of work, looking and feeling very sharp. Five other pages and I waited at the counter, taking turns for assignments. My first chore was with a tourist from Antwerp with one suitcase. After placing his luggage on a cart, I went up with him in the elevator, showed him to his room, carried the suitcase inside, and handed him the room key. He gave me a coin. I thanked him, and once outside I looked at the tip: one franc. By the end of a busy day, my tips totaled seven francs and ten cents.

It took me a few days to become proficient, but at the end of the first week I had nearly forty francs. On one very busy day, I earned thirty-seven francs! I counted the money four times before I really believed it. Papa was surprised and pleased. "That's just wonderful. Now you have the money you need and can save what you earn from now on."

My last week working at the hotel went by fast. I earned more than four hundred francs in just three weeks. When I left, the headman thanked me and said I could come back to work there anytime.

On the Saturday afternoon before the jamboree, I rushed around getting all my gear ready so I could leave the house at seven o'clock the next day. From the money I had earned, I took enough to cover the cost of the trip and another twenty francs "just in case," although there would be nowhere to spend it. Papa helped me pack my knapsack with everything I needed except for what I would wear the first day. Those clothes were spread out neatly on the floor. Even as excited as I was, I fell asleep immediately.

The next morning, after two rolls and a cup of cocoa, I was pronounced "mighty sharp" by Papa. After assurances that my money was safely packed in my knapsack, I descended the stairs. With the knapsack on my back and the group's triangular flag in my hand, I walked down the street feeling very good.

When everyone had assembled at the meeting place, we marched through the city and out to the highway in groups of three. The other two boys in my group were picked up by a man in one car, and in five minutes I was in a second car with Jeanette, a girl from the scout group, and two nice adults. Jeanette was my age and had been born in Brussels. Her parents came from Poland after the war. Small, with a big bunch of dark hair and pretty dark eyes, she always stayed close to me. I decided to be Jeanette's boyfriend.

We were dropped off at the entrance to the jamboree campground. After depositing our gear in the assigned tents, we wandered around the campground. Each group wore a different color uniform and had an identifying flag. The scouts ranged in age from ten to nineteen.

When all of our scout group had arrived, Willie gave us a copy of our itinerary and familiarized us with the camp's rules. According to the duty sheet, I would have night duty twice, K.P. (kitchen police) duty on three days, and four days in the cleaning crew. I would take part in the flag-raising ceremony once. To accomplish our assignments, we were divided into groups of four scouts. Jeanette and I were in the same group.

At an assembly of the entire camp, the camp director outlined the study groups and discussions we would have: politics, the world around us, and especially Zionism and Eretz Israel (the Land of Israel), which was now Palestine.

With all the excitement and novelty, the day passed rapidly and we went to bed early, quite exhausted. The sleeping bags and ground tarps softened the ground only a little.

In the morning we marched in the dark toward the toilets and washrooms. Each group had a limited time there before the next group arrived. After a very moving flag ceremony, we went to breakfast, which was served in several sittings. The first morning we had a three-hour orientation on kibbutz life, then a brief lunch period and an hour's rest.

The afternoon was for group athletics—no individual competition—featuring peopleball (catchball), soccer, and handball (which was not my game). When I told Willie that I'd been well trained in peopleball by Mr. Jacobson in Germany, his strategy was to play me as long as possible. We beat a group from Antwerp and a group from Liege in good time. The last game against a group from Paris took a long time, but we finally won it. Jeanette rewarded me with pats and kisses on my cheek.

After the evening meal, Jeanette, two boys from Antwerp, and I sat in front of our tent and talked about scouting and politics. David did most of the talking.

Each scout stood a one-hour watch during the night to prevent the theft of the group flag by other groups; at the end of the camp period, the group stealing the most flags was honored. My watch began at two o'clock in the early morning and the cold air kept me alert. I saw human figures in the dark, standing and walking around, and I heard various noises. But our flag was still flying at the end of my watch.

*****

The first week passed rapidly with my team winning its games and advancing to the semifinals. David and I had a few chances to talk and we became good friends.

On Monday of the second week, I had only two cleaning duty assignments and my participation in the flag ceremony, so I could concentrate on the games and Jeanette.

The team from Paris was really tough, but we managed to win after a game we thought would never end. And we won the next game against Antwerp, making it into the finals. The soccer winners were from Paris, and a group from Luxemburg won in handball. In the peopleball finals, our team played a team from Holland, whose members seemed older than us. After a hot, hard game, my teammate was eliminated, leaving me to face two opposing players. Somehow, I could hear Papa's voice saying, "Lutz, you can do it. Get them." In twenty minutes, I beat both opponents to win the championship for my team. Jeanette cried with happiness.

On Friday, I was one of the campers in the flag ceremony and so proud to be a part of it. In the evening, the awards ceremony took place. After many speeches, the closing ceremony began. Our team received a certificate of award and a big ovation. A large bonfire ended the ceremony, and afterward many of us stayed to dance the hora. Jeanette and I pledged to see each other often in the future.

On Saturday we cleaned our area, leaving the tents in place for those campers who would stay for another week. On Sunday morning, we had a little time to say our goodbyes and exchange addresses. David and I promised to stay in touch. (We kept our promise, but not in a way we could have imagined then.)

A truck arrived and departed as soon as we were aboard. Singing and talking about our experiences, we soon arrived at the scouts' meeting place in Brussels. I walked Jeanette to her home, ten minutes from where I lived, and we made a date for the next day.

Papa was surprised to see me, even though two weeks had elapsed. When I told him how much I enjoyed the jamboree and that some boys were staying for another week, he insisted that I go back for another week, too. After unpacking and repacking, I went to Jeanette's home to tell her about my plans.

The next day Papa woke me early and I departed once more, this time taking the streetcar to the outskirts of town. One of the boys I met in camp was on the streetcar, and we decide to hitchhike together. When we arrived at the camp, Willie spotted us and interceded for us with the camp management. Returning with a big smile, he signaled approval.

When he saw us, David was pleased and handed us information on the week's activities. The week passed with many lectures, discussions, readings, speeches, and long talks with David. I learned a lot from him and we became great friends, even with the difference in our ages. He was such a gentle soul and liked my attitude. He used to tell me that for a German, I was not very German!

On Sunday, we worked hard to clean the camp area, and when we were finished, no one would have known it had been a camp. At six o'clock, we piled into trucks and started homeward. Because our truck would pass within two blocks of my home, the driver detoured and dropped me at my door.

As soon as Papa left the next morning, I hurriedly unpacked and cleaned everything. By eleven o'clock, I was at Jeanette's home. Her father was at work and her mother had gone shopping, taking Jeanette's little brother. We hugged and kissed for a long time before I told her about my week at camp. I left in the early afternoon, promising to pick her up at five o'clock and take her to the scout meeting in the evening.

At the meeting place, everyone was laughing and greeting each other. Willie introduced me to two boys from Berlin who would be in Karl's group. One was Karl Kerslak and the other was Manfred Rieger.

Manfred, fifteen years old, was taller than I was with brown hair and straightforward-looking eyes; scouting didn't seem to be to his liking. He was staying with his stepmother; his father was in a camp in Germany. His real mother, not Jewish, was in Berlin. He had begun to learn his father's construction trade but never finished.

Karl, also fifteen, was a dandy—well dressed in an English-looking suit with wingtip shoes. Both his parents were in Brussels; his mother also was not Jewish. His father was some kind of an entrepreneur, and his mother had a huge ladies' and children's underwear store in Berlin. Karl seemed curious about what was going on in our group.

When I told Papa later about my two new friends, he told me that the Kerslaks were quite well known in Berlin and linked to various business and financial ventures, as well as racehorses.

The next day at Manfred's home, I met his stepmother. Overhearing their conversation, I could tell they didn't get along well. Manfred didn't take orders well and his voice was very loud. Outside, we ate ice cream and smoked cigarettes while he told me he wasn't going to remain with the Hanoar but would join the Trumpeldor group. It was considered radical and its members wore riding breeches and boots, usually black. I didn't understand the group's thinking and habits.

* * * * *

Papa thought it was time I learned to play billiards, so we went to a tavern where he always played. He had a beer and I drank a soda. I watched him play two games then joined him for my first game. Everything went well for a while, but then, despite Papa's warnings, I got careless. I pushed the cue too hard and made a large tear in the green cloth surface! Papa stopped breathing and gave me a serious look. After some discussion with the owner, Papa told me that the repair would take all the money I had saved. In addition, I would have to clean the tavern every morning for the next two weeks.

The first morning, getting up at 5:30 was difficult, but it took me only an hour and fifteen minutes to clean the tavern. After having something to eat I left to visit Karl, whose apartment was an hour's walk away.

In the hallway of the first-floor apartment, Karl introduced me to his mother, who greeted me in a long flowing robe, wearing heavy makeup. I was introduced to Mr. Kerslak and his friend, Mr. Kaslowsky, a huge man. Mr. Kerslak, about Papa's size but a little lighter, thought he knew my papa. While Mrs. Kerslak fixed us some hot cocoa, cold cuts, cheeses, and dark bread, Karl and I waited in his room. It was beautifully furnished, as were the other rooms in the apartment. When his mother took the empty tray away, Karl and I lit up cigarettes; his parents didn't mind, he said. Karl was so different from Manfred. His thoughts were devoted 50 percent to girls, 40 percent to business and money, and 10 percent to just dreaming. His fantasies were peculiar but I liked him.

As I left, Karl's mother invited Papa and me to dinner the next evening. When I got home, I excitedly told Papa about my visit to Karl's, and he agreed we could go there for dinner. In the meantime, Jeanette had left a message with him that she must see me in the morning.

As soon as I finished my cleaning at the tavern the next morning, I hurried to Jeanette's place. Boxes were everywhere and she was crying. Her family was leaving Belgium to live with relatives near Paris, she told me; they might even immigrate to the United States from there. She was happy to leave for Paris but quite unhappy that we would be apart. In her room, we hugged and kissed, but I was so sad. I hurriedly say goodbye to her parents and rushed home.

Papa listened to my unhappiness and sighed. "You know, you can go to America too. The consulate will take youngsters up to age fourteen if they have relatives there." I reminded him that I did not want to leave him.

That evening we rode the streetcar to Karl's house. While Papa and Mr. Kerslak got acquainted over sherry, I drew Karl aside to tell him not to say anything in front of Papa about my smoking. The meal was very nice. Papa and Mr. Kerslak had a fine time reminiscing about the past. We rode the streetcar home while Papa smiled a lot and sang softly.

In the morning I hurried home from the tavern so I could accompany Papa to a chess tournament where we would both play. I was proud to see my name on the roster behind Papa's. We both won our first five matches and also our semifinals. In the finals, I was eliminated after the first game. After a tense hour and twenty minutes, Papa finally won the final. At the conclusion of the games, certificates were given and we walked happily home, congratulating each other.

At the end of August I was back in school, but nothing exciting was happening there. At home, I read the newspaper to Papa. The political situation didn't look good. Letters from Mutti said conditions were intolerable. Naively, she wrote that the affidavit for the three of us to leave for the United States would be honored if Papa and I returned to Berlin to clarify why we had left Germany. When Papa read this, he laughed long and hard.

On September 1, 1939, Germany invaded Poland. World War II started three days later when England and France, Poland's allies, declared war on Germany. News was sketchy at first, with rumors and speculations everywhere. British and French forces were said to be massing along the Belgian-French border. On the 27th of the month, ten days after the occupation of the eastern part of Poland by Russian troops, Poland surrendered.

My life, however, went on as usual. Karl and Manfred and I became real buddies, meeting whenever we could.

Willie told me that I had to quit smoking or leave the scout organization. I kept smoking but made sure I didn't have nicotine breath or stained fingers. One night I arrived at home to find Papa sitting at the table with my cigarette holder near him. He angrily tore open all ten of the cigarettes I had in my case and threw the tobacco in the garbage pail. I wanted to drop through the floor. It took about a week before we were again comfortable with each other.

* * * * *

As the end of the school year approached, Papa frequently asked me about my plans for the future. I had to continue school until I was sixteen or take an apprentice position. When I told him I'd like to become an aeronautical engineer, he promised to see what the possibilities were.

Meanwhile, in the city, many Belgian soldiers were seen walking around and British military personnel drove around in their vehicles. Statues were covered to protect them in case of invasion.

I graduated from school on April 18, 1940, just after my fourteenth birthday. Papa had gotten me a job at a small airport; I was to start work on the first of June. The pay was low, but I'd be learning.

Chapter 10

I never took the job at the airport. Less than a month after I finished school on May 10, 1940, Germany declared war on the Benelux countries (Belgium, the Netherlands, and Luxembourg) and France. Papa—the only family I had in Brussels—was taken away from me, interned by the Belgian government just because he was a foreigner. At the age of fourteen, I found myself all alone.

When Papa was taken from Brussels, I walked all day searching for him. I first visited the Caserne du Petit Chateau, where Papa told me he would be, only to find out that he had already been transferred to Schaarbeck. Determined to find him, I headed to Schaarbeck, walking for more than two hours carrying a heavy suitcase. I wandered around, looking for Papa, for hours. Thousands of men had been assembled there, and many other people were also searching for their family members. I finally found someone who knew Papa, but I was too late—Papa had been taken away and no one could tell me where.

I dragged the suitcase back to the mansard, stunned and completely at a loss as to what to do. With no money, only two little papers to identify me, and no food, I didn't know where to turn. The city seemed deserted—no vehicles were on the streets, no streetcars were running, no shops were open. And I was very hungry.

I started searching the room, trying to find something, anything, that could help me. All I found were two passe-partouts, a type of master key, and two packs of cigarettes and a little liquor. I decided to check every apartment in the building, starting with the one next door.

The door opened very easily, but I found nothing. I continued through each apartment until I reached the ground floor, discovering only a few francs and an old piece of cheese. I headed for the rear apartment where the manager and owner lived. Papa had told me they made their own sausages, but I found only half a dozen very hard loaves of bread and some stale salami. I devoured the salami then I soaked the bread in water until it was soft enough to chew. After picking up some loose tobacco and cigarette papers I happened to see, I went back upstairs. My search activities had taken most of the day and I was tired enough to fall asleep.

The next day, after having a piece of soaked bread and a cigarette, I walked aimlessly along the nearly empty streets. The few people I saw eyed each other with suspicion. On the third day, the streets came alive with columns of people pulling small carts or carrying their belongings. I heard loud cannon fire and then explosions. People were crying that the Germans were coming and would kill everyone. A friend of Papa's disdainfully told me that was nonsense, that they wouldn't kill anyone who stayed behind, that people were panicking.

British troops marched by looking quite dejected. I heard that they had blown up all the bridges behind them to slow the Germans' advance, but the Germans repaired the bridges rapidly. Papa's friend handed me some bread and cigarettes and joined the column of people. So many people were in the streets trying to leave the city that military vehicles had to proceed very slowly.

For the next few days, I existed on bread and cigarettes. Only a few people seemed to be left—and no more English soldiers or vehicles. Where was the Belgian army? I wondered.

On the morning of the 17th, I stood in front of the building in disbelief. German vehicles were coming in waves—first armored trucks and smaller cars, then big trucks. German soldiers stood in the trucks with machine guns trained, prepared for resistance. They met none as they rolled by. Weakened by my lack of food, I soon fell asleep sitting with my back against the door of the building.

A boot kick in the thigh awakened me. I was startled to see a young German soldier—tall and blue-eyed with short-cropped blond hair. He held out his helmet and asked me if I had any water. I was so dumbfounded I couldn't speak and just shook my head. With an icy stare he marched away. I disappeared back upstairs and sat on the bed, very fearful.

I stayed inside for a day. Then, very hungry, I ventured outside to see columns of foot soldiers marching by, singing songs about conquest. Their heavy boots made a frightening clanking sound. Some women handed the soldiers flowers, but older men spat on the ground. It dawned on me that the Belgians had lost, the Germans had won, and conditions would be as bad here as they had been in Berlin. Belgians as well as Jews would suffer.

I wandered over to the tavern where Papa and I had played billiards. When Mieske, the owner's wife, recognized me, her face lit up. "It's you, Lutz, come in. What are you doing here?" When I told her about Papa, she had me sit down while she fixed me some food. Before I finished eating, she was called to help in the front room and left me. Curious, I peered into the smoke-filled front room. German soldiers lounged everywhere, smoking and talking. The owner handed me a bucket to empty behind the tavern. "Mieske told me about your papa," he said. "Why don't you stay here, help us a little, and make some money? We can give you food, too. And you can translate for us what these Germans say."

"I'm not going to speak German to them!" I said.

"You don't have to. Just listen and then tell me what they're saying. I'll tell everyone you are my son and you speak only French and Flemish."

I agreed and did little tasks to help out in the tavern, all the while listening to the German soldiers—mostly of lower ranks—boasting of their conquests. I heard that they crossed the Dutch border easily, although Rotterdam gave them some trouble. But with some treachery by local citizens, Holland's surrender and Belgium's, too, came quickly. The Germans were advancing everywhere. German and British planes were engaging in aerial fights. Civilians on the roads were strafed by German Stuka dive bombers; the Stukas would dive straight downward, making a howling sound and terrifying everybody. The soldiers laughed heartily as they recounted this part of the battle.

The soldiers finally left, and it took the three of us a long time to clean up the mess. When we finished, the three of us ate together in the back room. I agreed to come back early in the morning.

The walk back to the mansard was eerie—pitch dark with no electricity on the streets or in buildings. I groped my way up the stairs and didn't feel safe until I got inside the room.

Early the next morning, I walked deserted streets to the tavern. The door was already open, and after a breakfast of pancakes and coffee I started to do my chores. When everything was ready for business, we sat and waited, but nothing happened. After a while I said that since there was nothing to do I'd go home and see what the next day brought. Mieske fixed me a little bag of food and kissed me on the cheek.

I thanked them both and headed home. No one was in the streets. The world was at a standstill. Looking in the bag I found two sandwiches, a piece of cheese and a pack of cigarettes. On the bottom were two twenty-franc notes.

* * * * *

After another night of fitful sleep, noises awakened me. I went downstairs and saw many people walking in the street, carrying suitcases or pulling little carts. They looked worn out and dirty. Catching up with one man, I asked where they were coming from.

"From the border. It's chaos. Between the Germans and the English, we were a shooting gallery. I'd like to know where the Belgian and French soldiers are. People are hurt and dying and there is no help. We turned around and came back to the city. There is nothing to do but wait and see. How is it here?"

I told him that for two days Germans had passed through, but now everything was quiet.

We walked some distance together, then I wished him well and walked back home.

* * * * *

The next few days were quiet with only a few German vehicles passing. One day, many Belgian soldiers were marched through the city, guarded by German soldiers. Some were bandaged, some had canes, and all looked filthy and extremely tired. Tears ran down my face. I didn't think I could stand any more. I wandered the streets aimlessly for a long time, then went home.

As I passed the third floor, a door opened and a small man looked out. "Good afternoon. Aren't you Lutz, the boy who lives with his father in the mansard? Come in and tell us what's going on outside."

I stepped in and he closed the door. "I am Maurice Veillard and this is Claudine Pochet. Claudine, why don't you fix us some tea and something to eat, and Lutz can tell us what has happened since we left."

While Claudine prepared our tea, I looked at them. Maurice had fine hair parted at the side and a long nose; he was very slim and did not look athletic. Claudine was very nice looking, slim with short dark-blond hair. I told them everything that had occurred since May 10. They listened in silence, nodding. Maurice then said he expected hard times. He was born in 1890 and fought the Germans in the Great War, and he thought this war would be much worse. He hadn't lost his dislike of the Germans.

We talked for a while, then I said good night. I promised them I'd return in the morning to talk some more.

As I lay in bed that night, I silently thanked fate for having met Maurice and Claudine.

When I knocked on their door early in the morning, they were waiting for me. As we ate, I wondered where they were getting all the food. As if he guessed my thoughts, Maurice said they had picked up everything on their way back, and some of it they exchanged for at farm houses. Maurice asked if I was willing to go with him the next day to the outskirts of the city where the farms were.

I agreed, and after breakfast and a cigarette the following morning, Maurice and I headed out with knapsacks slung over our shoulders.

As the sun came up we could see it would be a nice day—clear and not too cold. Heading north out of Molenbeek, we marched at a good pace and soon were near the Kerslak family's home. I wondered how Karl and his family were surviving. To get out of the city and into the countryside took us nearly three hours. We began to see a few farms.

When we stopped to rest, Maurice shared his plan with me. "Let me do the talking." "We are father and son. My wife is very ill at home and your two younger sisters cannot take care of themselves. That's all anyone needs to know."

At the first place we tried, an older man opened the door and asked what we wanted. While Maurice explained, the man listened, then he gave us a sharp look and motioned for us to enter. In the kitchen, two women were busy at a stove. The man led us to a shed behind the house and told us to wait inside. A short time later, he reentered with a younger fellow, both carrying packages. Maurice put the packages in his knapsack and paid the men with some money and cartons of cigarettes. Maurice thanked them and we left without another word. Back on the street we found a secluded place to look at our packages. We found a big chunk of ham, some sausages, butter, and two loaves of bread. "Not bad, Lutz! I'll go to the next place alone while you hold the packages; people won't give us anything if they think we already have things."

At three more places we were able to obtain more meats and quite a few potatoes, too. We headed back to Maurice's place. It took us double the time to return because the haul was heavy and we had to stop often to rest. It was late afternoon when Claudine opened the door to us, giving a big sigh of relief to see us safe.

* * * * *

The days passed. The city slowly returned to normal, and some stores reopened. We had electricity, and a few streetcars began running—it gave me pleasure to hear their ringing bells. Of course, there was a greater military presence.

One morning there was a knock on my door. When I opened it, there was Karl, grinning at me. After we related what had happened to us since we last saw each other, Karl and I became business partners. His plan was simple: At the Gare du Nord (north train station), we would sell one picture postcard and three pencils for two francs to soldiers as they came out of the station. Karl's mother had advanced us 500 francs to buy our first supply.

I disagreed with Karl that soldiers need postcards and pencils.

"True," Karl agreed, "but under the postcard, we will have two porno photos, and for that we could ask *ten* francs."

He was right! We had a gold mine! As soon as we were in position, we sold out so fast we had to get more—much more. In two days we counted our profits and my eyes got as big as soccer balls! And Karl had other ideas. We repaid his mother and then contacted numerous people to obtain other merchandise to sell on the black market, which was growing rapidly in the city.

More military continued to arrive, so we had new buyers for our goods. Civilian authorities set up new laws and decrees, but they didn't bother us; and we didn't pay any attention. All we wanted was to make money, drink, eat and have a good time.

During that time, I didn't care if what I did was illegal or immoral. Money was flowing in. I was doing everything wrong: going with the wrong crowd, influenced by the wrong people and seeing things I shouldn't be seeing. I was growing up before my time.

* * * * *

Life went on. Black marketeering had its good days and bad days. The competition was heavy. Everyone was scrambling for a franc.

Maurice went back to being a maître d', and Claudine found work, too. Karl and I decided to operate separately for a while to become more independent. I got a job as a "Commie mixer"—a glorified title for a job doing everything—in a nightclub. I worked from eight in the evening until five in the morning for eighty francs a week plus tips. The first week I made 100 francs in tips, heard a lot of music, and gained much information. And there was entertainment—two nude dancers were the highlight of my evenings.

But by March 1941 it was all over. The nightclub was not a moneymaker. The two owners paid off everybody including merchants and other creditors, but had nothing left for themselves. I went back into partnership with Karl, but competition had increased and we weren't as successful, only able to just struggle along.

Chapter 11

When Germany went to war with Russia in June 1941, the situation in Belgium changed. New decrees from the German occupational government imposed many restrictions on the Jewish population, just as had happened in Germany. The German Military High Command issued an ordinance establishing a curfew for the Jews of Brussels, Antwerp, Charleroi, and Liege, and all Jews had to register. Commencing on August 29, 1941, the curfew spanned the hours between 8 P.M. and 7 A.M. At first, it wasn't too strictly enforced.

A second ordinance issued in January 1942 required all Jews to wear a yellow Star of David sewn on the left breast. The word "Juif" (French) or "Jude" (German) or "Jood" (Flemish) was to appear in the middle of the star. Some boycotting of Jewish businesses and restrictions on local travel by Jews were part of the ordinance.

My first reaction to the star was "They must be kidding." I looked like a pure Aryan Hitler Youth—blond and blue-eyed. With that star on me, Jews would think I was making fun of them. I refused to wear it.

On Friday morning, June 4, 1942, I stayed in bed as long as possible because no shops were open until later. I left my room at nine, hungry and broke, hoping to find someone to buy me breakfast or just a cup of filtered coffee. A beggar couldn't be choosey!

Looking up before crossing the street, I saw two men approaching, from the Gestapo I was sure. Gestapo men all looked alike—cheap suits, leather topcoats, felt hats, and the same peculiar inquisitive look. Just then, a streetcar went by. While the men waited to cross the street, I walked quickly in the opposite direction. At the end of the street, pausing at a shop window, I turned my head slightly to see them enter our apartment house. My heart, from somewhere below my

Lutz (age 15) with his friend Fred, Brussels, 1941

knees, chugged like a locomotive. Now what? I hadn't done anything wrong lately. Maybe they were not after me.

After twenty minutes they came out, walked across the street, turned the corner, and disappeared. I turned slowly, crossed to that corner, and peeked around to made sure they had gone. What a rotten way to start the day! I usually loved mornings, so full of life and energy, with the promise of new beginnings and with an absolutely intoxicating fragrance. Now this morning was ruined. I entered the house cautiously to make sure no one was waiting for me and then raced up the stairs. When I could breathe again, I opened the door.

A card had been slid under the door. Its face carried a big Gestapo seal. I'd been right! I turned it over to read the printing and the handwriting underneath. It was an official invitation to visit Gestapo headquarters on Avenue Louise "without fail" within three days. Such an invitation was no small matter; I'd have to give this considerable thought.

I closed the door and walked back downstairs. While I slowly walked to the business section of the city, I kept looking at the little card with its obnoxious seal.

Why me? What did I do? Or, maybe, what *didn't* I do? I hadn't been in any trouble lately, or at least none worthy of a formal invitation like this one!

I put the card in my pocket. I knew I'd eventually figure out what was happening, but at the moment I was too upset to make any sense of the matter.

It was still a beautiful morning, so warm and pleasant. I felt I could have walked forever. I decided to stop thinking about anything unpleasant—except my hunger. I walked a little faster to reach Karl's and my usual meeting place.

The Clef d'Or was a café on the Boulevard Ansbach—a place where the coffee was strong and the pastry very good. It was frequented by dealmakers and the well to do, but also those like me who were starving at the moment. It was one of three cafes where my friends and I met and tried to survive.

In these places, one could buy and sell almost anything. Deals ranged from expensive to cheap, high quality to bad black market merchandise, and from honest to shady. Also available were whores, pimps, male prostitutes, drugs, and even poker games in the back room where one could lose or win a fortune.

I visited because I had comrades there. Some had money and some didn't. Nevertheless, there was always somebody to pay for breakfast. They were a charitable bunch, and I felt very much at home with them.

As I approached the corner I stopped to check for traffic and saw Jean, the café owner, filling most of the café entrance. His arms folded over his chest, he moved his head from side to side. I walked toward him, raising my arm to greet him. Then I noticed that he was holding one thumb in the air. I recognized this signal—it meant "Don't come in." I nodded to show I understood and continued to walk.

As soon as I was out of sight, I took a deep breath and lit a cigarette. I continued walking and my mind raced. What was going on? Were the Gestapo after me? Jean had just made sure that I didn't enter the café at the wrong time. But why? All I could do was go on to one of the other meeting places. I hoped my empty stomach would wait until then. I decided I had to find my partner. Maybe he'd know something.

Café Van Bladel was a little classier—more expensive with a more diverse crowd. If one wanted to stay there awhile, one had to pay for the privilege. The black market flourished there because of the café's proximity to the train station where all the soldiers arrived and left. The soldiers, especially the staff sergeants, were the customers we wanted. They eagerly bought anything—stockings, coffee, cigarettes, butter, wine or hard liquor, gold, silver, or other items of value. Either they wanted it for themselves or they wanted to resell it at a good profit.

I passed Sarma, the big five-and-ten store, and marched into the café. Karl waved both arms, motioning for me to come to his table. He seemed quite agitated. At the table, the fantastic aroma of coffee assailed me.

"Good morning, Lutz, did you pass by the Clef d'Or?"

I nodded affirmatively, thinking that was a stupid question. He *knew* I'd go there first, but he was waiting for me to think of a clever answer.

"Karl, you could at least order me some coffee and food before I fall on my nose."

Café where Lutz and his friends operated their business in 1940

Karl ordered the coffee as I talked. When it came, he ordered the food while I slurped noisily. In between gratifying gulps, I told him everything that had happened after I left the house. He just stared and listened.

When the food came, Karl remained silent. He knew better than to speak while I stuffed myself. Finally finished, I leaned back and exhaled.

I showed him the Gestapo's card. He took it, turned it over, read it several times, and then turned it over several more times with a puzzled look on his face. We discussed the possible implications of the card without arriving at a plausible explanation.

We were still jabbering when Aaron, one of our pals, came in and headed toward our table.

"You know, Lutz," he said. "the Gestapo was asking about you. They've been at the Clef d'Or, searching the place. They seemed pretty anxious to get hold of you. Those guys looked very scary. You don't look too good either."

Karl and I glanced at each other and burst out laughing.

Before Aaron could feel insulted, I told him what I had already related to Karl. We must have been talking louder than we should have. It was suddenly very quiet in the café, and we realized that people had crowded around us to listen. When we finished our conversation, everyone sat down and began talking with each other about my situation. It was time for us to disappear before I had to repeat my story again.

To my surprise, Karl paid the whole bill. He must have been impressed by my troubles. Karl really wasn't stingy, just a bit hard to get money from sometimes.

Karl and I decided to go to our third meeting place, the Chez Nous café. We might find an answer to my question there.

The Chez Nous was a haven for gamblers, black marketeers, and dealers in all sorts of enterprises. It was a con artists' paradise and a place for aspiring politicians to be seen. A few thought it was a haven for some underground figures and resistance fighters, but not too many were aware of this rumor. At any given time, there would be a mixture of German and Austrian Jews and non-Jews, as well as representatives of other nationalities—people thrown together by Hitler's war. It was understood that everyone was in the same position and only by helping each other would we survive. Those without money could often put their expenses on a tab, or perhaps a generous soul would buy an unfortunate some food. Even the owner was involved, passing the hat for a few francs to help someone in dire need.

The food was good and plentiful, as was the coffee. Hot, strong tea was also served, and schnapps was available to drown one's sorrows for a while. Many of the café regulars knew my papa, and considering that I was one of the youngest and a witty big-mouth, they regarded me as a mascot.

As we walked toward the café, I turned to Karl. "You know, I'd rather go home first and see if anything else has happened. You want to come with me?"

Karl agreed and we headed in the opposite direction. As we neared the apartment house, Karl suggested we split up and walk on opposite sidewalks. If we saw nothing suspicious, we would meet in front of the building.

Since nothing appeared out of place, we walked into the building slowly and quietly. The concierge appeared from a rear apartment to tell us that two men had come by looking for me and asking questions about my papa and me. "Is everything all right?" she inquired.

I assured her that everything was fine. Fortunately, my rent was paid so there was no problem in that sense. I thanked her for the information and we started up the five flights of stairs. Karl began to breathe heavily. He was only sixteen and already his health was suffering because of cigarettes, liquor, and girls.

I opened the door to find another card with the same seal. This time the text read

> You are herewith ordered to appear and present yourself in person at the offices of the Geheime Staatspolizei, located on Avenue Louise in Brussels. The date of required presence shall be on the seventh of June 1942. No excuse will be accepted for not appearing.

It was signed, but I couldn't identify the signature.

Karl watched me while I read. He sighed. "Lutz, they mean it."

I nodded. My insides were in one big knot.

"You know, Karl, the concierge was right. Those two goons must have come back and when they didn't see their first card under the door, they left another one to make sure I understood."

With no idea as to what the cards really meant, we turned the second one over and over again, comparing it with the first one. Then we started back to the Chez Nous, hoping someone there would know. Arriving at the café, we made our way to a table where two men were playing chess. They both looked up and greeted me as we approached.

I introduced Karl, dropped the cards on the table, and explained what had happened earlier. While they were studying them, Karl and I went to the counter for coffee.

Karl was surprised I knew the two men. I told him I'd explain later.

Back at the table, the two men, Pierre and Michel, looked at each other and nodded slowly. Pierre stared at me.

"My little buddy," he said, "this is an invitation of the first class. You can't refuse. If you don't show up, they're going to come after you, and they'll find you. Then there will be real trouble!"

He explained that a military decree had been issued on March 3 through the Belgian National Work Office to secure workers for the Organization Todt, the engineering outfit for the Nazis. This process was directed by the Nazis, so anybody who received a card had better oblige.

Michel then looked around and murmured that they had a proposition for me. As we headed toward the back room to talk, he signaled the café owner to warn us if any "unfriendly" people came in. He turned to Karl and asked him not to come along for his own sake.

Karl was a bit insulted, but he left.

Michel told me I should keep my appointment with the Gestapo and look around while I was there remembering as many details as I could. Then I was to tell Michel and Pierre what I remembered so they could make composites of floor plans and maybe even maps.

I agreed. I had done some messenger work for these guys in the past, and I knew they belonged to a Belgian underground. I thought a Jewish resistance group was also involved, but when I asked questions, I was always told that the less I knew the better. They had helped me in the past without asking for any payment. Now I had the opportunity to return the favor, and I was glad to do it.

Michel instructed me to try to memorize the corridors, room numbers and layout, and most important, faces. Someone could then draw composite portraits from my descriptions. It was important for them to know who was in the building, especially those in command. We were to meet at the café Monday afternoon, right after my appointment.

I went back to the main room, sat at the counter, and ordered another coffee. Erwin, the owner, made it for me. He and his cousin Heinz, who owned the café, were from Berlin. They were great people who had helped me and others through some rough spots. I talked with Erwin for a while. Of course, he knew what was going on. He wouldn't let me pay for the coffee, so I thanked him and walked slowly home. It was going to be a long weekend.

Chapter 12

With Monday's dawn approaching, I got up to empty my ashtray and then lay down again. My stomach was so tight, it was as if I'd swallowed a cannonball. I felt like vomiting.

I got dressed and headed toward Avenue Louise for my appointment. The long walk gave me a chance to steady my nerves a bit. But the nearer I got to the building, the tighter my stomach got. Avenue Louise was gorgeous that day, but near the end of the street, the Gestapo building loomed. The huge swastika flag hanging from the edge of the roof gave me an eerie feeling.

I showed the guard at the door my invitation. He pointed to the courtyard and another guard. I crossed the yard, trying to commit the entrance layout to memory. SS men in black strode by, civilians rushed back and forth, and soldiers moved about. I could hear orders being given and snatches of conversations in German, sounding harsher than usual. I enjoyed being able to understand what they were saying when no one knew I understood.

As I approached the second guard, two SS men passed by, dragging someone. His head hung down and his clothing was tattered and blood stained. As they passed near me, the man lifted his head. His face was a bloody mess—I couldn't see his eyes. His head fell forward on his chest and the SS men continued to drag him through the courtyard. I could hardly breathe.

After examining my card, the guard led me into the building and through a hallway. Passing several doors, he stopped in front of one and knocked. From the inside, a metallic-sounding voice called *"Herein"* (Enter).

I had heard this voice before, but where? The guard opened the door and I walked in. The door closed behind me and I stood still, waiting. The office contained a desk, a filing cabinet, a large picture of the Fuehrer, and two chairs. The uniform of the man in front of me indicated he held the SS rank of *Sturmscharfuehrer* (sergeant major). In the German Criminal Police, to which he belonged, according to his insignias, his rank was *Meister Kriminalsecretaer* (master secretary for criminal affairs). His head was bent over a pile of papers at the large desk. I stood waiting, and as I stared at him, I became sure I knew him.

He looked up. Hans Frank! I had met him about a year ago when Mutti asked the Gestapo to check on my welfare.

He stared at me and then grinned: "Ah, the Posener boy. Time has passed quickly." He looked at the cards I handed him. "Good, good, this will be good for you. Work has never hurt anybody. We need young workers who are not afraid to get their hands dirty. We are winning the war, but we need to reinforce the coastline. Now the Belgian Work Office has nicely cooperated and the Organization Todt will treat all you fellows well. So, I want you to go to the Gare du Sud on June 24 at four o'clock in the afternoon. Bring all your belongings. Someone will be waiting for you, and other men will join your group."

I knew there was no use in saying anything. One must just listen and obey in situations like this—no questions asked and no talking back.

"Yes, sir, I'll be there." All the while I was mentally photographing the building and his office in my mind.

"That is all. Let's make sure you are at the station! By the way, I suppose your mother is still in Berlin?"

"I guess so, sir."

With that, I said goodbye and left, closing the door behind me with relief.

As I left, I looked around and was able to read the names on some of the doors. The building housed different units: the Gestapo— Geheime Staatspolizei (state secret police); the SD—Sicherheitsdienst (Internal Security Service, somewhat like the FBI and the CIA); and of course, the SS. I tried to memorize as much as I could.

Once outside the building, I felt about ten pounds lighter and was able to breathe easier. The building and its atmosphere had scared me, but I remembered the whole event well and could give a good description to Pierre and Michel. I wouldn't soon forget this little rendezvous.

Back on the street, I lit a cigarette and started walking, reviewing my visit. What a sly way of telling me what to do. I felt a terrible helplessness. Should I have objected? That would have made some difference! I was talking to myself, creating a whole dialogue between the Nazis and me, getting louder and louder and moving my arms and hands. The more I talked, the angrier I got and the faster I walked.

I arrived at the Chez Nous and stood outside, breathless. After a minute or so, my breathing eased and I entered. Karl waited at a corner table, obviously anxious. I sat down very calmly, ordered a coffee, and lit a cigarette.

Karl looked dumbfounded. "Lutz, start talking! What happened?"

People at nearby tables stopped eating and waited. I related my visit to the Gestapo office and then fell silent.

Karl whistled. "Are you going?"

"Now that's a stupid question! Would you like me to write them a letter saying 'Don't count on me. I'm indisposed'? I'd probably be picked up and put through a solo boxing match like the guy I saw in the Gestapo building courtyard today. Not me. I plan to keep my face as intact as possible. I've got another two weeks, and in the meantime something might come up. As of now, I'm planning to go. I might find myself a little closer to Papa. Who knows?"

Karl said perhaps I was right and invited me to his place. His mother wanted to see me and, of course, to hear about my meeting.

I said I needed some time to talk with Pierre and Michel before we went. I had to tell them what I knew. I was sure they were anxious to hear how my appointment went.

I walked toward the table where they were playing chess. Pierre gave me a surreptitious signal not to sit down, so I continued to the bar. When I sat down, I noticed a man resembling one of the two Gestapo men who had served me the "invitations."

As I paid for my coffee, I could see Karl in the mirror, talking to Pierre and Michel. He came over to me and said we should get going, and out we marched.

When we were outside, Karl said my friends wanted to meet me in fifteen minutes at the Sarma. I was to wait for them upstairs.

By the time we reached the Sarma, Pierre and Michel had already started eating. Karl and I ordered and while we were waiting I started to draw sketches of the Gestapo building with as many details as I could recall, inside and out.

When the waitress had brought the food and left, I explained all I had seen and everything that had happened. Pierre and Michel asked questions and took some notes. I agreed to see them later in the afternoon at Pierre's place. Someone would be there who could draw composites from my descriptions.

Karl and I took the streetcar to his place, riding in silence during the forty-five minute trip. His mother was waiting impatiently.

In the living room, good strong coffee was waiting. Karl's mother had also set out slices of dark bread with butter, cheese, and beef tartare. The latter, a traditional Berlin food, was my favorite. As we munched and sipped, I told Mrs. Kerslak the whole story. After I finished and she had asked a number of questions, she agreed that I would have to comply. I felt somewhat better knowing that an older person also felt I should report for the work assignment. Karl finally agreed, too.

Karl was now my best friend, and I appreciated his concern. He and his mother were always there when I needed help, even for just a little counseling. Both had been so generous with money that I was ashamed to ask them for help. I was reluctant to leave, but I knew Pierre and Michel would be waiting for me. I thanked Karl's mother for listening to my concerns and told Karl that I would meet him tomorrow at the usual place.

I boarded a bus and soon arrived at Pierre's place. He was waiting with Michel and another young man, who was introduced as the artist. I described Sergeant Major Frank and the others I had seen at the Gestapo office. When the artist had finished, I looked at the sketches to see if he had been able to translate my descriptions into recognizable faces. The likenesses were uncanny. Michel thanked the artist, who then left.

Pierre brought out some cognac and as we sipped we went over my story once again. As we talked, I was able to remember additional information. Pierre then inquired where I had met Frank.

I recalled that about a year before, in April, my stepmother wrote a letter from Berlin to the Gestapo in Brussels. She explained that the

Belgians interned her husband in 1940 but that her son was still living there. Innocently, she asked if someone would be kind enough to check on me and make sure that I was a good boy. I wondered, How ignorant could someone be to do something like that?

About a week after the Gestapo received that letter, they sent me a letter indicating that my mother had written to them and that it was of the utmost necessity for me to contact their office—which, at that time, wasn't located at the place where I had just had my meeting. Frank was very friendly but asked me a lot of questions while a woman in a German uniform typed our entire conversation. The last question he asked was whether I was working. I told him yes, but he told the woman to indicate that I was working at "wheeling and dealing."

When the woman had finished typing, Frank asked me to read the document and sign it. When I reached the last paragraph, I told him it was wrong and I wouldn't sign it. He gave me a withering look that made me think I had given my life away. However, he told the woman to strike the last sentence. Again he asked me to sign the paper, and that time I did. I also found out that the name Hans Frank was a pseudonym.

He dismissed me, telling me to stay out of trouble. I hadn't seen him again—until my meeting—but I knew I'd never forget him.

Pierre looked thoughtful. He said with my knowledge of languages—I spoke so fluently and without an accent—I could be of enormous help to his organization. He added that I really didn't have anything to lose since, he gathered, I was leaving anyway. He said it wouldn't be difficult work and I'd be doing something worthwhile.

I agreed to help. Pierre said we should meet at his place again the following day, at the same time, and he'd fill me in. He cautioned me not to say a word to anyone about what had happened.

On my way home I was in deep thought. What a stressful day it had been. I began to think that these events could change my whole life!

* * * * *

I awoke early, feeling fantastic. Still in bed, I ate a piece of chocolate, had a cigarette, and reflected on the previous day's events. I felt so good I decided to walk around until it was time to meet Pierre and Michel. By the time I arrived at their place, my legs were weary.

Waiting with Pierre and Michel was a trim, well-dressed man with a compact build who looked very much like a business executive. He was quite a contrast to Pierre and Michel, who resembled Russian farmers in their casual dress. It was hard to believe they were in the resistance.

With a map spread out on the table, the room assumed an aura of a military command post. I was shown certain sections of the city and then specific corners and streets. I was to carry mail from one place to another, picking it up and dropping it off at different locations.

Mr. Gerard, as he was introduced to me, explained my assignment. "There will always be instructions included with material you pick up so you won't ever be at a loss as to what to do. And don't worry about getting in touch with us; we will contact you. You have a password sequence: Anyone approaching you will say 'Boulevard.' To this, you reply 'Avenue' and each of you will then say '*Rue, quoi.*'

"Only the four of us in this room and your individual contact will know this password sequence. This is all you need to know. This way, if you are caught, you really don't know anything. I advise you not to tell a soul about this. Remember, with your silence, you save lives."

＊ ＊ ＊ ＊ ＊

The next morning on the way to meet Karl at the café, I confirmed my intention not to tell him, or anyone, anything about my new assignment. I would just have to be evasive and pacify him, which probably wouldn't be too difficult since we were very occupied with making money. Times were lean and business was not too good. I could always manage to scrounge food, but money was a lot harder to get.

I noticed a number of people wearing yellow stars. In the evening hours, fewer people were on the streets. The curfew was being enforced more strictly. Everyone was afraid of being stopped and subjected to questioning. It was understood that the Germans were aided in these activities by the Flemish and Walloonian SS. (Walloons came from Southern Belgium.) It was said that those men would sell their mothers if they could got a good price or a medal.

＊ ＊ ＊ ＊ ＊

Three days later I received my first assignment. I was to walk on Rue Neuve in front of Nicholas Church. A young man came toward me and took both my hands in his, shaking them vigorously.

"Hello, hello, how are you doing?" And then, softly, he said, "Boulevard."

"Avenue," was my reply.

And both of us said at the same time, *"Rue, quoi."*

Handing me an envelope, he immediately walked away.

I continued toward Sarma and once there I went upstairs to the men's room and locked the door. I opened the envelope and read the instructions:

> Go to Rue de pont Neuf, corner of Rue aux Fleurs. Right on the corner is a novelty store. Enter it, leave the envelope on the counter and say loudly, "I'll be back later." Then, just leave. That's all. Burn the instructions at the nearest urinal and flush the ashes down the toilet.

I did exactly as instructed. As I walked away from the store, someone I had never seen before passed me, and as he drew abreast of me said "Thanks, buddy." That shook me. I hadn't realized that someone would be watching. My knees wobbled a bit with the excitement of it all.

About a week later, I made a similar run. I was approached in the same manner as before but at a different place. This errand was to be a little more complicated. I had to deliver a small package in Kockelberg. That meant taking the streetcar.

I stepped into a crowded car and squeezed into a corner. The riders were mostly soldiers, one of them a sergeant. The sergeant's bulk nearly hid a small man. From where I stood I was able to observe some of his movements. His shoulders moved slightly, very slowly, and a holstered gun appeared close to his face. He slid the holster and gun into a shopping bag beside his leg, bent over, and pulled something over the top of the bag's contents. Straightening up, he noticed me watching his actions and smiled. I smiled back. After a few minutes he made his way to the exit, pulled the cord for the car to stop, and jumped off.

Church from which Lutz carried messages

Three more stops and it would be my turn to get off. The car was not as crowded now and it was easy to make my way to the door. Just as I reached the exit, I heard a loud yell in German: "My belt has been cut! Where is my revolver and holster?"

While the sergeant was ranting and giving orders, I slipped out of the streetcar. My drop-off place was only a block and a half away. After delivering the package in the same manner as before, I returned to town.

Chapter 13

My last night in the mansard I lay awake worrying and fighting the bedbugs. The fat, red-brown bloodsuckers caused bites that itched terribly. I scratched them so hard they hurt, stinging unbelievably and leaving big red welts.

I had cleaned and disinfected the bed two months ago, but reinforcements were coming in hordes. Unable to get comfortable, I got up and walked around for a while.

Soon the sun would rise and another day start. I couldn't guess what the day would bring. I had a piece of chocolate and a cigarette. If I puffed hard, I thought, my bedbug enemies might think it was tear gas and leave me alone. I needed some time to think.

Back on the bed, pillow adjusted and somewhat comfortable, I munched the last of the chocolate, then took a deep puff and slowly exhaled, staring into darkness. Slow to awaken, my mind started to spin.

I had unanswered questions and a very uneasy feeling in my stomach. My head felt very light. At any moment I thought I could stop breathing altogether.

The faint dawn let me see a little more, but I didn't need the light. I could close my eyes and describe every inch, corner, nook, and crevice of this room. When Papa looked for a place for us to live, he was mainly concerned with finding the least expensive one. He paid twenty-five francs a month, not bad for those days. The war had driven the price up to seventy-five francs, which I thought was too much.

The lone window in the room opened toward the roof with an upward push. Papa loved the crispness of the fresh night air. He felt it was healthy to sleep with the window open. In winter, though, the temperature dropped below zero. In the morning it was not only very cold, but the window couldn't be closed—it was frozen open. While he lay in bed, laughing, I would drag myself out of bed to start the fire.

The toilet was between floors and at night we used a pail. Placed next to the window and partially filled with water, the contents of the pail froze during the night. Papa had made it my job to empty it. Now there was no one else to do it.

I learned a lot about survival and life from Papa that would come in handy in the future. It was hard to believe he'd been gone two and a half years—I missed him and wondered how he was. I wished he was here to help me at that moment.

* * * * *

I didn't own much—just one suitcase and what I was wearing. I'd sold or pawned almost everything: Papa's two suits, the shirts and shoes, items the landlady had stored in the armoire, the goose down bedding that Mama had sent us from Berlin in 1939. The place was practically stripped.

I went quickly down the stairs to give Maurice and Claudine some pictures and other personal items to keep until I returned. They'd been so nice to me in the past. Since they were not Jewish, my belongings would be pretty safe, even in those unstable times.

I left my key on the table and went down the stairs very quietly, softly, so I wouldn't attract anyone's attention. I didn't feel like talking. I eased down the hall and through the door. Then, at the corner of the street I looked back once with a sigh and went on my way.

I had said goodbye to most of my acquaintances over the past two days, but I wanted to say goodbye to Karl and a few others I had come to know pretty well. I trudged slowly to the Clef d'Or. People who frequented the café had put up a collection box for me. When I was there the prior night to say goodbye to another good friend, Manfred, they gave me the contents, a nice sum. I was thankful for their generosity. Some didn't even know me, but when asked to contribute for a young Jewish boy, they gave. All Jewish refugees seem ready to help someone in need. In bad times and misery, everyone sticks together.

Manfred and I had visited for a while and promised to keep in touch if possible. I didn't mention my trip to the Gestapo or the assignments I had carried out during the past few weeks. Now that I looked back, I realized how dangerous a position I had been in. I don't know what would've happened had I been caught with the packages I delivered.

At the Clef d'Or, faithful Karl was waiting for me. Manfred had also stopped by. I was so glad to see them. When they asked how I was, I said I actually felt great now that all the waiting was behind me.

Manfred wished me well then headed off to work. Karl and I ate in silence and then made small talk while we smoked. At eleven o'clock, Karl shook my hand. "So long, Lutz. I'll see you soon, I hope."

"Bye, Karl. Give my best to your mother. Thank her for everything."

He disappeared. I was alone and I felt as if I had lost an arm and a leg. I paid my bill, picked up my suitcase, and left. I couldn't sit any longer.

Since I didn't have to report until four o'clock, I decided to tour some of the city. It was warm and balmy—such a pleasant day. I walked slowly up and down a number of streets, feeling very unburdened. People were moving about, preoccupied with their own affairs. If I hadn't seen uniforms, I wouldn't have believed there was a war going on. But people were dying on battlefields and in prisons, hospitals, and camps. The thought jerked me back to reality.

At the Gare du Sud, I began to feel nervous. Inside, civilian men were clustered together. German soldiers with backpacks stood nearby with rifles over their shoulders. I showed my cards to the ticket taker and he pointed toward the group of men.

There was Frank from the Gestapo office. He saw me and motioned me to come to him. "I see you made it. Very good. I was counting on that. We don't want any trouble, right?"

"Yes sir. I mean, no sir, we don't want any trouble."

"You will be the youngest in this transport. The other men are all much older and are from Antwerp. They speak only Flemish and Jewish [Yiddish] so make yourself useful by translating. Keep your nose clean and everything should be all right."

I agreed and joined the group of men and got a puzzled look from them. I looked like them but they heard me speaking in German to the man in charge. I knew they probably didn't trust me. I put my case down and sat on it.

One of the men came over and introduced himself as Mr. Mandelbaum. In Flemish he asked, "Do you have any idea when we are supposed to leave?"

"No, none whatsoever. I am Lutz Posener."

Mr. Mandelbaum expressed surprise at hearing a Jewish name, so I explained that the reason I spoke German was because I was born in Berlin. I told him that besides Flemish and German I spoke French and Yiddish. He returned to the group and it was apparent he was speaking of me. The men turned around and smiled at me.

Mr. Mandelbaum returned and asked if, on behalf of the group, I would be their spokesman and translator. I quickly consented to do so.

I picked up my case and started toward the group, but a loudspeaker stopped me. A voice speaking in German told everybody to line up in rows of five. A sergeant came over and looked at me. "Hey, little one, explain to these men what they are supposed to do. Looks like not one of these pigs understands anything."

I hated his sarcastic tone of voice, and words spoken in this manner in German sound twice as bad. I turned toward the group and explained what we were to do. After about an hour, we had lined up and were counted twice; there were forty-five of us. During the count, the group was joined by another man and Frank commented on that: "Well, these birds will soon learn punctuality. That I can guarantee."

Fortunately, nobody understood and I was not about to translate. But I was beginning to be sorry I was there.

The train slowly entered the station and came to a halt. Several German soldiers jumped on the steps of one car and prevented civilians from boarding. Our group was motioned aboard, however. I entered one of the compartments, hoisted my suitcase into an overhead rack, and took a window seat to watch the rest of the group board. Mr. Mandelbaum took a seat across from me, saving six seats for others in the group. We waited. A soldier checked our compartment, and many others remained on the pavement. Inside, it was a beehive; everybody wanted to know where we were going. We had no answers.

With a loud whistle, the train pulled out of the station slowly and then fell into a monotonous rhythm: one, two, three; one, two, three. I was asleep almost immediately.

A marvelous smell woke me and with half-closed eyes I saw Mr. Mandelbaum's smiling face. He opened a bag and my eyes popped open.

"I guess, Lutz—that's the name, right?—this smell would wake anybody. Come, share with me."

He filled a cup with hot coffee and handed it to me; he also gave me some of his food. When we had eaten, he asked me about myself.

I told him I had come to Belgium in December 1938. Papa and I crossed the border illegally with two young men and a woman we knew. Papa had been interned in May 1940 and was sent to Gurs in southern France. I hadn't heard from him since then.

When I mentioned that I had recently turned sixteen, Mr. Mandelbaum said he had a sixteen-year-old son at home who wanted to be a tailor like him. He didn't know if he should have left him, but he wasn't given much choice.

He asked if I thought the Germans would keep their word and release us after three months. I expressed surprise, saying I hadn't heard anything about that.

Apparently, when he appeared at the Gestapo offices, some Belgians from the labor boards were there. They said that the Organization Todt needed workers to help in the war effort; each group would work, get paid, and be released in three months for a new group.

I replied that I was the only one from Brussels and I never spoke with any Belgians. I laughed derisively at the idea of Germans keeping their word. I reminded him that to the Germans, we Jews were just parasites.

I dozed off. When I awoke, most of the others were sleeping. I slept pretty well, even though the compartment wasn't too comfortable. Dawn appeared on the horizon. I stretched and stepped out of the compartment as quietly as I could and went to the toilet at the end of the aisle.

Standing at the window near our compartment, I opened it to have a smoke and some fresh air. What a beautiful countryside! I had no idea where we were. Admiring the sight, I didn't hear the guard approaching.

His voice startled me. "The window must be closed, or else a few birds might get the idea of flying away."

I closed the window and returned to the compartment, where everyone was now awake.

Mr. Mandelbaum shared the rest of his food and coffee with me, which was very much appreciated. While we smoked, I watched the scenery roll by. We must have been close to the French border. I stepped outside and asked some men standing there if they knew where we were, but they could only guess, too. With nothing else to learn, I went back inside and sat down across from Mr. Mandelbaum.

I told him that the landscape was very familiar—I knew I'd been there before. I would keep my eyes open the next time we passed a town. Although I couldn't be sure, it seemed as if we were heading toward the coast.

Mr. Mandelbaum asked why I thought that. I told him that the Germans were always talking about workers helping their war effort. That probably included building fortifications, especially if the Organization Todt was sponsoring the work, and that had to mean the coast—either Calais or Boulogne-sur-Mer. I knew that the Organization Todt had trucks full of building materials going to those cities.

We rode in silence until we felt the train slowing. We were moving into a station. The sign read "Boulogne-sur-Mer."

I realized I'd been there before. It was a port in northern France on the English Channel, right across from Dover.

The doors opened with a bang and everyone was ordered out. We gathered our belongings and stepped onto the platform. A bit chilly, it was five o'clock in the morning. I was stiff all over. We lined up in rows of five abreast and the sergeant counted us as if we were sheep. Although we were all curious about where we were going, we remained quiet. Silence seemed to be required.

We were ordered to board two trucks. As the sun came up, we slowly proceeded through the town. The coastline and ocean were breathtaking! The city seemed deserted and there was no traffic on the highway. It was Sunday, and people must have been in church or still in bed. It was June 27, 1942.

As we approached a fenced compound, two guards in German army uniforms jumped down to open the gates. When the trucks halted, we were surrounded by soldiers who shouted for us to get out. Scrambling to hold on to our luggage, we jumped down and stood bunched together in the dirt beside the trucks. The camp seemed to have been hastily constructed. Sort of square, almost the size of a football field, it was surrounded by barbed wire. No guards stood at the perimeter, so I thought the enclosure might be electrically charged. I saw two long wooden barracks near the fence, another one across the square, and a fourth one, larger, to the left of that. There was only one gate.

Fine gravel covered a sand base, not too evenly. When it rained, it would be a mess underfoot. During cold weather the wind probably blew through with a vengeance, and in the summer there would be no protection from the sun. Altogether it was a very unappealing and desolate place.

A wooden box somewhat like a playpen sat next to a long trough with faucets. At the far corner of the last barracks was a tent.

Four men exited one of the barracks and approached us. Two looked like Berlin police *Wachtmeister* in blue uniforms. Black SS insignias on their breast pockets indicated they were regular policemen assigned to oversee work camps in occupied territories. The blond, pleasant one would be nice looking out of uniform. The other had black hair and a mean expression. The other two, in civilian clothes, looked more like us.

A regular army sergeant joined them as they came toward us. The blond looked us over, obviously amused, and gave an order to stand at attention. I was already at attention, but the others weren't since they didn't understand German. The blond paced in front of us with an ironic smile. Turning to those with him, he spoke rapidly. "This looks like a pig sty. That's all we need. Oh, well, a little sport will shake the lead out of those bones."

Two guards motioned for us to line up in rows of five in the middle of the square, and the blond shouted his orders: "Everybody lie down! Everybody stand up! Down! Up!" This caused chaos for a while until our group watched and imitated me. They had a tough time; the SS and guards were very amused.

Then the blond shouted, "At top speed, go, go!" We started to jog, only to have him order us to lie down and get up again. All were huffing and puffing; two had collapsed and fainted, some lay prone, and the rest struggled along. During the forty-five minute period, the guards shouted, prodded, and kicked anyone not fast enough. When the abuse finally stopped, one man was coughing and spitting blood, and half of the group lay flat on the ground, unable to move. I tried to help some of the men who couldn't move. My suit was torn and I was filthy, covered with dust, hands cut and bleeding. I was so angry. The only reason for this lesson was to show us who ruled the camp, and to top it, six men died of heart attacks.

We returned to our pile of luggage and waited to be assigned to quarters. The man in charge of this activity was Ernst Schlesinger, an old friend of my family, but he didn't recognize me. Calling out names, he designated either Barracks One or Two. He called my name, looked at me with a jerky motion, squinted, and said "Barracks One." I picked up my luggage and walked to Barracks One.

Three-tiered bunks accommodating 180 men lined the long sides of the barracks. The private alcove opposite the entrance was an office for the barracks chief.

Max, the barracks elder or second in command after the barracks chief, who is the *Blockaelteste*, introduced himself to me and led me to a tier in the middle of the barracks and instructed me. "Take the bottom, it is more practical. You have time to get settled and cleaned up. Then look around and become familiar with the camp. You must be a Berliner from your accent. I am from Cologne. We'll got along fine if you follow the rules." With that, he marched out to direct the others to their places.

Alone for a moment, I looked around. There was no blanket on the bunk—only a straw mattress and fleas having a good time. I wanted to get cleaned up, but since barracks assignments were still being made, I decided to clean my boots first and put my belongings away. With that done, I went out.

I walked toward the wooden box I saw earlier. It was a huge toilet consisting of a big hole in the ground, a wooden square on top, with planks placed across it to provide rudimentary seating. One could easily fall in if not careful. I was surprised that this facility was all open, not only because of the odor but because in warm weather, all sorts of diseases could thrive. No paper was provided. Along the trough was a sign: "Cleanliness is a duty, but drinking will destroy you." I found out later that if one of the SS guards walked past someone sitting there and didn't like the man's face, the guard would push the man in, hold him down with his rifle butt, and within two minutes he would be dead.

I turned on a faucet and knew why we shouldn't drink the water. It was foul smelling. It was also ice cold and there was no soap. I cleaned up as best I could, thinking that the camp couldn't last long with such conditions.

Returning to the barracks, I was startled to see the blond SS man and Schlesinger near the entrance. I halted and stood at attention. The blond one looked me over and said in German, "Are you a Jew?"

"Yes, sir, Sergeant."

Looking surprised, he looked at me again. "Your father is a Jew?"

"Yes, sir, Sergeant."

"Your mother a Jewess?"

"Yes, sir, Sergeant."

"What? The whole family Jews?"

"Yes, sir, Sergeant."

"Where were you born, then?"

"In Berlin, Sergeant, sir."

He shook his head. "I will never believe that you are a Jew. Something isn't right here," and dismissed me.

Inside, I sat on my bunk with my knees shaking. As I sat alone, Ernst walked up to me and said, "Lutz, you're about the last person I expected today. How are you anyway? Even here, it's good to see you."

He explained that although he recognized me earlier, he had to be cautious. He inquired whether my father was still in Gurs. With a heavy heart, I told him I hadn't heard from Papa since 1940, and no one who had returned from Gurs knew him.

Ernst began to tell me about the camp. He said that he and the man in the bunk next to me had been there only two weeks, but they were considered "old timers" or "old inmates."

When I expressed surprise at the term "inmates," Ernst insisted, "That's what we're called, what we are, no matter what they say. *Schutzhaeftlinge* [protective custody inmates] is the official name."

Naively, I asked why it was called a working camp if we were really prisoners. Ernst observed that the expression "working camp" sounded better than "concentration camp."

My hope for a short stay in the camp was fading. "One of the men I came here with said he was told that after three months we would return home and a new bunch would take our place."

"What a joke! This place is for Jews, and the Germans are not about to release anybody. Nobody knows what will happen, probably not even the SS here. All I can say is since we're here, we have to work and try to survive as best we can. The bastards in Berlin don't seem to know what to do with the Jews yet, or if they do, they're not saying. For now, let me tell you the do's and don'ts.

"The hygiene here is nil, and there aren't any medical supplies. Don't drink unboiled water. You can wash, but there is no soap unless you can scrounge some. The same goes for toilet paper. We have a first aid kit, but don't break a leg because there isn't enough in the kit to care for much of anything.

"Most important is food. You get a quarter pound of bread, three quarters of an ounce of margarine, and a pint of coffee in the morning. At noon, a quart of soup consisting of boiled water and a few leaves. At night, another quart of soup, a little thicker. You won't get fat—it's not home cooking.

"The sleeping quarters are not the Grand Hotel. Our barracks have 100 men and they're out working now."

"On Sunday?"

"Yes. I am sure the Germans are trying to find more days to put in a work week. The SS doesn't care about Sundays or about you or your needs. They're concerned about the Fuehrer, the Reich, and their own pockets. Otherwise, they don't care. You are cheap labor. If anything happens to you, it is just one less to feed. You see, the OT [Organization Todt] pays the SS so much per hour for each laborer. One-third goes to Berlin, one-third toward overhead (practically zero), and one-third they keep to use for bribes, payoffs, and good times. So, with everybody under control, it is like a concentration camp. Being born German, you understand this better than the others who've never dealt with Germans. A good deal of hatred develops and that's what is needed to survive. These Belgians are a pretty nice bunch and I don't like to see them mistreated. The SS take full advantage of their position. In a way, I am glad you're here. One needs a countryman to talk to, even a young one like you. And also remember, the two SS men have the power to do as they please with you. If they shoot you, who cares?"

"The same goes for me," I said. "I wanted to ask you about my papa, but I guess you don't know either where he is now."

"No. The last time we were together was in Gurs. I went to St. Cyprien, ran away from there, and returned to Brussels. They didn't come after me because I am only half Jewish. Down south, the Germans and Vichy government decided to let all non-Jews and non-Communists go and keep the rest. They even herded some families together. It was a mess."

"I know. I heard that Papa had lost a lot of weight in three months but was okay otherwise. He needed underwear and other items, so I sent a large package with half his things. It wasn't easy. The German military postal office clerk sent me to the field gendarmes to get approval. They tore the package apart, not believing it was my papa's used clothing, and had me repack it. I never heard whether he got it or not."

"Most packages are never delivered. It is all a scam. We could have used a lot of things. With so many in the camp, it is easy to lose track of friends, and you don't want to make new ones for fear of becoming involved. It is easy to become a loner. There were several camps in the area, and I think your papa was in one of them. I think he was in Bordeaux as an infirmary corpsman at one time, but that's all I know.

"Relax today, Lutz. Tomorrow you'll go out on a work detail. You'll get to know the others. If you need anything, yell so I can hear you."

"Thanks. With your help, I guess I can tolerate this vacation spot. How are the SS and guards toward us?"

"The guards are not bad, not good either—just morons. One or two *Feldwebel* (army sergeants) are sadistic. Watch out for them; they can do whatever they please with you and nobody will bother them.

The *Wachtmeister* with the SS insignia are big wheels and commanders in chief. The blond SS man you met likes you; he thinks you can't be a Jew and are on some kind of undercover mission. Let him think that. He told me, 'I like that little guy. He's not like you people, he's much more like us Germans. I wonder what he is doing here. But I would've been told. Something's puzzling, Schlesinger, but take good care of him.'

"Who knows, Lutz? You are the youngest, and maybe he thinks of you as a mascot. It is the other SS guy you want to stay away from. He's got a mean streak; he's miserable and spiteful. He knows the blond likes you and that means he'll play some vengeful games. There is some sort of rivalry between them. He might try to use you as a pawn, but I know you'll be able to maneuver around him.

"Most of the inmates feel depressed, knowing there is no way out. And we are expecting three or four more transports from Brussels."

"Maybe we'll meet some friends, Ernst, and we can help each other."

"In this type of situation, humans fall apart easily, and you might not be able to count on all of them, maybe only a few."

"We'll just have to rely on ourselves." I lowered my voice. "What are the chances of walking out of this paradise?"

"You mean escape?"

"Yes. Any possibility?"

"Haven't had too much time to think about it, but it could be done. Where would we go if we did?"

"I thought the south, maybe find my papa."

"That's crazy—too far and too close to the French-Spanish border. What would we do if we did get there—go from one camp to another trying to find him? Not too brilliant."

"You're right. Maybe we could hide someplace until the war blows over. How long could it last?"

"The war would go on for a while yet. People are so afraid of the Germans, they won't hide people, especially Jews. I like the idea, though. We could join the resistance, live in the hills or forests. Would the resistance accept us? Let's think about it. On the work detail, we'll have contact with the French and get some information. Then we'll talk about it again."

He left me, walking toward the infirmary. I went to my bunk and fell asleep.

"Get out of that bunk! This is no sanitorium or convalescent home where one rests after lunch. It is not a resort. Up, up!"

I jerked upright and stood at attention.

With a devastating look, a mean-faced sergeant told me there would be no daytime naps.

"No, Sergeant, sir! It will never happen again."

He marched out and I took a deep breath. Before I could exhale, another sergeant came in, looking me up and down.

"So, you are the one. Jew pigs work here and you will be useful. I am watching out that no one cheats. I don't care who you are. My eye is on you."

Feeling degraded, I straightened my bunk and went outside. Mr. Mandelbaum was standing at the far end of the barracks.

"Greetings, Mr. Mandelbaum. How are you doing?"

"Okay, Lutz, but I surely did not expect a place like this. A disgrace. Animals live better!"

"Don't take it too hard. It'll be all right somehow."

"Do you know the barracks chief? I saw you talking with him."

"Yes, he's an old family friend. He gave me some pointers about the camp. Otherwise, he didn't know too much. He said we'll go out to work tomorrow. When the workers come back tonight, we might find out more about our situation."

About seven o'clock, three columns of men marched into camp, five abreast. They looked pitiful, miserable, ragged, filthy, and exhausted. Everyone exited the barracks and watched in silence.

"Oh, Lutz, this is terrible. I can't stand looking at them. I'll never be able to take this life."

"Mr. M., sure you'll make it. We all will. They might look worse than they really are." I was lying, of course.

As soon as the returning workers were in the barracks, we were ordered to assemble outside for a head count. After both sergeants had entered numbers on their clipboards, the count was reported to the two SS men waiting nearby. They seemed satisfied and ordered the workers to be dismissed.

Men who had arrived that morning attempted to talk with the exhausted returning workers but got nowhere. In the barracks, Ernst was holding a ladle over a big barrel, waiting for everyone to form an orderly line. He scooped a ladle of soup into each man's bowl. Those who didn't have one were issued one with the warning that if it was lost, the soup would have to be held in our hands.

I got my soup and went outside, where it was less crowded. Hungry as I was, I could hardly swallow the stuff. Mr. Mandelbaum tried to eat but couldn't. He offered his soup to me, and I took it. I was so hungry I could eat anything.

"Lutz, you are fortunate to be young because you will handle all this easier."

"Mr. Mandelbaum, this isn't the time to be particular. To survive, I have to eat. I'll just close my nose."

I finished, smoked a cigarette in silence, and took our bowls to the trough to clean them. The water was so cold, washing was impossible. A little fellow next to me watched with a smile on his lips.

"You'll never clean it that way. Use some sand, but rinse it well or it will clean your insides, too."

Pleased to know a survival trick, I took the cleaned bowls back to where Mr. Mandelbaum was sitting. Accepting his thanks, I went inside to get ready to sleep. The barracks was filled now, with everyone talking at once. As I put my bowl away, I heard a voice.

"Do I see right or are my glasses fogged up? Is that you, Lutz Posener, my *Voelkerball* [peopleball] player?"

Swinging around, I saw an inmate in his late twenties with heavy horn-rimmed glasses and a big smile. I didn't recognize him.

The inmate frowned. "Ah, I'm saddened. You don't remember me. I'm David Stolowitz. I met you in Brussels in July '39. I was a group leader for the Antwerp Hanoar Hatzioni. Because of you, we lost the peopleball contest at the gathering. But I did enjoy watching you play and wished you were on my team. We chatted after the game, and later, after the dinner and speeches, we talked outside while everyone else was dancing inside."

My memory of that time slowly returned. I recalled David talking about Palestine and idealism and trying to convince me that I belonged in a kibbutz. He told me I could go with a youth transport and that the living in Palestine was great.

David said it was obvious I hadn't taken his advice. He had been at the camp about a week. Although he was sorry I had been sent to that miserable place, he was glad to see me and hoped we could help each other.

I said that I had managed to get some information from Schlesinger, whom I'd known for a long time. David said that was good fortune. Schlesinger was respected by the SS, which might help a little.

When I asked about David's family, he said his wife and young son were with his parents in Antwerp. His wife, Rosa, had no parents of her own.

I then inquired about the work I might be doing. David said he shoveled sand and leveled areas where the Germans wanted to build bunkers. Unlucky workers were assigned to mixing sand and cement to make concrete blocks. It was hard work and with the meager food they received, everyone was exhausted by nightfall.

The *Meister* (German work bosses) apparently thought they would win the war next month. They behaved like world masters. The guards weren't any better. The Germans who were second in command to the *Meister* were really first-class devils. If they didn't like the way someone was working, they beat him with a stick and the guards looked the other way. David cautioned me to stay out of their way.

I said, only half joking, "Hey, David, haven't you heard of sabotage? Let's work with 'hands at rest and eyes wide open.' From now on, we're brothers in joy and sorrow."

Suddenly, German voices shouted. It was time for everybody to be quiet and go to bed. Despite the hard bed, I fell asleep immediately.

Chapter 14

Bong, bong, bong! Was I hearing cow bells? I thought I was on a farm, but then I heard rude shouts and sticks banging on our wooden bunks.

"Let's go, let's go. Scram, scram! Are all of you heavenly dogs hard of hearing? C'mon, let's go, let's go. This ain't no hotel here. Move, move!" The orders, shouted in German, were verbally abusive.

It seemed like the middle of the night to me, but I heard Max say it was already five o'clock.

David shook me. "Come on, Lutz, or you'll really catch it. Can't be slow in the morning!"

It dawned on me where I was. I moved like a bullet—making the bed and stowing my belongings. David and I walked to the trough to wash but had to wait in line. Rather than wait, I tried to use the toilet, but I was too inhibited and nothing happened. Back at the trough, where David had saved my place, I brushed my teeth and washed my face, the cold water shocking me totally awake. It was still dark.

We got our bowls and joined the long food line. David told me that many didn't wash before they ate, or even afterward. Ernst and Max appeared with two workers carrying a box with our bread and oleo rations. Two others carried a kettle with the coffee. The line moved rapidly.

We took our food to the side of the barracks. I didn't like eating outside, but it was forbidden to eat inside the barracks when it was made up. I was told that the two inmates who sweep reported anyone who didn't obey the rules. I finished, looked at David, and asked when we'd get the main course.

He shook his head. "That's it, Lutz."

Suddenly, I had an urge to use the toilet. When I got there, all inhibitions were gone. I felt a lot better. Mr. Mandelbaum was there also, and I shared some scrounged paper with him. We walked back to the barracks together. I couldn't believe that one could get used to this awful place so fast.

I introduced Mr. Mandelbaum to David, who was sitting on the barracks steps, just as Max came by. Max told us to move toward the *Appellplatz* (counting place).

As we walked briskly, I asked David if he thought he could arrange that I stay with him or in the same working group. He said he'd do what he could.

When everyone was assembled, Ernst gave the order to stand at attention—hands to one's side, heads high, motionless and silent. A sergeant counted down the ranks and then counted back up. When the count was finished, we were ordered into columns. David told the guard that I was new and he was supposed to get me started. The guard nodded. As soon as the columns were formed, we marched out of the camp through the open gate and toward the highway. I paid attention to the countryside and landmarks. The information might come in handy sometime.

After a forty-five minute march, we arrived at the work site. The *Meister* and his assistants were waiting. We picked up shovels, picks, and rakes and received instructions. A whistle blew to mark the starting time. We would hear it again at lunchtime and at the end of the workday. It was daylight, and we could see we were not far from the shore. We would probably be able to see the coast of England on a clear day. A foreman showed us what to do and we started. David loosened the ground with a pick and I used a shovel. I thought we were digging a hole so a foundation could be laid for a bunker.

I had never done any real manual labor, so it wasn't easy. The soil was like granite. The sun came up and I began to sweat, so I started to take my outer clothes off.

David shook his head. "You don't want to do that. You'll burn to a crisp and be sick as a dog. Besides, a little sweat never hurt anybody."

Between shoveling and leveling the soil, I was able to smoke and took a look around. Others were doing the same. One guard walked back and forth, another sat on top of a hill overseeing the work site, and the foreman constantly checked our progress. We didn't have much opportunity to just walk away, I realized.

David was a workhorse. He was about five-foot eleven with a muscular build, dark hair, and a nice-looking face. His eyeglass lenses were very thick, and he told me his eyesight was poor. He was gentle and agreeable, and I was lucky to have him for a friend.

Making sure I wouldn't be overheard, I told David not to work so fast. I asked him if he was trying to win the Germans' war all by himself.

He admitted that he tended to work too quickly. He asked me to watch him to make sure he worked at the "proper" pace.

About eleven o'clock, a guard directed two inmates to get the soup for lunch. They returned about forty-five minutes later, struggling with a fifty-liter kettle. Two wooden sticks through the handles allowed the inmates to carry the kettle, but it was so heavy that it swayed from side to side. If they lost control of it, we would have no lunch! But they managed to set the kettle down near the guard.

At noon the whistle blew and we dropped our tools, grabbed our bowls, and formed a line. As I started to eat, I looked at David and said that the only thing good about the food was that it was hot. I looked at the soup and sarcastically exclaimed, "Oh, I found a leaf!"

David smiled. "Eat it. You need whatever nourishment you can get."

Ernst was right—I'd never get fat at camp. But at least the soup filled my stomach. I finished and lit a cigarette.

Several French workers were sitting nearby, but they stayed by themselves. David indicated they were jobbers who got picked up any day there was work. He said they were a "poor bunch," but they would barter with us when they could.

When I asked what they had that we needed, David said they might trade food and cigarettes for money or jewels and other treats. Sometimes they even had alcohol. It was a good idea to be on good terms with them as we might need them one day.

The whistle blew and we returned to work. An hour later the foreman and a guard approached me and asked if I spoke German.

When I said I did, he asked me to follow him. He wanted me to translate his orders to the men who were unloading the cement wagon.

I put down my shovel and went with him to the open door of a railroad car loaded with sacks of cement. Two men took the sacks from the railroad car to two inmates who shouldered them and stacked them nearby.

The guard addressed me. "Tell them to work faster—it all has to be unloaded today—and not to tear the sacks."

I relayed this to the workers and caught the eye of one of them. He smiled faintly and winked at me. The others nodded. The foreman walked me back. Picking up my shovel, I whispered to David that one could really do a lot of sabotage there.

He studied my face, trying to tell if I was truly serious. He warned, "Be sure of what you're doing, Lutz. I don't think you can count on many of these guys." I acknowledged the risk but vowed to do what I could to slow down the war effort.

The first workday passed. At the six o'clock whistle, our cleaned tools were counted, inspected, and stored in a shed. The lineup was counted and marched back to the camp, joined by other groups along the way. Counted again in the camp, we scrambled for the evening meal, a slightly thicker soup than at lunch. Mr. Mandelbaum joined us and ate ravenously. I finished my cigarette and, at David's urging, attempted to clean myself up. Despite the straw mattress, I was soon asleep.

I awoke in the morning in the same position, stiff and aching. David and I were still in yesterday's clothes. We made our bunks, cleaned the area, and rapidly consumed our meager breakfast. I was worried: I was almost out of cigarettes—a necessity!

Shortly we were on the way to the work site under a sun that would be scorching soon. The worker next to me was a trumpeter from Antwerp. He was very thin and didn't look Jewish. In fact, he told me he didn't know he was a Jew until he was picked up and told so.

When I asked how that was possible, he said his parents were not religious and died when he was very young. They never told him he was Jewish and they had nothing Jewish in their home. He was placed with Catholic foster parents, so his background came as a shock. He didn't understand why he was there.

He then offered me some loose tobacco and I accepted it gratefully.

The morning passed and after gulping the noonday soup, I rolled a cigarette. That simple task reminded me of when I used to roll Papa's cigarettes for him. Seeing my less-than-perfect technique, a nearby worker grinned and proceeded to show me how to roll one and watch out for the foreman at the same time. I practiced for an hour and became pretty adept.

At nightfall back at the camp, we ate and prepared for bed, agreeing that the days were bearable and the routine somewhat comforting.

*****

The third day, David and I were assigned to unload the cement. It was blistering hot so I was stripped to my shorts when a cement sack broke and poured over me. With no way to wash it off, I continued to work, feeling miserable. In the afternoon, the *Meister* brought a bucket of water, which David poured slowly over me. I felt better, but the cement still stuck to me. My hair hung in long dirty strands.

As we entered the camp after the workday, the black-haired SS man spotted me and yelled, "You, dumbhead, come over here, and make it fast."

I ran over and stood at attention, and the SS man called for the barber. In the barracks, the barber started to clip my hair with dull clippers, pulling some of the hair out. When I winced and protested that I was not a sheep, he just told me to be quiet.

My beautiful blond curls fell to the ground. The barber continued until my head was smooth. What a weird feeling I had as I rubbed my hand over my shaven head. A small mirror revealed how ugly I looked, and I felt helpless and outcast. I swallowed my tears and my anger.

David commiserated with me. "It'll grow back, Lutz. Besides, everyone's head is to be shaved."

The barber shaved quite a few men, and I supposed the rest would be done tomorrow. I tried to clean up, forgetting all about my evening soup. In my bunk, I fell asleep immediately.

*****

My fourth day in the camp was the hottest yet. I worked in my shorts, and my skin was nicely browned. Others had been badly burned, but not David, whose olive-hued skin was very tan. Our clothes were so filthy they almost stood alone. We had no way to get them really clean. I planned to asked Ernst that night if he had any suggestions.

The day passed and as we assembled in the camp for the evening count, two inmates brought Ernst in, practically carrying him. He was badly sunburned, blistered all over his arms, face, and upper body. When the count was completed, we rushed him to the so-called infirmary. A *Sanitaeter* (medic) covered his burned skin with cold compresses.

Ernst smiled faintly, shivering with fever. He said he felt like the biggest ignoramus around. We assured him that we loved him and asked if there was anything he needed, but he said he was fine.

Back at the barracks, David handed me my soup and asked about Ernst. I said I'd never seen blisters like his. I also told David he was right; I'd better be careful about sunburn.

So far, I'd been too busy adjusting to life in the camp to think about leaving, but I hadn't given up the thought of devising a plan. At that moment, though, all I wanted to do was sleep.

* * * * *

The next morning before I could go to the infirmary to check on Ernst, I saw him approaching. I was surprised to see him on his feet. He said he would stay inside that day and be fine by evening. Then, good-naturedly, he told me to get moving.

At the work site, I told David that Ernst still looked bad but had weathered the crisis. While leaning on my shovel, I heard the foreman shout, "Move, move! We need to get these bunkers ready. This isn't a sanitarium here!"

Under my breath I responded, "The less ready they are, the better."

"What did you say, you lazy piece, you?"

"Ah, nothing. I didn't say anything."

"Well, all right." And he walked away.

I turned to David. "I guess I'll have to watch it. These Krauts keep their ears open."

We worked on. My arms itched. The itching had awakened me during the night, and now it was starting again. David said I had crab lice, as did many other inmates, because of the straw and dirt and the

As we were being counted that night at the camp, a sergeant started hitting a man so hard he keeled over into the mud. As he lay there, the sergeant repeatedly kicked him in the head and ribs, yelling for him to get up. He didn't so the sergeant picked him up and threw him to the ground. The man landed heavily, groaned, and sighed one last breath. We were hypnotized by the scene, and I clenched my fists tightly. David noticed and motioned me to stop doing that.

The guard marched up and down in front of us. "This will happen to all of you if I see you looking at me like he did."

I felt like killing him, but I was scared and just stood motionless. We were dismissed, and two inmates took the dead man's body to the infirmary.

The bread we got was wet and had a terrible taste. We ate it anyway because we were so hungry. After we ate, I showed my hands and arms to Ernst. He couldn't identify my problem but said he'd try to find out the next day and let me know.

In the meantime, the ooze from my blisters dried and then stuck to my clothes. No one else seemed to have blisters or show signs of a fever or the shivers. I hadn't taken my clothes off in two days and felt so dirty. Miserable—wet and itching—I tried to fall asleep.

The next day it had stopped raining. Even though it was cold, I worked at the site stripped down to allow my clothes to dry. By then the itching had spread all over my legs. And the more I scratched, the more I hurt.

In the evening, I washed as best I could and went to the infirmary. The medic gave me a cream I hoped would help. I smeared it all over me, put on my last set of underwear, and went to bed.

In the morning I was in worse shape than ever. Cursing and swearing, I returned to the infirmary and demanded to see the medic. Told he was not available, I loudly insisted I had to see him. When he came in, I told him I was worse, and he said, "Well, complain to the SS. I don't know what else to tell you."

Enraged, I left the infirmary and met Ernst on my way back to the barracks. When I told him what the medic suggested, he agreed I should talk to the SS about my problem. I decided to wait until evening, and I worked at the site throughout the day feeling very uncomfortable, not helped by a fine mist that fell all day.

Ernst walked with me to the SS office. Thankfully, it was the blond sergeant who came to speak with me. "What's the matter, peewee?"

Ernst explained and I rolled up my shirt sleeves. He took one looked and said with disgust, "Oh, yes. That is the mange or scabies— very, very contagious. Horrible! Tomorrow is Saturday and you might as well stay inside the camp, and on Sunday it is off to the hospital.

"In the meantime, stay away from everybody, understood? I can't afford to have you contaminate everybody. That's *all* I need now. First, two dead, then seven in the hospital already, then another dead one, and now this. Nothing but a nuisance, these Jews. One more time, keep away from everybody."

"Yes, sir." With that, Ernst and I retreated.

Ernst told me I should be happy. A stay at the hospital meant being away from the camp. It would give me a chance to recuperate as well as a little bit of freedom. I was lucky in a way because the SS men were paranoid about contagious diseases, especially skin conditions.

* * * * *

I slept well but awoke itching. When the others left for the work site, I crawled into my bunk. Ernst had somehow excused himself from work for the day, and together we ate our midday soup and some bread he had saved. He agreed I should try to get information on the progress of the war and whatever else was going on outside while I was in the hospital. For his part, Ernst would try to argue his way into escorting other sick inmates to the hospital so we could talk there. When he left me, I fell asleep again.

Chapter 15

When Ernst woke me the next morning for roll call, I was itching again, and there were no more bandages for my sores. I was afraid to take my clothes off; everything stuck to my skin! I tried to get ready for the day and gathered my few belongings. Most of my clothes had been thrown away because they couldn't be cleaned to wear again. It was easier to travel light, I told myself. I looked forward to my trip to the hospital. Another inmate from the camp was also going to the hospital; his knee was very swollen, and he could hardly walk.

I said goodbye to Ernst, Max, and Mr. Mandelbaum. After giving me a big hug, David choked back tears and left quickly. I felt I was losing a part of myself, abandoned again. After the count, the work detail marched out. David waved, and I waved back. One of the guards yelled, "What do you think you're doing? This isn't a summer camp. Get your junk together and get over to the truck!"

When my suitcase was thrown onto the truck, I helped the man with the bad knee. As soon as we were settled, the blond SS officer walked over. I jumped to the ground and stood at attention.

The sergeant was almost friendly. "Just watch it, peewee, and keep your hands off the nurses at the hospital."

After assuring him I would do as he said, I climbed back in the truck, and we slowly moved out of the camp and onto the highway to Boulogne-sur-Mer. What a great feeling it was to be out of the camp! My spirits climbed and some energy crept back into my body. I breathed deeply—the sea air was intoxicating.

The truck pulled up before a brick building that looked like an old fortress. A Red Cross flag flew and a big sign said "Hospital St. Louis." Nuns dressed in long black robes, heads covered with black veils, walked by, their hands hidden in sleeve folds. I had read about these cloisters. Two orderlies appeared and placed my companion on a stretcher. A nun observed me as I hopped down. A guard pointed at me and said to her, "That one, he's a Frenchman. Yes, yes, Frenchman."

The nun approached and asked if I was French. I told her that although I wasn't, I could speak the language. She explained that the hospital had dire need of a translator as the staff couldn't understand what the inmates were saying about their illnesses.

The truck left and I followed the nun into an office. I was free. No more guards!

The nun introduced herself as Sister St. Augustine, and then left me with the clerk to fill out forms.

As I finished, Sister St. Augustine returned with another nun and announced, "This is Sister St. Benoit who will take you to her pavilion."

"How do you do, Sister Benoit. My name is Lutz Posener."

"Lutz? That's a German name, isn't it? Your French is so fluent, no one would ever guess."

Somewhat hesitantly, I explained my background. I felt somewhat awkward in her presence.

She sensed my uneasiness. "You needn't felt strange. We are of the Catholic Dominican order and professional nurses. We help the sick and our devotion is to God."

I picked up my suitcase and we walked outside into an enormous courtyard. Passing through an archway, we entered the pavilion and walked through a doorway into a hall. The sister opened a door and I saw three beds. Everything was immaculate. I took the bed nearest the huge window that overlooked the yard.

When I showed her the contents of my suitcase, she was repelled and told me that I should remove any personal items because the clothing had to be destroyed. I did so and she left with the suitcase. Throwing myself on the bed was a mistake; my clothing ripped away from my skin. But as painful as it is, I felt I was floating on air. It was so silent and peaceful here, I thought, I wanted to stay forever.

Soon the sister returned with towels and a tray of bottles, tubes, and gauze pads. She said a nice, hot bath would help my skin.

Down the corridor, we stopped at a door posted "Shower Rooms." A very strong disinfectant odor drifted toward me, as well as another smell. When I asked about the odor I couldn't identify, the sister said it was sulphur ointment, which was very healing for the skin.

Removing my clothing was very painful, and the sister suggested I soak it off in the tub. The water was so hot and stinging to my sores that I swore, forgetting about the sister's presence. But soon the water loosened my shirt and it could be peeled off. I apologized for my outburst.

The sister, thankfully, was not offended. She told me to finish removing my clothing and excused herself for a moment.

After removing the rest of my clothes easily, I lolled in the tub. The sister returned while I was standing up, trying to add a little cold water. Noticing my embarrassment, she put me at ease. "Don't concern yourself; I've seen naked men before. Nursing is my vocation and the human body is part of my profession."

She spread an ointment over my body and started to scrub me with a bristle brush. I cringed with pain, but she said it was the only way to get rid of the problem.

She ran fresh water into the tub and I sat down, feeling much better. When I dried off, the sister smeared me with sulphur and wound bandages all over me so I looked like a mummy. The pajamas she offered were three sizes too large, as were the slippers, but they felt wonderful. I looked so funny she grinned. Back in my room, I apologized again, climbed between the sheets, and fell asleep.

* * * * *

The next morning I sensed someone approaching my bed and opened my eyes to see Sister St. Benoit's smiling face. It was only 6:30, but I'd had a wonderful night's sleep.

After taking my pulse and temperature, the sister left to bring me breakfast. I checked my arms and legs and almost all the sores were healed. Waiting for breakfast, I watched the sun slowly rise. A few nuns crossed the courtyard and went about their business.

Breakfast arrived on a tray and smelled delicious—Cream of Wheat hot cereal, two French rolls with butter and jam, milk, and coffee. I couldn't remember ever being sick enough to have breakfast in bed, but it was quite wonderful. The food disappeared rapidly and I leaned back to enjoy a cigarette. When Sister St. Benoit returned for the tray, I learned that smoking was permitted only in the hallway and out of doors. She had a second item of unwelcome news: I had to have another bath to continue treatment of my sores. The bath was not as painful as the previous day's, but the odor was still pretty unpleasant. Afterward, I returned to bed very groggy and slept until early afternoon.

Putting on the robe Sister St. Benoit had left for me, I went into the hallway for a cigarette. Kitchen workers and cleaning women with carts all smiled and greeted me. The afternoon passed pleasantly. At six o'clock the sister came back to take my pulse and temperature.

I was feeling so good I wanted to see what was outside the building. "May I walk outside? Tomorrow?"

"The doctor will examine you tomorrow. Meantime, more food and rest. I'll bring you a book to read so the time will pass faster."

Sister brought me *The Count of Monte Cristo* by Alexandre Dumas. I'd read it twice in school, but it helped the evening pass. I fell asleep with the lights on.

In the morning I waited for the doctor's arrival. A young man with a pleasant smile, he introduced himself. "Good morning I am Dr. Buzet. How are you today?"

"Much better today; my sores are nearly gone and the itching, too. When might I go outside?"

He examined my arms and legs, nodding approval.

"When the sores are completely healed in a day or two, you will be able to go outside. I am sure you'd like to visit with other camp inmates. Perhaps I could use you as an interpreter. You speak several languages?"

I told him of my background and fluency in German, French, and Flemish. I mentioned that I could also converse in Yiddish and manage quite well in Hebrew.

"An uncommon talent. Maybe I can find a way to keep you here permanently as an interpreter. More of your people will be coming here, I am sure. In the meantime, rest up. When you go out Thursday you can acquaint yourself with your surroundings. Sister St. Benoit will be caring for you while I am away for a few days."

What wonderful news! Maybe I wouldn't have to go back to the camp! Maybe I could even find a way to leave here!

* * * * *

Thursday finally arrived. Sister St. Benoit pronounced me cured, and I dressed in the clothes she brought me. I felt human again—face shaved and hair (what was left!) combed. Outside I went to the grassy, flowered courtyard with its bushes and pathways. I walked the paths, greeted other convalescents, and finally sat down on a bench, tired. The hospital gave the impression of being a twelfth-century castle.

Later after more rest and some dinner, I walked the hallways, smoking. My spirits were returning and I started to think about how to quietly discuss leaving with others who might have similar thoughts. I had mixed feelings, though, because everyone had been so nice to me here, particularly Sister St. Benoit. She was a unique person; always kind and gentle, never perturbed or mad.

The next day I was directed to another building where there were others from the camp. The clean, bright room held twenty-four beds. A sister led me to the bed of an elderly man.

"Mr. Labitsky, this is the young fellow I told you about." Puzzlement showed on his face because he didn't understand what she said.

"I'll translate, Sister, and then visit for a while with him." I was able to relay to the sister that Mr. Labitsky was comfortable and needed nothing. To me he indicated one complaint, however: the tall nun who was second in command was thoroughly anti-Semitic. In fact, she hated everyone in the whole world who wasn't a devout Catholic. No one liked her, he said, and he warned me to avoid her.

We met many men from the camp, all in their midfifties. None spoke French, but all could converse with me in Yiddish. Most of them had migrated from Poland to Belgium in 1919–20, and many were really sick. After some discussion, we decided to go to the office the following day to make their needs better known.

On the way back to my room I met the young lady from the office, and I told her that some of us would be in the administrative building office in the morning so our records could be updated.

"Fine," she said. "We need someone who can help us translate for them."

I slowly walked through the lovely grounds. How lucky I was to be there.

* * * * *

The next day at ten o'clock, we crowded into the office. Only the young lady was there. It took all day to process everyone. The men left and the young lady thanked me with a smile, agreeing to put in a good word with Dr. Buzet about my helpfulness with the inmates so I could stay there permanently.

Heading back to my room, I almost collided with Sister St. Benoit. When I told her how well the day went she reminded me that doing something for others does something for ourselves. She promised to asked Dr. Buzet to help me stay at the hospital as well.

In the morning, the sister told me I was to have breakfast with Dr. Buzet, and I sped to the nearby building where medical and administrative personnel and some of the sisters were billeted. Supplies and equipment were stored there, too. Another nearby building housed the operating rooms, facilities, and recovery rooms.

The doctor was pleased to see my recovery. When we were seated outside to enjoy the fine morning, the food arrived. I ate until I was stuffed and leaned back to enjoy a cigarette the doctor thoughtfully provided. I thanked the doctor for the food and cigarettes and for the good treatment all the men were receiving.

The doctor said that Mademoiselle Perrault, the office secretary, had given me a glowing reference. Both Sister St. Benoit and he were impressed with me, and he'd been able to persuade the Mother Superior to keep me there as long as possible.

I was so happy I choked on the cigarette and began to cough. When I was able to breathe again, the doctor set forth the ground rules for my stay at the hospital.

They expected many more inmates from the camp. I could help by setting up more beds and storing equipment and supplies. I would be a liaison to translate and relay patients' needs and complaints. Most important, I was to ensure that patients did not leave the hospital or steal anything.

I assured him that I could handle the responsibility.

The doctor had one final warning: I was to stay out of sight when any SS guards were around. He didn't want any questions arising about me.

When he was sure I understood what was expected of me, he told me to meet him at eleven o'clock in front of my pavilion. I was to begin my new job then.

It had happened! I was staying! I wouldn't have to go back to the camp! I smoked another cigarette to calm down and began to think. This job was a big responsibility, but I could do it. The doctor also said that there were to be no escapes, so I set aside any thoughts I had about leaving—at least for the time being.

When the doctor took me on his rounds, I soon realized that I must take care to interpret exactly. The task wasn't as easy as I had thought. Rounds took up quite a bit of the day—each inmate had an opportunity to tell the doctor exactly what his condition was and ask questions. When we were finished, the doctor dismissed me and told me we would do rounds together the next day.

I went back to my room and devoured the tray of food the sister had left, had a cigarette, and drifted off to sleep.

Chapter 16

The sister took my temperature and pulse and pronounced me fit for my new job. I made rounds again with Dr. Buzet and became more familiar with the hospital and the staff. Soon we were finished and the rest of the day was mine!

Across the courtyard, Sister St. Benoit was standing with several nuns. She motioned me to come to her. As I walked toward the group, I saw a very tiny sister standing in the center of the group. Sister St. Benoit introduced me. "Reverend Mother, this is Lutz Posener, the young boy I told you about."

"Oh, yes," the tiny nun nodded her head and squinted at me. She must have been eighty years old. She shook my hand and welcomed me. With that, two of the nuns supported her as they walked toward the building.

One of the sisters, the tallest, looked down at me with a fixed stare. "Of course, we have rules and regulations here that everyone must follow. That includes all prisoners, Jews or not. I suppose you are a Jew like the others, even though you don't look like one."

Mr. Labitsky was right. She had no liking for Jews. I began to boil inside!

"Yes, Sister, I am Jewish. And the camp inmates are able to follow your rules, just like everyone else. I don't think it is too kind of you to jump on my comrades because they can't understand you. If you have any complaints or my comrades don't respond fast enough for you, just let me know and I'll deal with it. I am very able to handle all this."

"Well," she sputtered. "I give the orders here!" She strode away.

I had better watch out for her, I said to myself. She could be trouble, and we certainly don't need any trouble right now.

Sister St. Benoit caught up with me later. "The Reverend Mother was pleased to meet you. But I saw you had words with Sister Theresa. She doesn't like any of you, nor does she like many other people. Avoid her. I shouldn't say this, but she can be very troublesome."

She took me on a tour of the rest of the hospital and grounds. We entered the surgical building, which also contained recovery rooms and labs. Everything was so clean. The odor of disinfectant mixed with the smell of ether unsettled my stomach. We continued to the morgue. Two bodies were lying on cement slabs. One was only half covered. I began to feel nauseated. Aware of my discomfort, the sister walked me quickly to the exit.

We continued our tour and when we had seen everything, the sister left me sitting on a bench, enjoying the fine sunshine. On a nearby bench sat a young, attractive woman. She was wearing a long robe and her left hand was fully bandaged. She stood up to leave, and as she walked by she gave me a big smile. I smiled back and felt warm inside. She was my height, rather thin, with dark blond, straight hair. I decided to try to meet her tomorrow. I wondered how old she was.

As soon as Doctor Buzet and I finished making rounds the next day, I walked through the garden, hoping to see the young woman. There she was, even prettier than I remembered. She was still in the robe but her bandage looked smaller. Our paths crossed and we both looked up at the same time. She smiled and my heart pounded. I smiled back and stuttered, "Good day, mademoiselle. How, er, how are you?"

"Fine, thank you. You must be the fellow who interprets for the men from the camp. My name is Louise."

As we walked along the path, she saw me looking at her hand and told me that she neglected an infected hangnail until her whole hand was swollen. Dr. Buzet had to cut one of her fingers off in order to save her arm.

"I am alive and I can do without a finger. But my husband is very upset, and our daughter doesn't know yet."

I was disappointed—she had a husband and daughter. I told her how I came to be in the hospital and about my new job with Dr. Buzet. Just then her husband, Jean, and daughter, Nicolette, came by and she introduced me. Jean was a steel worker, unemployed since there was no work. Louise and Jean were born and raised in Boulogne-sur-Mer, so they could be very helpful if any of the inmates were to try to escape.

During the day, a basement in the building nearby was set up to receive seventeen more camp inmates who had been injured. By the time we were finished, thirty inmates could be accommodated. The orderlies started to bring them in on stretchers. I was kept very busy answering questions and helping to get them settled. A large part of my time was spent trying to find out if any of the inmates' friends and relatives had also arrived at the hospital.

By Sunday, everyone was settled and it was peaceful. I was getting along very well with everyone except Sister Theresa. I thought I could feel comfortable here forever, but I knew I must not get complacent.

* * * * *

September was approaching and ninety-five inmates were in the hospital. I had been there for more than a month. On Monday, we buried the eleventh hospitalized inmate to die in a small section of the local cemetery reserved for Jews. We always managed to gather a minion (ten men), required to conduct any kind of a service, according to Jewish law. This was a chance to be outside the hospital walls. Sister St. Benoit warned me to be cautious and reminded me that I was responsible for keeping the men from escaping. Even so, it was exciting to be in the city and to talk to people.

We left the hospital, walking behind the funeral carriage drawn by two horses. Uphill and downhill we trudged to the cemetery and then followed the path to the Jewish section. It was old and not well kept. One of us led the service, saying the eulogy and prayers and the traditional prayer for the dead, the *Kaddish*. Then the earth was shoveled back into the ground.

On the way back to the hospital, we stopped at a tavern and had a brandy. Everyone who attended the burial arrived back at the hospital without incident.

The next day an inmate's leg was to be amputated and Dr. Buzet let me watch the operation. Clothed in a white gown and mask, I stood behind a window-like frame in the operating room. Three big lights focused on a rotating table in the center of the room. When three sisters completed their preparations, the unconscious patient was wheeled in and placed on the table, and his leg was swabbed with strong disinfectant. Dr. Buzet and his assistant entered. At the first cut, blood began to ooze out. Unpleasant as this was to watch, I was able to remain until the doctor began to saw the leg off. I barely made it to a nearby bathroom before I vomited. Surgery was not for me!

Soon Dr. Buzet came out of the operating room and handed me a sheet-wrapped object. I knew what it was. He said we were taking it to the morgue—that I had to become used to seeing things like that.

We entered a small, windowless building next to the morgue with a chimney rising from the roof. A simple altar stood against one wall with a crucifix hanging above it. An orderly in a white coat took the package from my hands, opened one of the three iron doors set into one wall, and placed the package inside on a tray. Flames erupted under the tray and the door was closed. An unfamiliar odor hit me.

By now I was shaking and in tears. I asked the doctor why he wanted me to go through that awful experience. He replied that he wanted to toughen me and that I should get used to such encounters.

Still revolted by the morning's events, I started back to my room. Louise was waiting on a bench outside to tell me she would be discharged the next day. Handing me a slip of paper with her address on it, she said, "If you need help, please come to us. If you have free time in the city, visit us."

*****

The next day I felt better, although I hadn't gotten over the previous day's shock.

After rounds, one of the inmates was waiting for me at the pavilion. He handed me a package. "This is from all of us—a little token of our appreciation for everything you do for us."

Back in my room, I opened the package on the bed. Inside were cake, some cookies, chocolate, candies, and three packs of cigarettes. I was delighted to receive such a treat!

I was lying on my bed around noontime when Sister St. Benoit entered with a young man. He was nice looking and had a muscular build. She introduced me to Joseph Janowsky, from the camp, my new roommate. He spoke French and was eighteen years old. He announced that Ernst Schlesinger and David sent their greetings; Ernst said he'd try to see me one day. Many more people were in the camp and conditions had gotten worse.

We talked as we ate lunch and throughout the afternoon. All the treats disappeared as well. Joseph (or Jossel, as I called him) and I were old friends by supper time.

* * * * *

In the morning we talked some more. Jossel told me that inmates could receive packages now. This explained the one the patients gave me.

Sister St. Benoit came to tell me I was wanted in the office— four more inmates had arrived from the camp. As Jossel and I entered the hallway outside the office, I saw Maxel, an old acquaintance, on a stretcher against the wall. His face was very pale and his eyes were closed. Before the orderlies took him away, I grasped his hand; he opened his eyes for a moment. "What a surprise to see you, Lutzel," he said, then closed his eyes again.

Jossel asked how I knew Maxel. I told him that our families were friends in Berlin and I knew him in Brussels, too. He was older, twenty-three. Noticing my concerned expression, Jossel insisted that I go see my old friend. He said he'd stay to help with the new people from the camp.

Rushing into the pavilion, I bumped into Sister St. Benoit. "Where's the new one, Sister? What's wrong with him?"

She told me Maxel was in the last room on the second floor and that he was sedated and sleeping. She didn't know what was wrong— the doctor couldn't see him until the following morning.

I peeked into Maxel's room and tiptoed away. The other newcomers had been settled in their beds, so Jossel and I spent the day talking and walking around the grounds.

* * * * *

After a bad nightmare-filled night, I was up early to go on rounds with Dr. Buzet. After lunch he told me that Maxel was very, very ill. Dysentery had left him so weak he hadn't any strength left to fight it. Dr. Buzet couldn't assure me Maxel would get better. When I entered the room to see him, he was sitting up, eating pudding, but he was obviously very ill.

I tried to use my cheeriest voice. "They'll pep you up here," I assured him. I told him to get some rest and we'd talk the following day.

When I got back to my room, Jossel showed me two packages of treats one of the inmates had brought by. We spent the afternoon snacking and talking. Just before supper, I visited with some of the patients. The amputee was feeling stronger and I could finally face him.

The September air in the mornings and evenings was cool and fragrant, but the days were still sunny and warm. Leaves were turning brownish red.

I went to see Maxel at noon. He hadn't been able to eat much of his lunch and didn't look any better. We talked for a while until he fell asleep.

Later, as I sat on the steps outside, a French gendarme appeared, leading a group of twelve women accompanied by two policewomen. One woman, young and very pretty, looked straight at me and smiled. My face became very red and warm. I stared at the group as it entered one of the buildings.

One of the orderlies slapped me on the back. "Don't bother with any of them. They're all prostitutes with diseases. They'll be in isolation on the top floor of that building until they get well. Then it's back on the streets until the next time."

When I saw Dr. Buzet, I asked him about Maxel. The doctor said Maxel was worse and the medication didn't seem to help. I should just sit with him and not talk too much because he needed lots of rest. The doctor didn't know if Maxel would get better.

I had received a bar of Cote d'Or chocolate, and I took it with me the next time I visited Maxel. He refused it but wanted to talk so I helped him sit up. He said my name, sighed, and fell back limp. For a moment I didn't realize what had happened. Then for a long time I sat in the chair, staring at him. Sister St. Benoit came in and looked at us, then leaning over, she shut Maxel's eyelids. I left the room angry at God for taking poor Maxel and I spent the rest of the day in a depressed daze.

Chapter 17

On the day of Maxel's burial, we marched to the cemetery at ten o'clock. As the coffin was lowered into the ground I wanted to scream, "It isn't fair, it isn't right!" I grabbed a shovel and worked furiously, which lessened some of my anger and grief.

On the way back from the cemetery, we stopped at the tavern. After four shots of cognac, I was inspired to sing the French national anthem in German. The others dragged me back to my room and put me to bed.

One day after rounds, I found a letter on my pillow addressed to "Monsieur Frize" (Mr. Curly). It was written in French.

> My dear friend,
>
> I am the young girl among the women who arrived the other day who smiled at you. I am twenty-four years old and I think you're awfully cute. I'd like to get to know you. The messenger is here to take this to you. If you write me a note, he will bring it to me.
>
> Many kisses,
> Yvonne

I looked out the window toward her building. There she was, waving. She threw a kiss.

When I turned away from the window, Jossel was grinning at me.

I was a bit embarrassed. "Why, you knew all along, Jossel!"

"Oh, yes," he said nonchalantly. "I got the letter first, sniffed it, and put it on your pillow."

I sat down to write a note to Yvonne. I was sure we would find a way to meet, and in the meantime we could exchange notes through the messenger. He was outside when I finished and I handed him my note as casually as I could.

We kept this up for three days. Every free moment I had I looked at her window and waved. She was there every time, waving back at me. Even my sadness about Maxel couldn't overcome my longing to be with Yvonne.

One morning Yvonne's note said she was to be taken to the x-ray department at ten o'clock that day. She wondered if I could meet her there. I could hardly wait!

I was there by 9:45, pacing back and forth. At 9:55, six women arrived, including Yvonne. Her paperwork was completed first and when the guard became busy with the others, she walked toward me and extended her hand. "Good morning, Lutz, my curly friend. Finally I can see you up close."

I squeezed her hand—it was so warm and soft. "Bonjour, Yvonne. I am so happy to make your acquaintance."

We stood as if glued to the floor, gazing at each other. My face was glowing warmly! We decided to try to find some way to be alone with each other.

I floated out of the building in a dream! Later, when I approached Sister St. Benoit about my spending time with Yvonne, I stuttered and swallowed hard but she finally understood what I was asking. "If the policewoman doesn't mind, then you and Yvonne can visit in the last room at the end of the hallway."

Late in the afternoon, the sister returned. "All right, she'll be here tomorrow at two o'clock. I've found a small radio so you can listen to music. You can have two hours, not more. Play the radio softly. And one more thing: her tests were negative, so she's all right."

I looked at my shoes, speechless. I finally muttered, "Thank you, Sister." I ran to my room and told Jossel, who just smiled.

* * * * *

I spent a lot of time preparing the room, which contained a couch with a small table and two chairs. At the appointed time, the radio was playing soft music. I'd brought two chocolate bars, a large piece of cake, and a package of Des Gauloises cigarettes. Two roses stolen from the garden were in a drinking glass.

The door opened and Yvonne entered. Sister St. Benoit, behind her, nodded her head and closed the door.

I hugged Yvonne and gave her the traditional French three kisses on the cheeks. She held me close, warm lips on mine. I was really floating. I lit her cigarette and mine.

She told me she had had only two boyfriends. One got married and the other was a prisoner of war in Germany. She was certain that when he came back and found out what she had to do to survive, he wouldn't want her.

I told her I understood, that it hadn't been easy for me, either. To me, she was a nice girl and a good person.

We ate the cake and listened to the radio. Before long, the announcer gave the time—it was already time for Yvonne to leave. I gave her the chocolate and, after one more embrace, opened the door. The police-woman was already waiting.

I straightened the room and returned to my own room. Jossel grinned. I cautioned him not to say a word or he'd break the spell—I loved the world!

He said I might feel differently tomorrow. Dr. Buzet wanted me to have breakfast with him in the morning.

* * * * *

The next morning, Dr. Buzet said he hoped I had a good time with Yvonne. Somewhat mysteriously, he said she might be helpful to me in the future.

We finished eating and began to smoke. The doctor spoke to me frankly, saying the idea of going south to find my papa was foolish at the moment. The Germans were emptying the camps in the south, bringing all the inmates up north. All Jews in France were being rounded up and placed in camps near Paris. This was happening in Belgium and Holland and in other occupied countries, too.

The whole country was swarming with Nazis. Traveling or moving about was not safe, and my situation with the hospital couldn't last forever. The doctor said that the sergeant asked for me whenever he brought inmates to the hospital. He suggested trying to make the sergeant believe I had escaped, but he wanted to know if I had any other ideas how to avoid going back to the camp.

He invited me to dinner the following Saturday for a talk. I agreed happily. A restaurant would be a nice change from the hospital, and I would meet his sister. All week as I went about my duties, I was thinking about my future.

Jossel was well and on Friday he left to go back to the camp. After he and some others left it was lonely, but I had a new roommate and my duties kept me very busy.

* * * * *

Saturday evening arrived and Dr. Buzet met me in front of the building. He informed me that we would be dining at one of Boulogne's best fish restaurants.

The evening was cool and the sea breeze hit me as we walked through the town. Boulogne-sur-Mer, located on the English Channel about twenty miles southwest of the town of Calais, was an important fishing port. An old town dating back to the thirteenth century, its commerce also included cement plants, foundries, and textile factories, as well as cordage, earthenware, and footwear manufacturers. The Germans occupied the town in 1940 and built many fortifications along the seashore.

At the crowded restaurant, Dr. Buzet was greeted by everyone, who looked at me quizzically. The place was heavy with smoke and a great aroma of fish and wine. A waiter led us to a table where a woman was seated. She was tall and about forty-five years of age.

The doctor introduced me to his sister, Francoise LeFleur. Then he told me to order whatever I wanted and not to be bashful. I eagerly asked for bouillabaisse and a pot of mussels.

While we waited for the food, Dr. Buzet told Francoise what we had talked about at the hospital. She hinted she might possibly hide me. Then, leaning toward me, she asked in a low voice, "How about joining the underground? They could always use a runner or messenger. With your looks and languages, you'd be very valuable to the Maquis."

The food arrived. It was the best I'd eaten in a long time and I finished every bite. Our glasses were filled with wine and Dr. Buzet toasted a better life, the defeat of the German army, and lasting peace.

When the plates were removed, Dr. Buzet ordered cognac. While we sipped and smoked, the café door opened and four German officers entered and seated themselves at the next table. They ordered food and drinks and started talking about the war. I listened in.

Francoise watched me. "Louis—I shall call you that; it's not so Germanic—can you understand them?"

I nodded and indicated that they were talking about some orders from their headquarters in Berlin. As the Germans continued to discuss the war, I translated for Dr. Buzet and Francoise. Soon their conversation turned to mundane matters.

Francoise brought up a new subject. "Doctor told me you have a little girlfriend in the hospital who's leaving tomorrow. I hope you know where she can be reached."

The doctor looked sheepish. "Ah, yes, Louis. I didn't have a chance to tell you."

Francoise continued, "I'd like you to visit her here in the city— Doctor will give you permission. You and she could pass as my children. I'd take you to a place frequented by many Germans where you could listen to their conversations. The information you pick up would be very helpful to some people I know. We can get passes for you to be out after curfew. Your friend would have to agree and we'd need to be sure she can be trusted."

Of course I agreed to help. I would have an opportunity to pass on valuable information and, best of all, be with Yvonne overnight.

Outside, Francoise kissed me on both cheeks and said good night. As the doctor and I headed back to the hospital, I thanked him for a great evening and wondered what would come of the evening's conversations.

Chapter 18

In the morning, I sent a note to Yvonne saying that I had to see her. She replied that I should meet her at noon in the room next to the office.

She was already waiting for me when I arrived. When I related to her what had taken place when I dined with the doctor and his sister, she agreed to work with us.

Before leaving, she gave me her address. I found Dr. Buzet and told him the good news. In his quarters, he handed me a curfew pass, a hospital in and out pass, and a paper stating I was on the hospital staff.

He told me not to eat supper since I would be eating at the restaurant later. Most importantly, I was not to ever speak German except in extreme circumstances. It was important people didn't know I understood what is being said.

I approached the front gate of the hospital at five o'clock. The security guard nodded at my pass and I was out! Even if I wasn't really free, I felt great. It didn't take me long to reach the address Yvonne had given me. It was an old four-story building whose stairs were in very bad condition. As with many old buildings, it had a peculiar odor.

When I found number three on the second floor, I knocked gently. The door opened slightly and Yvonne peeked out, then she threw the door open to pull me inside for a bear hug.

Yvonne offered me a cognac. We sat and smoked and sipped, waiting for Francoise. Yvonne rushed me into the toilet room to hide when we heard a knock, but when I heard Francoise's voice, I came back into the living room.

"Hello, Francoise. This is Yvonne. She is willing to help."

"Good. You will both be able to pass as my children. You are Louis now, not Lutz, and you must not speak a word of German. Listen well, but don't be obvious about it. Remember all you can about what is said."

We walked for fifteen minutes and arrived at an unimportant-looking restaurant. Not imposing inside, either, it was full and busy already. Deliberately, the maitre d' seated us near a group of German civilians who were discussing nothing of importance. I ordered a pot of mussels, garlic bread, and salad. The ladies ordered beef and vegetables.

As we ate, I gathered from the conversation at the next table that the men were all newly arrived from Berlin. Some were members of the Gestapo and the others belonged to the Sicherheitsdienst (Security Service), a political cleanup crew for the Reich. One or two were high-ranking SS men. They began to talk about future events. I couldn't believe what I was hearing!

The Germans paid the waiter and left. As I started to speak, Francoise gave me a warning glance.

When the Germans' table was cleared and reset, five middle-ranking SS men sat down and made small talk among themselves. One, a lieutenant, stared at us—particularly me. I turned to Francoise and suggested that we had better leave now. I didn't like the attention I was getting.

As we started to leave, the lieutenant came over and my heart dropped into my shoes.

"Heil Hitler."

I slowly looked at him. "Hello."

"We do know each other, don't we?"

In French I asked him what he was saying. He looked at me in disbelief.

"I am sure that I know you. You can't fool me, even with that French jabbering."

I remained silent. He shook his head and returned to his seat. Yvonne and I left quickly, and Francoise joined us after a word with the maitre d'. We walked to Yvonne's place, taking care that no one followed us. I was still shaking when we sat down in the living room. After a cognac and a cigarette I was ready to tell them what I'd heard.

They asked if I knew the officer who had spoken to me. I admitted that it was possible I'd met him, but I didn't recognize him.

I explained that the Germans who were in civilian clothes were high-ranking officers. They discussed heavy artillery, new orders, and assignments. One topic was a program for a "final solution"—what would be done with the Jews in Germany and all over Europe. They felt that the Jews were the real enemy, and they were making plans to get rid of them. There was talk of a mass migration out of Germany. One of the men had said the program would involve an estimated 9.75 million Jews.

Francoise was astonished. "How calculated! I know people who can use this information. I must leave now. Doctor will let you know when we will do this again."

As soon as the door closed, Yvonne locked and chained it. We spent the night in each other's arms.

When day came, Yvonne made coffee and put out some croissants while I got dressed. We smiled at each other as we ate. After a long kiss and a big hug I walked back toward the hospital feeling absolutely marvelous.

The doctor was looking for me. I told him that Francoise had said the evening went very well, and he agreed to update my pass to give me another night away from the hospital.

About five o'clock, my room and belongings left in good order, I passed through the gate without incident. I thought I made a pretty good Frenchman: a beret to hide my blond hair, worker's plain clothing, and Des Gauloises cigarettes. I sat down on a bench to watch the sun disappear below the water's horizon, then walked along the piers. Three rather large German navy ships were anchored as well as a few smaller ones and many little French fishing barges. Most of the gray buildings across from the pier had flags with swastikas hanging from their roofs. It seemed all the buildings were occupied by German military. Trucks with army signs were parked everywhere, and tarpaulins covered all the truck beds. Every thirty meters or so, an armed guard paced back and forth.

I turned left and moved inland, away from the piers, window shopping until I realized I was being followed. The person trailing me didn't look German. When I speeded up, he did too. When I stopped, he stopped. I tried to get a look at him when I stopped before a tavern window.

"Don't look around; just listen," said a voice right beside me.

"Walk to the next street, Louis. Turn left at the third door and go in. It'll be open. Wait there." He walked on.

I felt better. He knew my new name, so he must be a friend of Francoise's. The door opened when I knocked and a flashlight blinded me.

"Hello, Louis. Sorry, but this was the best way to approach you."

"How did you know me? I thought I looked like everybody else."

"A mutual friend knew you'd be in town tonight. I followed you when you left the hospital. You can call me Paul. Can you help us translate some information we will be getting? It would be of tremendous help and won't take long."

"Yes, I can do that."

"Our contact is a German officer. We think he is okay but he speaks only German. He's been with us only a short time, so don't make any comments. Just translate what he gives us."

We headed toward Yvonne's place. It was very dark with only a few dim street lanterns. He led me to a building a block away from Yvonne's and up to the second floor. The door opened to his knock and we were allowed to enter after his identity was confirmed. A dark hallway led through another door. We waited.

A voice said,"Good evening, gentlemen."

I responded in German.

Paul became anxious. "Let's not waste time. Louis, ask him if he has the maps for the bunkers along the coastline."

The officer unrolled the maps on the table and began to tell me what they meant. His German voice made me nervous. The maps revealed strategic points where bunkers and shore batteries were installed. Paul held a flashlight in one hand and wrote the information I translated for him with the other. When we finished Paul told me to thank the soldier and tell him someone would be in touch with him. Paul rolled up the maps and held them under his arm.

We were guided down the stairs. Before we reached the outside door, Paul said that if we were stopped, he would give me the maps and act as a decoy. In that event, I was to take the maps to the person I planned to visit that night. He said he had an uneasy feeling and that he distrusted the German.

We walked briskly down the street but had not gone far when we saw four men in uniform approaching. The uniforms indicated they were field police.

Behind us, shadowy figures were emerging from the building we just left. We heard three gunshots.

"Here, Louis. Take the maps and go that way. I'll try to distract them by going in the opposite direction. If they're still following you, get rid of the maps if you can, but don't let them see you do it."

He started running. All four of the police followed him. I walked in the opposite direction as quickly and quietly as I could, and when I thought I was out of their sight, I began to run. Everything was quiet when I stopped to catch my breath. But then I heard shouts and the rapid fire of a burp gun. I ran toward the hospital until I was so winded I couldn't run any farther. When my breathing slowed a bit, I approached the gate and showed my pass to the guard. I was dripping with perspiration, and he inspected me with a puzzled look but waved me through.

I sat on the bench outside the pavilion until my breathing was normal and then tiptoed into my room. With the maps pushed to the farthest corner under my bed, I undressed in the dark. Surprisingly, my heart slowed its beating and before long I was asleep.

I awoke early and relived the past night's events. Dressing hurriedly, I went to the doctor's quarters.

Dr. Buzet inquired as to why I looked so terrible and why I was there so early. I fell into a chair and lit a cigarette. Blurting out the whole story, I saw he wasn't surprised by what I told him.

The doctor confirmed my guess that he was involved in the resistance and asked me to show him the maps. He scanned the maps and written information, turned to me, and exulted, "This is pure gold! Do you realize how important this material is? Now, for the bad news. The

German soldier was shot and Paul was apprehended as he tried to evade arrest and presumably killed."

Tears came to my eyes. Paul had led them away from me, otherwise he'd be alive now.

Dr. Buzet expressed his sorrow too. But he explained that Paul knew the risks and how important this information was to us. The doctor instructed me to get some rest and to see him after the evening meal tonight. He promised to have someone take a message to Yvonne to let her know why I wasn't with her last night and couldn't come tonight.

In my room I lazed and slept for most of the day. At four o'clock, the sister woke me to tell me Dr. Buzet wouldn't be able to see me tonight after all. Instead, after supper, I paced and smoked outside the pavilion. I hoped Yvonne had received my message.

* * * * *

In the morning, as I left the building, one of the nuns hurried to tell me that Dr. Buzet must see me in his quarters right away and that he was very angry. When I entered his quarters he was standing in the middle of the room.

"Lutz, can you imagine? I never lock my door. I've always trusted everyone. Someone was in my quarters last night. All of my tobacco is gone and some bread, butter, and marmalade I keep in my cupboard. Nothing else is missing. I don't understand it—there is plenty of food here in the hospital. I know it was one of the inmates. Filthy foreign Jews!"

He stopped, realizing what he had said. Apologizing profusely, he ordered me to tell the inmates not to leave their buildings. I was to be held responsible for the incident and must find out who did it. Outside the building, my eyes filled with tears. I was angry that I'd let the doctor talk to me that way, and I had lost my respect for him. I would find whoever took his food and tobacco, but I would no longer count on him for personal help.

By the end of the day, I had gotten nowhere.

* * * * *

Three more days went by, and I was not any closer to finding out who the thief was. I had alienated most of the inmates by telling them they couldn't leave their buildings.

By Sunday morning, I had questioned all the inmates and hadn't found any of the items that were taken. I was mentally composing my report to Dr. Buzet when there was a rap at the door.

Two inmates I know entered with a man I had never seen before. A small, thin, middle-aged man, he was very pale and frightened.

The man told me in Yiddish that he was sorry and didn't know why he stole the items. He looked so woeful and wan I felt sorry for him. I assured him that the doctor wouldn't be too upset—something I was not at all sure would be the case. When they left, I walked to the doctor's quarters and reported my findings to him.

"I accept your explanation and the man's apology and apologize for my behavior. But the fact remains, it did happen. To set an example, both of you are to go back to the camp."

"I don't think that's fair. I didn't do anything, and I can't be expected to control all these inmates."

"I'm sorry your stay has to end like this, but it will be a deterrent for the other inmates so such an incident won't happen again."

What could I say? I accepted my fate with resignation. I thanked him for keeping me there as long as he had.

By the time I returned to the pavilion, everyone seemed to know I was being sent back to the camp. Sister St. Benoit was indignant and said she'd ask to the Reverend Mother to intercede.

Later in the evening she sadly reported that Dr. Buzet was in charge and the Reverend Mother could do nothing. All the nuns but one were very unhappy with Dr. Buzet's decision. Their prayers went with me, they said. I felt very sad because I had become quite attached to the doctor.

Chapter 19

On Wednesday, I had packed and said goodbye to everyone. I hoped Yvonne would get my message that I was being returned to the camp. The man who took the items from Dr. Buzet's quarters and six other inmates were being returned to the camp as well.

Sister St. Benoit came to my room to say a final goodbye. Clutching both my hands and unable to hold back her tears, she shook her head, and then she left.

Eight of us waited at the front gate, our paperwork finished. The truck arrived and three sick inmates were removed. The guards—I'd never seen them before—picked up our papers and herded us into the truck. The doctor sadly waved goodbye as the truck moved out.

We reached the camp and were driven through the gate, halting at the infirmary. I had forgotten just how horrible this place looked. And the sergeant was the same one!

"Move, move! Down, down with you, quickly, quickly. This is not a resort area." He looked at me. "What have we here? The tender one is back from his long trip. All that good life had to end eventually."

I jumped from the truck and landed in front of him.

"Now we shall see if his hands haven't gotten too tender and if he hasn't forgotten the word 'work.'"

The barracks door opened and the blond SS guard came out, followed by Ernst. The SS man walked over to me and said, "Well, peewee, back home again?"

Turning to Ernst, he went on, "Schlesinger, he looks first-rate. I am sure he was at a spa. With that, he walked off accompanied by the sergeant.

Ernst indicated I would be housed in my old barracks and I entered to find a place to sleep. A note was pinned to the bed I had before: "Welcome to Mother's featherbed." It was signed by David.

Ernst, who had lost a lot of weight and didn't look too well, smiled at me. I stored my belongings quickly and joined Ernst in his alcove. He had smuggled in some schnapps and we drank a toast: "L' chaim" (To life). I told him all that had happened to me since I left the camp.

Ernst said that at the camp, the Germans still commanded the show. I would be back on work detail the next day. Ernst suggested that maybe I could hear some of the Germans' conversations and bring him some news.

There was less food, and it was usually rotten. Everything was filthy. Many were dying. French civilians came every three days and took the bodies away—no one knew where. The new SS guards were sadistic and had come from other camps. The sergeant was kind compared to them. Ernst warned me not to trust anyone, and not to do anything foolish.

Lunch wasn't any better than it used to be. The day passed while I waited to see David when he returned from the work site.

Finally, the truck arrived and he jumped down to hug me. His eyes were moist. After the count was finished and we were dismissed, David and I lined up for evening rations. As we ate quietly, I glanced at him. He looked like Ernst, worn and tired. We finished, washed our bowls, and sat down outside so I could have a smoke. When I had told him all that had happened to me, he brought me up to date on what had happened while I was away.

He said life had gotten much harder there. His work group had to walk seven kilometers (about four and a half miles) to the work site and get up an hour and a half earlier. His group was rousted out of bed by 4:30 and didn't get back to camp until 7:30 or 8:00. That day's ride in the truck was an exception.

* * * * *

We were awakened at 4:30 the next morning.

"Get out of those feathers, men. Let's start moving, you sleepyheads."

Before I could get up I felt a burning sensation on my backside as the sergeant whacked me with a rubber hose. I jerked to a sitting position and saw his grinning face. "That wakes even a dead man. Out!"

As he continued on through the barracks, ranting, David and I rushed to dress, wash, and use the toilet and then we ate our morning food.

By 5:30 we were marching in formation out the gate and onto the highway. Before we reached the work site, it was pouring rain and we were soaked. Although we were issued tools, the inmates just stood around and tried to keep warm. The guards, foremen, and *Meister* were all in nearby sheds keeping dry.

At noontime, the two men bringing the large soup kettle slipped on the muddy slope and fell down. The lid snapped off and rolled away. The kettle itself tipped over and our lunch washed away. We watched, speechless. A guard started beating the men as they lay on the ground. When they tried to rise, he hit them even harder. They stopped moving after a while.

"You stupid pigs can't even carry a little kettle! Stupid Jew dogs. Now you all can swallow dirt, and anyone who doesn't like it can receive the same portion as these two. Let's go, let's go. You two, lift up the kettle so we can take it back. You two there, lift up these two filthy creatures and sit them against the sand pile."

Some men bent over the two prostrate men and one shook his head. "They're dead, both of them."

"Come on, Lutz," said David. "There is nothing we can do."

I felt nothing but hatred for the guards.

We worked through the rest of the day and by nightfall were exhausted and starving. The hike back was uncomfortable. David and three others carried the dead men on stretchers.

The evening soup, thin as it was, helped warm us. We stripped to our underwear and hung our sodden clothes everywhere in the barracks, hoping they would dry overnight, but it was so cold they were still wet the next morning.

We had to wear them anyway. My nice Canadian boots I got at the hospital were ruined—so stiff it hurt to walk in them. The ground outside looked like a lake with a few small islands. Even the bread we got for the morning meal was wet.

Although it stopped raining, the next few days passed uncomfortably. David and I talked incessantly about escaping, which we knew would be nearly impossible. German military men were everywhere, we didn't have any contacts who would help, and we had no safe place to hide.

Rain and cold weather had taken their toll. Many inmates were sick with high fevers, sore throats, and coughs. Some were so ill they couldn't stand, and the word was that many were dying. The food, which was always inedible, had gotten worse, if that was possible. The soup tasted like sawdust.

All my clothes were ruined. My boots were so worn that my feet had became very sore. Worst of all, I was itching between my fingers, and I had sticky blisters again. Spots were developing on my arms and legs.

Two days later, my skin was so miserable I went to see Ernst. I showed him my arms and legs.

"I'll have to put you on the hospital list. In a way, I am glad; that work group you're in will get you killed eventually. I'll talk with the blond SS man and by Wednesday you'll be back at the hospital in Boulogne. Take it easy till then."

* * * * *

Wednesday morning came and I was ready by 7:30. With a sad goodbye to David, I climbed in the truck.

We were dropped off at the hospital's front office, and I felt like I'd come home again. Dr. Buzet was there with a big grin on his face. "Lutz, my dear little friend, how happy I am to see you again. I hope you have forgiven me for the past. This time, you will not leave the hospital for any reason."

I was happy to hear that, but I had not forgotten, and I was not so quick to forgive. I rushed to the pavilion. It was wonderful to walk along the paths and see the fall colors. Sister St. Benoit knew I was coming and was waiting with a pleasant smile.

"We all missed you. Your old bed is waiting. Put your things away, and you'll have a hot sulphur bath and some clean clothing."

Two other men were in the room, but they were not from the camp. I stowed my belongings, put on the hospital robe, and went for my bath.

* * * * *

For the next three days, I did nothing but sleep, eat, and take baths. No one bothered me.

On Sunday, Dr. Buzet made rounds. He checked the two others in my room and stopped at my bed. Deciding that I'd had enough rest, he invited me to his place for some breakfast.

It was good to get back into my clothes again. The sister had cleaned them and shined my boots. My skin was clearing but was still tender. When I arrived at Dr. Buzet's quarters, a pretty young woman was there, about twenty-two years old. She told me her name was Alice and then served me some coffee while I waited for Dr. Buzet.

When the doctor arrived, I complimented him on his new maid. He assured me that she would remain with him and that I would not be able to kidnap her to the pavilion. When we finished the excellent meal, Dr. Buzet told me what was going on in the hospital and in Boulogne.

He said he was still involved in the resistance and in sabotage, enough to hurt the German war effort. Yvonne had disappeared; no one had heard anything about her.

He promised to do his best to keep me there permanently. If anyone asked about my health, I should say that I was better but not quite cured. He asked that I join him at the Sunday services in the chapel, especially that day. The Reverend Mother and all the nuns would see me there, as would the priest, which would help to keep me at the hospital.

Remembering what Papa had said about visiting other religious houses of worship, I agreed.

We walked to the chapel, which was located at the rear of the hospital grounds and found the service was starting as we entered. During the service the priest was aided by an assistant on each side and several teenage boys. The priest sang portions of the service aloud, but I thought a cantor had a better voice.

I looked around the church as unobtrusively as possible. The walls were hung with many religious paintings, some featuring Christ. Statues lined the sides of the chapel. The altar, which took up all of the far end looked very similar to a *shul* (although a *shul* would not have an art gallery). A large cross was flanked by many burning candles. I didn't understand what was being said during the service—everything was spoken in a foreign language.

Dr. Buzet noticed my puzzlement and told me that the service was conducted in Latin.

Alice joined us in the pew as the service continued. Some parts were not very different from a Hebrew service. The Reverend Mother, Sister St. Benoit, Sister Theresa, and all the other nuns were there. The sermon's theme was loving one's neighbor and taking care of one's fellow humans—an ironic theme, I thought, although the priest seemed sincere. When the service ended, the Reverend Mother walked up the aisle and nodded at me. She took my arm and we walked apart from the crowd.

"So nice to have you back and to see you in the chapel. After all, God is God to everybody. We hope to keep you here. The camp is very bad, no?"

"Yes, Reverend Mother, very bad. All the more, I appreciate the help of everyone here."

As we neared the group of nuns waiting at the chapel entrance, I grinned at Sister Theresa. The Reverend Mother thanked me for walking with her and asked me to come by to chat with her again the next day.

I met Alice on my way back to my room. "My day off is tomorrow. Maybe we could spend some time together, Lutz. I have a room all to myself in the service quarters building—room nine. Two o'clock?"

I felt very happy as I watched her walk away.

When I passed Sister St. Benoit's room, I saw the door ajar. I wished to tell her of the Reverend Mother's invitation to visit her. Standing in the doorway, I called the sister's name several times, but got no answer. I pushed the door open and saw that she was hanging laundry outside.

When she finished and came back inside, she saw me. She invited me in.

The room was very plain. It had white-washed walls, a small single bed, a table with a small lamp, a side chair, and an armchair. There was a cross on the wall above the bed and a picture of Jesus as a baby, held by his mother.

The sister explained that she and the others lived very simply since their lives were devoted to God. They didn't need worldly goods. They worked and prayed all the time to remain free of sin.

When she left to get me some coffee, I went to the window to look at the clothes on the line. I was intrigued by tiny anklets and wristlets, long white underwear, and other garments I didn't recognize. All immaculate, all cotton—they must have to be ironed, I thought.

After a time, she looked at me shyly, and admitted that she knew very little about my faith. Interested in learning, she suggested that maybe next Sunday after services we could walk and I could tell her something about the Jewish faith.

Finally it was Monday, at two o'clock! I knocked on Alice's door. She invited me in and asked what I wanted to drink.

When I chose wine, she told me to uncork the bottle of red wine and pour two glasses. Time slipped by as we sat and talked. I grew tired and became aware my words sounded like nonsense, repetitious and silly. Alice suggested I lie down and then put a pillow under my head. Before long, we were under the covers, so warm we had no need for clothing.

Before dawn, Alice awakened me because she had to leave for work. She invited me to come back that evening after dinner.

The early morning air was cold when I left her building.

* * * * *

The next five days passed pleasantly. Each night I was at Alice's and each day I spent reading and visiting with inmates from the camp and sometimes walking with the Reverend Mother.

On Sunday morning, a recent inmate from the camp rushed to my room. He had heard that all inmates were to be returned to the camp. The SS was forming a transport to return us, but someone had overheard the doctor say that some inmates would die if they were transported.

I found the doctor and asked if it was true. He said that all he knew was that a guard said to be ready to evacuate the sick at a moment's notice.

The transport arrived later in the day to return well inmates to the camp. One of the returnees agreed to tell Ernst to try to come by the hospital to see me on his next trip into Boulogne.

* * * * *

Early the next morning my door opened and Ernst entered. He had gotten a ride on a camp truck with one of the sergeants who had business in Boulogne. After we exchanged greetings, he told me that it was true—the camp was to be closed in six or seven days. All inmates in the hospital were to be returned to the camp before that time. The rumor was that all inmates in our camp and the one in Calais were to be returned to Belgium and released or maybe relocated to another camp.

I was stunned. I guessed my stay at the hospital was too good to last. In the late afternoon I visited Dr. Buzet in his quarters and told him the news.

He didn't want to get my hopes up but he thought it might be possible for them to keep me here. He said he would talk to some people and see what could be done.

Even with this upsetting news, I still wanted to be with Alice that night. She welcomed me and locked the door.

I left Alice's room as the sun came up in the morning. I was tired and apprehensive of what the next few days would mean to me and the other camp inmates.

Sister St. Benoit was just coming from church services and stopped to tell me that there had been some discussion on how to keep me at the hospital. Throughout the day, my mind was in turmoil, but my thoughts yielded no solution.

* * * *

On Monday, I talked with many of the hospitalized inmates. We agreed that all we could do was try to be emotionally ready to return to camp.

At lunch, Sister St. Benoit told me that the sisters were fearful of German reprisals if they were to help the inmates or attempt to delay their return to the camp. She said Sister Theresa had reported the situation to the bishop, and his response was that the Church could compromise itself by becoming involved. This was not good news but not entirely unexpected. I thanked her for what she and the others had tried to do. She told me not to despair, that God was watching over us.

Chapter 20

Very early the next morning, October 29, 1942, I was shaken awake by Sister St. Benoit. "Lutz, please get dressed quickly and meet me outside my room."

It was only 5:15 A.M., but I was dressed and in front of her room in minutes. Tears were in her eyes.

"Early this morning, German soldiers from the camp arrived in three trucks. The one in charge woke Dr. Buzet and tried to give him instructions in German. As you know, Dr. Buzet speaks very little German and he could not understand what the soldier was saying. He wants you to translate for him."

I rushed to the doctor's quarters. He and the leader were waiting for me.

"Finally, someone who understands something. Well, you little Berliner, tell the doctor that everybody has to be ready to leave in three hours. I mean all the inmates, whether they can walk or not. No questions. All we know is that you are all to go back to Brussels. The camp is dissolved."

When I told him this, Dr. Buzet said seventeen of the men shouldn't be moved and another five could not be moved under any circumstances; some were operated on only yesterday.

I relayed this, but the leader shook his head at both of us. "It doesn't matter. We will move them all right. Everybody goes, without exception." He turned and walked away.

With a sigh, Dr. Buzet told me to inform the patients that they were to assemble in the courtyard, ready for the move. They received the news with apprehension.

I packed my few belongings in a travel bag and then went to help those who needed assistance. In two hours, all of them were waiting in the courtyard. The windows were filled with sad faces, watching us. The Reverend Mother bid me goodbye. Sister St. Benoit whispered that she would hide me, but I couldn't let her do that; it would jeopardize everyone at the hospital.

When the trucks arrived, the tailgates were dropped and we started to board amidst the shouts of the soldiers to hurry. Many inmates were in great pain but were boarded nevertheless. The lead soldier went into the office with Dr. Buzet to complete the paperwork. In a few minutes they reappeared.

With a serious expression, Dr. Buzet thanked me for all my help. I was sorry I had to leave. I had learned much from the kind doctor, whom by this time I had forgiven.

I hopped into the truck. The tailgate latches were checked, and we slowly rolled out of the portal and headed toward the camp. The sisters waved. Alice stood quietly.

The sky was gray and overcast, and we were cold. I wondered if I should have hidden and tried to stay or run away. I suddenly realized I forgot to say goodbye to Alice in all the excitement. I also forgot to eat breakfast!

We neared the camp but didn't enter. The trucks drove onto a siding where a train waited and armed soldiers paced back and forth. Metal plates on chains around their necks identified them as *Feld Gendarmerie* (field police). These were the infamous troops who arrested people and took them across the border and into prison.

Ernst Schlesinger appeared. "Hey, Lutzel, I thought you'd have walked away from the hospital."

"Maybe a mistake, but I didn't. Where's David?"

"I don't know. Nor do I know where we're going; no one does. Maybe Brussels."

When everyone was aboard the train, Ernst headed toward the first car. The blond SS officer ordered me to walk with him. Stopping before a lieutenant, he pointed to me and announced, "This is him. Keep an eye on him. I don't think he's a Jew and he might be helpful to us." He left me with the lieutenant, who had a very unpleasant look on his face.

"So, you're not a Jew, huh? I don't care what you are. You're just a parasite and I step on parasites." He raised his arm, and in a split second, he'd struck me with the back of his hand. I felt a burning sensation on my face. "I am in command here and if you don't get onto the train right now, you'll be sorry."

I leaped on and the door shut behind me. The lock clicked. I put my bag on a top rack in a compartment and sat down. Seven others already sat on the two benches, and I took the last place next to the door by the aisle. My face was very sore.

One man recognized me as the interpreter from the hospital. He asked if I knew where they were taking us. I told him I'd heard we were going to Brussels to be released but that it was probably just a rumor.

The men started to eat the bread rations issued at camp that morning. I puffed on a cigarette, hoping my hunger pangs would go away, and looked down the length of the aisle. A familiar head emerged from among those milling around outside compartments.

"Hey. Hey, Jossel! Over here!"

He saw me, waved, and made his way to me.

"Hi! What happened to your face?"

"That lieutenant from the field police backhanded me—almost got me in the eye. I guess he thought that the blond SS had something going with me. I'd like to meet him another time!"

Jossel said there was an empty seat in his compartment, so I retrieved my bag and followed him. He even had a piece of bread for me. The train had not moved yet. We speculated that we were waiting for the inmates from the camp in Calais.

Suddenly the train lurched and moved a foot or two. We felt another little push and concluded we must be hooking on cars from the Calais camp. The locomotive hissed and the train moved forward slowly.

I settled down for a nap, but before I was fully asleep, I heard Ernst Schlesinger's voice: "Well, well, always sleeping!"

"Ernst, am I glad to see you! Sit down. We have some questions for you. Where are we going and when is the food coming?"

He said we were headed for Brussels, with no stops along the way. We were traveling as inconspicuously as possible so we wouldn't attract the attention of the civilian populace. He didn't know what would happen when we reached Brussels or if we'd be fed.

He pointed to my face. "I see you've met the lieutenant in charge of this car. He's a fervent Jew hater and very sadistic. He looks for people to pick on, so stay out of his sight. There has been a hint that we won't stop in Brussels but go on toward the east. All of the camps in the south of France have been closed, and the Jews have been transported elsewhere, but no one seems to know exactly where. Now, Lutz, I know you—don't try to escape from this train. There are too many guards and you'll be shot if you try. Don't trust any of them. I'll get back to you when I have more information."

When he had left, Jossel nudged me. "Boy, you're full of surprises. I didn't know you knew anyone who had any position in this operation."

"He is a friend of my father's from Berlin, and he's known me since I was small."

I went back to sleep. When I awoke, my back ached from the hard bench. It was dark and cold and I guessed we wouldn't be fed.

Jossel and I woke up very early the next morning. The train was still moving through the countryside. During the night the temperature fell and we were stiff with the cold. In the restroom, we ran our hands under the faucet to warm them. After I had a cigarette we returned to the compartment. There was still no food and nothing to read for distraction, so I slept through most of the day and night.

* * * * *

Early on the morning of the third day, the train slowed and I went out into the aisle to see what was happening. A guard came by and waved me back into the compartment.

After a while, Ernst and two other men came down the aisle carrying a steaming barrel. Each of us got one cup of something that smelled like coffee but tasted weak without much flavor. It was not much, but it was something. When I went into the aisle for my morning cigarette, the terrain outside seemed familiar. Ernst confirmed my feeling that we were near Brussels, but he told me to be careful; the number of guards had been increased, and they had orders to keep us quiet and on the train.

Toward the end of the day we entered the suburbs of Brussels. Excited, I headed out of the compartment to look out an aisle window. No sooner did I open the door than two guards pushed me back inside and pulled the window shades down. One guard remained outside our door. The train slowed, and we heard the hissing of locomotives and orders being shouted. I thought we must be inside the station, but the train continued to creep along. Soon the voices and sounds of the station seemed to be coming from behind us.

The train came to a halt. Guards shouted something unintelligible. I managed to slip under the shade and put my nose against the window. When my eyes became used to the darkness, I saw we were in an open field with many railroad tracks. There were wagons in the distance. While I stood at the window, a train of cattle cars slowly rolled by on the next track. It stopped suddenly and I realized what I was seeing: there were people jammed inside!

I eased the window open and saw a woman's face through an opening in the side of one car. She asked me where we were from, and I told her we were coming from northern France. She indicated that her car held men, women, and children from Brussels, Antwerp, and other towns in Belgium. They had been told they were being resettled at camps in the east.

A guard appeared and I hurriedly closed the window and sat down. When I could look out again, the train had moved on and I could not see the woman any longer. I heard a child crying in misery. After a series of shoves and clanks, we started moving again, the other train probably a part of our train now. I didn't understand what was happening.

I surmised that "east" meant Poland. I remembered when Polish Jews in Berlin were deported to Poland in 1938. They were paraded through the streets, miserable, and no one did anything, no one moved. I understood how they felt.

A guard opened the door and ordered us to raise the shades. It was pitch dark, so we couldn't see anything. We sat in silence, apprehensive and depressed.

After a while Jossel left to use the toilet. When he came back he reported that people were jumping out of the windows because the guards were all up in the front part of the train. We discussed whether we should do the same. When I said there would be no place for me to go if I left the train, Jossel said I could stay with his family. The constant drizzle wouldn't make escaping easy. The border couldn't be too far ahead of us, we concluded, so if we were going to leave the train we should do it soon. Someone mentioned that the Albert Channel and the Meuse River were just ahead.

We donned extra clothes so we'd be warm and wouldn't have to carry them. Sometime around one o'clock we were ready. Jossel opened the window and jumped. Many others were jumping out, too. When I jumped, I landed on gravel near the train. As I straightened up, a large silhouette in a German uniform loomed in front of me. A plaque around the neck of the soldier caught the light—a field policeman! Because of the dark and rain, he couldn't see me very well. I threw my small bag over my shoulder and snapped to attention. I hoped he would think the outline of the bag slung over my shoulder resembled a burp gun.

Taking a chance, I addressed him in the most authoritative voice I could: "Order from the Commandant. I have to go toward the front."

"*Ja, ja* (Yes, yes)," was the policeman's response.

I marched away from him, toward the front of the train, which was standing still now. I tried to put some distance between me and the train. The embankment was strewn with barbed wire, so my progress was very slow.

I heard someone whispering to me. "Lutz, Lutz. Over here." Jossel was caught on some barbed wire. When I lifted several twists of the wire, he slipped down the hill. The train was still stopped and we could see several German helmets moving around. We backed down the embankment as quietly as possible, but at the bottom, our boots hit gravel and the sound broke the silence.

"Halt, halt. Stop or we'll shoot."

"Let's run for it!" As we ran we heard bullets hit the wall of a nearby house. We were faster than our pursuers and didn't stop until the shouts faded. After a while we saw a farmhouse and several outbuildings, including a barn with a loft. We climbed a ladder into the loft and covered ourselves with straw. It took some time before our breathing became normal. Many dogs were barking; if they came after us, we would certainly be caught.

We heard voices not too far from the barn. "Only the devil knows where they scampered off to. It is too dark. We can't see anything. Let's go or else we will never find our way back." The footsteps grew fainter, but it took me a long time to stop shaking.

Chapter 21

We woke to the sound of voices. Smoothing our clothes, we climbed down from the loft.

Jossel said he'd do the talking. His plan was to try to exchange some of our extra clothing for money and directions back to Brussels.

We met a young farmer in his twenties. As he walked us to the farmhouse we were joined by two other men. In the house, an elderly man and woman sat at a table. On a nearby sofa a young woman held a child in her arms.

The older man asked where we were from and what we were doing here.

Jossel explained, then the old man and one of the younger men went into another room to talk. The old woman brought us coffee, and when the men returned they said we had a deal. A map was spread on the table and the men showed us where we were and how to get to the railway station, where we would board for Liege. We left all our extra clothing with the family. Thanking them for their help, we said goodbye and left.

On our way to the train station, we kept glancing back to be sure we were not being followed. Our supposed benefactors could still betray us, so we had to be watchful. After watching activities at the train station for a while, we entered separately. Jossel purchased two tickets and slipped one to me. There were only a few soldiers who seemed to be waiting for a train.

We walked to the gate one at a time. Our tickets were taken and punched.

We boarded the train and entered a compartment. In a few minutes the train pulled out of the station and we were on our way. We had the compartment to ourselves—only the conductor entered to take our tickets. By two o'clock we were in Liege.

At the nearest public bath we indulged ourselves in tubs of wonderful hot water, then shaves and haircuts. Looking in the mirror, I was shocked at how I'd aged.

At a nearby restaurant we ordered large meals. When our plates were empty, we were so stuffed we could hardly move.

Jossel counted our money. "Lutz, we have exactly three francs seventy-five left. Take it. My girlfriend will have money for me."

We decided to go to the train station to avoid attracting unwanted attention. We sat down to wait for the Brussels train in the nearly empty station.

Jossel decided that when we arrived in Brussels, we should separate and meet outside the Gare du Nord at the number 36 streetcar stop. We would be in Brussels by 8:50 P.M. and at his girlfriend's house by 9:40.

Finally, we were able to board and the train moved out. The pretty city of Liege passed by our window. Along the way many travelers boarded. When we arrived in Brussels I mingled with passengers leaving the train and tried not to stand out. German soldiers stood next to Belgian railroad men at the exit gate. Everyone was subjected to scrutiny, but I passed from the station without incident.

Jossel rejoined me at the streetcar stop just as one came to a stop. We boarded and sat separately and left the streetcar separately. We met again in front of his girlfriend's house. We had made it!

Jossel knocked three times very softly. In a moment, a frightened voice asked "Who is it?"

"It's me—Joseph."

"Oh, my God, my God. It can't be!"

The door opened and a pretty dark-haired girl stared at us. Barefoot and clad in a nightgown, she fell into Jossel's arms. Many kisses and tears later, she noticed me and invited me inside.

Jossel introduced me to Stephy and then asked about their parents.

She had terrible news. Her parents and Jossel's were picked up and sent to Malines and then somewhere in the east. Many other people had been picked up too. There was no place to hide if you didn't have a lot of money. Even then, the Flemish and Walloonian SS helped the

Germans. Many people took bribes and betrayed Jews. Anyone caught hiding Jews was taken to Gestapo headquarters on Avenue Louise and beaten. I was so exhausted after our escape I slept deeply, despite the makeshift bed made from chairs pushed together.

The next morning after coffee, bread, and a cigarette, I said goodbye and stepped outside. My clothes were thin and I felt the cold. My warm clothing was in my travel bag, which I lost when I helped Jossel out of the barbed wire.

I decided to try to find my old partner, Karl. It was early as I started toward the Gare du Nord, keeping to side streets. I had no yellow star to wear and no legal papers, so I didn't want to be stopped and questioned by anyone.

I knew the city well and cut through alleys to reach Boulevard Ansbach. My stomach growled. I hoped Karl had some food. Vehicles passed by in increasing numbers, and many people were walking to work. A reflection in a store window revealed I looked like a disheveled bum. My hair was cropped short; a dirty shirt, pants, and jacket hung on me; and I wore very dirty boots. Maybe my appearance would help. I didn't think Germans picked up bums!

Many uniformed men patrolled the Gare du Nord area. I tried to looked nonchalant as I walked along and then boarded a streetcar nearby.

I paid my fare to Schaarbeck and stood near the door, ready to leave should anyone stop me. Most of the passengers were women. Four men sat in back, two of them in German uniforms. By the time I got off, only the four men and two of the women remained.

Anxiously, I hastened to Karl's place. In front of the house I studied the tenant list. He was still here! I pushed the button under his name and stepped back, looking upward to a window on the second floor. It opened and Karl's head popped out.

"Lutz! I'll be right down!"

The front door opened, and Karl stood there in pajamas. He gave me a bear hug.

"Come on up, you *petzele*" (a Yiddish term of endearment meaning 'little person'). My mother can't believe it's you."

As Karl's mother fixed breakfast we sat, smoked, and talked. Neither commented on my shabby appearance. A pot of coffee and plates of meat, cheese, and bread were served.

Soon there was nothing left. Leaning back, I had another cigarette and told them what had happened to me since I left Brussels. They stared at me, appalled.

Then they told me how it was in Belgium now. All Jews, even Belgian Jews who were not bothered in the past, were being picked up. Queen Mother Elisabeth had requested that the Germans not pick up children of Belgian birth and descent. The Germans supposedly agreed, but they had gone back on their word. It was rumored all Jews in Belgium were to be picked up for deportation to Poland. Anyone caught hiding Jews would be deported also, so it was difficult to hide.

When Karl's mother went into the kitchen he whispered, "We've been told my papa was arrested in Portugal and shot for espionage. We did not know he had been involved in resistance activities. My mother is safe as a Gentile, but she is frightened for me since half-Jews are being picked up, too."

Returning, his mother asked where I planned to go. I really didn't know. I asked Karl if any of our old friends were left.

He cautioned that I'd have to be very careful in looking for them. He gave me Manfred's address and told me the bus stopped near his place. He was working for a Germany company where no one knew he was half Jewish.

We talked all afternoon and into early evening. After another meal, I gave Karl's mother a hug. She had tears in her eyes. I thanked her for everything, and then Karl and I went downstairs and outside. He pressed some money into my hand, saying it was from his mother.

Karl went back into the house, and I waited for the bus. When it came, I boarded and got a transfer slip to change buses at the Gare du Nord. Many Germans were in the station, but I didn't have any trouble crossing the square to board another bus. Before long, the conductor indicated that my stop was coming up.

I followed Karl's directions easily and found the apartment house where Manfred lived. None of the names resembled his; perhaps he was not using his real name. Taking a chance, I pushed the bell for the second floor. Sure enough, a window opened and Manfred's head emerged. "Stay there, I'll be right down."

The window closed and in a moment the main door opened. I was momentarily blinded by a flashlight. "Lutz, are you crazy? How did you get here?" I got a big hug and a whiff of alcohol. "Come on up. I can't believe it's you."

We entered and he locked the door after us. He was in pajamas and I could see he'd had a bit too much to drink. From another room a woman's voice called to him.

Manfred walked toward the voice and opened a door. A half-dressed woman was sitting up in bed. Manfred explained who I was. Handing me a pillow and blanket so I could make myself a bed, he warned me not to make any noise.

In the morning, I was shaken awake and looked up into Manfred's eyes. He was on his way to work. He instructed me to stay inside all day, be quiet, and not answer the doorbell or open the door to anybody.

I watched him disappear around the corner and then started looking around. In the small kitchenette I fixed something to eat. Searching for a smoke I went into the bedroom and saw a package of German cigarettes on the dresser. Returning to the living room I noticed a small sign hanging on the front door:

> When you come through this door, your greeting should be Heil Hitler.

I wondered where he got that from and why he would hang it up. He seemed to be the same old Manfred, but there must be a reason. I decided to ask him that night.

A bath and fresh clothes would be wonderful, but I didn't dare run the water, so there was nothing to do but sleep. It was dark when I awakened. Hearing footsteps, I jumped up and flattened myself beside the front door. A key turned in the lock and Manfred entered.

"It's me, Lutz." I stepped away from the door as he turned a light on.

After we had eaten and talked awhile, Manfred told me he could keep me only a few days because the Germans where he worked often came over.

I told him I understood and asked him about the sign on the door. A bit embarrassed, he explained that it showed his German coworkers that he was a German, too.

I told Manfred that I needed a bath so he filled the tub and suggested that I soak my underwear off because it was sticking to my sores. I stretched out in the delicious hot water and Manfred gently washed the sores. After a soft toweling, a slathering of Nivea cream, and bandaging over the sores, I dressed in borrowed underwear. Manfred promised to try to find a doctor for me.

In the living room we discussed my options. After some thought we agreed that Gustav Herz, an old friend who still ran the Diana Bar, might be able to help me. It was worth a try, anyway.

As we settled down for the night, I expressed curiosity about the woman who was there the night before. He said that she wasn't his girlfriend; she came over only once in a while and spent the night.

I was more comfortable than I'd been in several days. Sleep came easily, even on the living room floor.

In the morning, Manfred again emphasized that I must make no noise and should stay inside. He returned in the late afternoon, closed the curtain, and turned on a small table lamp. After a meal of dark bread with salami and ersatz coffee, we relaxed with a smoke.

He said he'd talked with a Belgian doctor who was willing to look at my eczema on Thursday—for free. The doctor felt it was his patriotic duty. Manfred would take me there, but we had to be very careful going to his place because he was most likely being watched.

* * * * *

On Thursday night, we took the streetcar and got off after five minutes. The fresh air felt good. We stopped in front of an ordinary-looking building and Manfred rang the doorbell. A small square in the door opened and eyes peered out at us. In French a voice asked what we wanted. After telling them who we were, the door opened and we were led into a sparsely furnished room with an examining table, a small cabinet, a large light on a stand, and two pieces of equipment hanging on the wall.

A short man in a white coat entered. He greeted Manfred and then looked at my sores. He asked me what I was treated with before and what effect it had. After I told him I'd been given sulphur baths and was covered with sulphur ointment, he said he wouldn't be able to provide those for me, but he'd treat me with ultraviolet light.

After putting on protective glasses, I lay on the table. The doctor positioned a lamp to shine on my whole body. After five minutes, he returned and covered my sores with ointment and then bandaged them. He instructed me to leave the bandages in place for three days and come back to see him Monday evening.

As we left, Manfred looked up and down the street to be sure no one saw us. We rode the streetcar in silence, speaking only when we had entered his apartment. I told him I'd be gone by morning.

Manfred apologized. "Lutz, I feel terrible not to be able to let you stay here, but I have no choice."

"That's okay, Manfred. I understand. I appreciate your letting me stay for a whole week."

Chapter 22

In the morning we said goodbye hurriedly, promising to keep in touch, and Manfred went to work. About 3 P.M., I left the building and walked down the street in the November cold.

My clothes were clean but well worn. My shoes were another matter: the soles had small holes that would soon be larger. I had only ten francs in my pocket.

I tried to avoid anyone in German uniforms and others who might be too interested in me. It was nearly five o'clock when I approached the Diana Bar. A uniformed doorman stood in front of the half-open door, through which German music and laughter floated.

I greeted him, gave him my name, identified myself as a personal friend of the boss, and asked him to tell him I was here.

The doorman looked at me suspiciously but walked to the stairs leading to the basement. While I waited, I saw three high-ranking German officers talking with girls in evening gowns. Two bartenders stood behind a shiny bar. When the doorman returned he led me down the hall, pointed to a door, and indicated he was waiting for me.

Gustav Herz got up from behind a large desk to shake my hand. "Lutz, you don't look the greatest, but at least you're alive. Many of our people haven't come back. How about some good coffee?"

As we drank I told him what had happened to me since I left Brussels. Leaning back with a cigarette, he said "I wish I could help, but I have no contacts. All I do is work in the bar; I even live here. However, I can give you some money to tide you over." He handed me seven one-hundred-franc bills. "Here, at least this will help some. If you are ever in dire need, come by. Otherwise, it is not a good idea to hang around the bar. Gestapo are here frequently. If you must come, tell the doorman you want to see the officer, and he'll know you want to see me. Now, take care." We shook hands.

Out on the street, I squeezed the bills in my pocket. I was suddenly hungry. I headed toward a Hungarian restaurant near Boulevard Ansbach. Inside there were only two waitresses and a woman behind the cash register.

The woman led me to a corner table and handed me a menu. I ordered the paprika stew with steamed potatoes, soup, rolls, and pudding she recommended.

At the cash register later, the manager stared at me, and asked if we knew each other.

I told her no, left a tip, and stepped out into the street. I needed to find a room somewhere that wouldn't attract German attention. The hotel near the red lantern district might do, I thought.

I passed the north station with caution and walked down a side street. At the hotel desk, I asked the concierge for a room. He eyed me and asked if I was eighteen. I assured him I was and told him the owner could vouch for me.

He went in the back and returned shortly. Apparently, the old madame had looked through the peephole and approved my stay. I registered and paid sixty francs for the night. The concierge handed me a key. "Second floor, last room on the left."

As I climbed the stairs and walked down the hall, I listened for German voices but heard none. The room wasn't very attractive—a small bed, a nightstand, a commode with a basin and pitcher—but it was cheap. I closed the door, put the key in the lock, and hung my jacket over it.

Removing my clothes, I peeked under the bandages. My sores still looked bad and the bandages probably wouldn't last until Monday. Putting off that problem, I climbed into the bed. It felt wonderful; the sheets were clean and cool and the down cover was soft. I was soon asleep.

The next morning I dressed and walked downstairs. The concierge wasn't there, but the old madame was. She looked at me. I winked and in French asked for the room for another night. I gave her sixty francs and then headed toward some familiar places in town.

Rue Neuve was crowded with people walking. This was good because it allowed me to slowly scout around for old friends without attracting attention. I peered through the window of a coffee shop. It was nearly full and I made my way to a table. When the waitress handed me a menu, her eyes opened wide amd she smiled. Holding the menu, I looked around but didn't recognize anybody. When the waitress returned to take my order, she dropped a piece of paper in front of me. I covered it with my hand and ordered my food.

I took a magazine from the rack and opened the piece of paper inside it.

"I can't believe it is you, Lutz. Meet me outside at four when my shift ends." There was no signature.

When the waitress brought my food, I smiled and nodded. When finished, I left a tip, paid the cashier, and went outside. I purposely had left my cigarettes and matches at my table. Sure enough, the waitress rushed outside with them. As she handed them to me she whispered, "See you tonight."

Walking away, I tried to remember who she was. I spent the rest of the day trying to find old friends but had no success. At four o'clock I was waiting outside the coffee shop when the waitress came out. She kissed me on both cheeks and put her arm in mine, and we walked away.

"Lutz, you don't remember me. I am Margot from the Café Patou."

"Margot, how good of you to remember me."

"Lutz, how could I forget you? When I needed somebody, you helped without asking any questions."

Suddenly, I remembered. She was a lesbian with a small daughter who lived with a female prostitute. I had met Margot in the Café Patou, a place frequented by prostitutes, pimps, and other unsavory people. Margot had been beaten and her little girl was very sick at the time. She had no money or family, but I was able to help her.

We headed for the Café Patou, which Margot said hadn't changed much.

When we arrived there, her roommate, Julia, was waiting. She shook my hand enthusiastically.

Inside, Julia ordered aperitifs. When I finished telling them about my ordeal, Margot said they could put me up for a night once in a while. Their concierge had many German friends so they had to be very careful.

I thanked them and said if I got in trouble, I'd gratefully accept their offer.

By now the café was nearly full. A man approached our table and my heart started to beat faster, but he just wanted to talk with Julia, who followed him out of the café. I offered to walk Margot home. When I said good night to her in front of her apartment, she reminded me that I should talk to her if I needed help.

I went back to the Hungarian restaurant. It was early and there were few diners. The manager led me to a table in the rear and sat down across from me. She finally remembered who I was and asked why I hadn't admitted knowing her when I was in there the other day. I explained that I was always very cautious. I wasn't sure how she would react, so I let her take the first step. She told me that I could come by when I ran out of money and was hungry.

After a good meal I returned directly to the hotel, not lingering outside because of the cold. The key was handed to me without comment.

*****

The next day was Sunday and I paid for one more night. At the coffee shop, Margot led me to a table. She said I should walk up and down the boulevard. That way, perhaps I'd find people who remembered me and who could help me.

I thanked her for her suggestion, but for some reason, I just wanted to sit in the coffee shop for a while. Perhaps I was feeling a little hopeless about my situation, or perhaps I just wanted to pretend nothing was wrong.

Margot kept my cup filled with coffee and I passed three hours reading a magazine. Toward noon, the café became busy so I left and found a movie house. The movie was idiotic, but I had a warm place to sleep. When I left in the late afternoon, the streets were thronged with walkers, many of them in German uniforms.

Hungry again, I approached the Hungarian restaurant, but the manager motioned me to walk on by. Although I didn't see anything suspicious, I kept going and had dinner at a place near the north station.

* * * * *

In the morning, the old madame told me I couldn't stay at the hotel any longer because military police inspections were planned and SS men were checking for deserters.

My money was shrinking. At the automat in the railway station, I bought three sandwiches and a cup of coffee from a vending machine then went back to walk the boulevard in search of friendly faces. When I returned—cold, tired, and hungry—to the automat, the place was full of German uniforms, so I left without any food.

At the doctor's office that evening, he saw that my sores were worse, not better. After a lengthy treatment with the lamp, he covered me with a heavy layer of ointment and bandages and said it was very dangerous for me to be there—he was being watched closely. He begged me not to mention his name to anyone and then told me to come back Thursday evening.

I had dinner in the automat and then looked for lodging. I saw a vacancy sign at a hotel in the red lantern district. I paid seventy-five francs for a room that had seen better days. Leaving my clothes on to keep warm, I tried to sleep.

Sometime during the night, I was awakened by shouts in German and loud knocking on doors. On went my boots and jacket. At a soft knock, I opened the door and the front desk clerk rushed in. He quickly told me the Gestapo was looking for anyone who was not legal, then he gave me a shove out the window. We landed on the grass and ran into an alley. Squatting behind a large garbage can, we tried to control our breathing.

It seemed like hours before a woman called to him. We got up slowly, cramped from crouching in one position, and entered the hotel. The desk clerk looked at me slyly. "I knew when you came in last night that a raid would get you up in a hurry. Who are you?"

I gave him the name of someone who had died in Boulogne.

"Go back to sleep. They won't be back."

But soon there was another commotion. This time I was much faster and again hid behind the garbage can. When the noise died down, I went to the front of the hotel and spotted two German guards posted there. I went back behind the garbage can and somehow fell asleep. I woke up stiff with a cat sniffing me.

After a sandwich and a hot drink at the automat, I walked through the district, trying to locate another hotel for the night. Finally, at an old, run-down hotel I paid 200 francs for four nights. I was given a receipt and a key. For another 50 francs a night, I could have had the company of a "lady."

With somewhere to stay for four nights, I could concentrate on finding something long term. I wandered the streets and found myself in front of the Clef d'Or. Jean, the owner, stood behind the counter and at first had the most surprised look on his face. It turned into a broad smile.

"Lutz!" He stepped from behind the counter and gave me a bear hug. "Come in the back room and have some coffee. Tell me where you've been."

When the coffee was in front of us and we'd lit cigarettes, I told him what had happened to me and the predicament that I faced.

"Well, there is one thing I can do for you. Come in every morning and sometimes during the day. There'll always be hot coffee and a piece of bread for you. But you know, a lot of people come in here, so we must be very careful. I'll call you Jeffke. Please speak only French. If anyone asks any questions, you live with your mother and work here occasionally."

In response to my question, he said he hadn't seen any of my old friends except one. Klara Loeb had moved into the building. She had become a prostitute in order to survive.

* * * * *

Thursday night I returned to the doctor's office, my condition not really any better. Although the doctor treated me, I didn't think he wanted me to come back.

Friday morning, with no place to go and my money running out, Jean handed me 500 francs, donated by some "old-timers" he talked to. I accepted it with relief and heartfelt appreciation—I could keep my room at the hotel through the end of the month.

"Jean, thank you. What can I say? This will get me through the month."

Chapter 23

The month passed and I hadn't found permanent lodging yet. Out of money, I had to leave the hotel. For the next two weeks I slept in courtyards, on benches in the park, and most of the time, in alleys behind garbage cans. Many times I slipped in open doors after dark to sleep in apartment hallways.

I couldn't go to the Clef d'Or. Jean said quite a few Gestapo men had been coming in and the café was being closely watched. I could still visit the Hungarian restaurant, where the manager fed me leftovers in the back room.

My clothes hadn't been off in two weeks. The soles of my boots were worn off and I was walking on my socks—they wouldn't last long.

Hordes of Gestapo were everywhere as well as German military police. Many people were stopped for identification checks. I looked so bad and smelled so awful, no one bothered me!

After a particularly bad night spent in an alley, I started to walk to Karl's place. After traveling two blocks, I realized I'd never make it there on foot. On a busy corner I begged passersby for money. One lady stopped, looked at me, and handed me a ten-franc bill. "What is this war doing to us, especially the children?"

I thanked her with a warm feeling of relief; I could take the streetcar. When I boarded and took a seat, I handed the conductor the money without looking up. He gave me change and a one-way ticket. It was so warm in the car I fell asleep.

The conductor woke me up. "End of the line. Where did you want to get off?"

"Schaarbeck."

"Okay, you can ride back with me, but don't fall asleep and miss your stop again."

I managed to keep awake and left the car in front of Karl's place. When I rang the bell, he looked out the window and buzzed me in without speaking. His mother looked at me with a horrified expression. "Oh, Lutz, this is terrible; you look simply awful." Karl shook my hand and held it.

I apologized for barging in. I just didn't know where to go and what to do anymore.

Mrs. Kerslak ran a bath while Karl and I smoked a cigarette. In the bathroom, I tried to remove all my clothes but gave up with my underwear. It would have to soak off in the tub.

After I spent an hour in the tub, asleep most of the time, Karl came in with some of his clothes. He left and I started to dry myself. My old sores were worse than ever and there were some new ones. After some tucking in, the clothes looked decent. Karl even gave me some shoes that fit pretty well when stuffing was pushed into the toes.

We spent a nice evening just talking. In the morning, I rode the streetcar, paying with some money Karl's mother had slipped into my jacket pocket. Happily, Manfred was home when I arrived at his place, and he agreed to let me stay there.

The next day we visited the Belgian doctor again. Manfred waited nervously outside. The doctor treated me again and agreed that my sores were much worse, but he couldn't suggest any other treatment. As we left, the nurse told Manfred that the doctor could not see me anymore. The Gestapo were watching who he treated. I spent one more night with Manfred, then I went back to sleeping in alleys.

The next time I went to the Clef d'Or, Jean took me into the back room immediately. "Manfred has been picked up. Be careful. He might mention your name if he is interrogated."

I was too shocked to say anything. When Jean left to wait on customers, I just sat there, thinking.

Later, Jean returned and said he had been told that Karl and his mother would be at the café tomorrow at noon and they'd like to see me.

* * * * *

The next day was Sunday and I was at the café early. When Karl and his mother arrived, Jean brought us coffee and something to eat.

As we talked, two men entered and took a table near the back. After a few minutes, one of the men came to our table and spoke to us.

"Mrs. Kerslak and Karl. We are from the Gestapo and have to take your son with us for about two hours. Just a few questions and then he can come back here." My legs were shaking. Karl said goodbye to us and went outside with the men, where a car was waiting in front of the café. Karl and the two men got in and the car drove off.

Very distressed, Mrs. Kerslak turned to me. "Lutz, did you know those men were coming here? No, of course you didn't. Why did they take him? You know they won't bring him back today."

I told her the story Jean's friend had told me. We made arrangements to meet the next day at the streetcar stop outside the café and to go to Gestapo headquarters together.

* * * * *

The next morning I waited outside Gestapo headquarters while Mrs. Kerslak was inside, inquiring about Karl. When she emerged two hours later, she said, "There is nothing I can do. He and the others will be turned over to the Belgian courts for action. I will be notified when the trial begins and ends."

We rode the streetcar in silence. Before I got off at the Gare du Nord, Mrs. Kerslak told me to check at the Clef d'Or, where she would leave messages for me when she had more information.

At the hotel in the middle of the night, there was a knock on the door. "Out, out. The police are here to check every room."

I was out of bed in a flash and into my clothes. When I opened the door, a man was waiting. "Come on out the back door and down the fire escape." We waited in the cold over an hour and then cautiously reentered. The rest of the night passed uneventfully.

When I left in the morning, the concierge told me, "Better not come back, they will be here every night."

The Hungarian restaurant was closed and the sign on the door indicated it wouldn't reopen soon, that the owner was on a long vacation. As I started to walk away, two men followed me. I rounded the corner and started to run. I looked over my shoulder and saw they were still following me. I ran through the courtyard of a large house, toward the five-and-ten store on Rue Neuve, and hid. They walked right by my hiding place, looking around, but didn't see me.

Later, saving only enough money for a room that night, I bought a loaf of bread at the local bakery. After it was gone, I would have to beg again.

No one was left I could call on for help. Begging on street corners, I got a little change, but although it was Christmastime, people were not very charitable. Since I didn't have any money for cigarettes, I picked up cigarette butts from the street. By taking the butts apart and rolling the loose tobacco in toilet paper, I could make a passable cigarette.

For quite some time, whenever I passed the Clef d'Or, Jean would wave me on and I would keep walking. One day not long after Christmas, he didn't signal me and when I went in, he handed me something to eat. He said his place was being watched, so I should always walk by unless he signaled for me to come in.

I asked if he knew what had happened to Manfred and Karl, but there was nothing he could tell me.

* * * * *

The new year, 1943, didn't start out well. The Diana Bar was closed. When I visited Karl's mother in mid-January, she told me that the Belgian court had made an "unconfirmed decision." The Germans took care of the Dutchman in their own way. Marcel Cohen was to be taken to a work camp but was beaten to death on the way there by the SS. Karl and Manfred both received prison sentences, and Mrs. Kerslak would not be able to see her son. After a meal and overnight stay at Mrs. Kerslak's place, she and I agreed to leave messages for each other with Jean.

In February I ran into Klara, who was living above the Clef d'Or. We talked the evening away and she let me stay the night. It was nice to be warm again.

As I walked by the automat one day, someone called my name. I pretended I didn't hear her. Then, right behind me, a voice said, "Lutz Posener, I know it has been a long time and you know my mother better than you know me. I am Roeschen Butow, Rosa's daughter. Let's go somewhere and have some coffee."

I spun around to face her. "I can't believe it! I'd love some coffee, but I don't have a penny," I confessed.

"Oh, that's okay. I have enough for coffee for the two of us."

When we were seated at a table in the five-and-ten store's restaurant, she confided that she and her mother had become estranged because of her choice of a boyfriend. When she and the boyfriend separated, she had no means of earning a living and was forced into prostitution. When her mother realized how her daughter was earning her living, she just walked away. Roeschen had been living in a basement apartment with an Austrian named Eduard who was a deserter from the German army.

When I told her of my desperate situation, she said that if I could scrape together 250 francs I could rent a room in the building where she was living. I didn't know how I could come up with such an amount. We agreed to meet every afternoon in front of the automat.

* * * * *

Jean told me he would try to start a collection for me and Mrs. Kerslak gave me 50 francs. After six days, I had 200 francs—50 francs short. Suddenly I remembered a middle-aged homosexual who had shown some interest in me a long time ago. I rang the bell at the apartment house where I knew he had lived. He was still there and invited me in for coffee. He looked the same. He smiled as I explained my situation to him, then I realized my foolishness and started to leave.

"It's all right, little fellow. I understand. You can stay here tonight and I'll lend you some money." He put his arm around me and walked me to the bedroom. "Do you wear a nightshirt?"

My mind raced. How was I going to get out of this? He closed the bedroom door and started to undress.

"Which side of the bed would you like?"

"It doesn't matter." I pretended to take off my shoes. By then he was nude. He turned his back to me. Looking around the room I saw a statue and picked it up, walked up behind him, and hit him behind the ear. He fell on his face without a sound. I was afraid I had killed him, but thankfully, he had a pulse.

I went through his pockets and found some bills. There were more on the nightstand. Stuffing them into my jacket, I tiptoed out the door. The stairs creaked, but no one stopped me.

After running four blocks, I counted the bills—395 francs. It was a nice sum, but I hoped I didn't have to make robbing people a habit!

Roeschen was waiting in the cold for me.

"Were you able to get the 250?" Looking at my fistful of bills, she asked, "Did you make a killing?"

"Don't say that. It is too close to the truth! Let's meet Eduard and get some food."

Eduard was waiting for us at a café where prostitutes spent time with their pimps. Belgian and German authorities didn't bother anyone there. Roeschen introduced me to a man with an Austrian accent.

When the food and beer arrived, we ate rapidly. They were as hungry as I was. After dinner, I paid the bill. We then walked for a half hour to Roeschen and Eduard's place.

The building had four stories. It was pitch dark inside until a door opened, throwing light into the hallway. A small man came out into the hallway. After Eduard identified himself, the man invited us inside.

We entered a small living room, poorly lit and with a heavy cigarette odor. I was introduced to Pauline, who squeezed my hand harder than necessary and gave me a faint smile.

I was given a room on the top floor with a window that reminded me of our mansard. A light hung from the ceiling. I had a bed, a nightstand, a basin with a water pitcher, and a bucket to use as a toilet at night.

Emile handed me the key and told me not to stay out too late in the evenings. The linen would be changed every two weeks and the next rent was due March 15.

The next day, Roeschen, Eduard, and I went to a café around the corner for breakfast. This time we shared the bill; I didn't have too much money left. Eduard and I walked Roeschen toward the north station, where she would go to work. After we left her, Eduard and I drank beer at a bar nearby. He told me about himself and why he deserted. I didn't understand why he loved Roeschen, a little Jewish girl. He was not her pimp, but she was still a prostitute who supported him. I gave them credit for doing what they felt was right.

* * * * *

Late in February the waiter at the café indicated to me that Eduard and Roeschen hadn't been in for a few days. At my knock, Eduard answered his door, half-dressed. The room was dark and musty. He told me that Roeschen wasn't well, and I barely heard her say "Hello, Lutz" from the bed. Roeschen had pneumonia—fever, chills, a cough, and pain in her chest.

At her request, Eduard and I went to a nearby pharmacy to see if we could buy something to make her more comfortable. Eduard didn't want to go inside because he might be recognized as a deserter. The pharmacist gave me two medications. We rushed back because it was long after curfew.

* * * * *

One night after Roeschen was much better and back at work, I was jolted out of bed by a loud knock on the door. "Who is there?"

"It's me—Emile. Open up. The Germans are raiding the place. Put something on and let's go out the window."

Since I was smaller, I went first and then helped him onto the roof and across to another building. Just then we heard German voices. "Where are you going? That is not the way to Palestine."

We eluded whoever was speaking and lowered ourselves through a roof window into the next building, into the presence of an old man.

Again, we heard the German voice, but it was fainter: "No, I don't see anyone. They probably scrammed, but we will find them somewhere else. After all, we caught some Jews and, of course, the Austrian deserter. So, all in all, we didn't do too badly."

Emile had placed his hand over the old man's mouth. "Shh, not a word." The man nodded his head. We heard the sound of motor vehicles leaving and started to breathe easier.

"I'm sorry," Emile said to the old man, "Let me clean up the mess we made."

"Not necessary. Don't worry about it. I am glad the Germans didn't find you." And he gave us each a cigarette.

After a while we cautiously went downstairs and out the front door. We separated and went off in different directions.

When I entered the apartment building late in the afternoon, an unhappy Pauline and her friend Flora stood on the stairway. They said Emile had come back too soon. As he entered the building, the Germans came in right behind him. All of them were taken to Gestapo headquarters and interrogated. Emile was beaten. He and Roeschen were being detained, and Pauline thought Eduard would be shot without a trial.

Pauline insisted that I move out because the Germans would be back. I got my topcoat, gave Pauline my key, and left, although I had no idea where to go.

Chapter 24

I was back on the streets for a week. By the first of March the weather began to warm up, but I was worn out, my sores were really hurting, and I hadn't eaten in three days.

Walking on the boulevard I tried to ignore someone calling my name. A quick glance over my shoulder showed me it was Cherie Coco, a tall, mulatto prostitute. With a slight motion, she told me to follow her into a nearby building.

At her place—one well-furnished room with a bed, a small couch, and an alcove with a stove—Cherie told me to sit down while she prepared some food.

We met in 1940 when I had just started in the black market business. She asked Karl and me to get her some cigarettes for a client. Cherie had come from the Belgian Congo with her parents, and when they died, she was raised in a foster home. Prostitution paid well because she was a novelty for most men. She was young, good looking, and black. We became friends, partly because I felt we had a common situation. Both of us were looked down upon—she because she was black and I because I was a Jew.

Once a deal Karl and I had with her went awry. Her client took the merchandise without paying her, although she had already paid us a considerable sum. We gave her back most of her money, keeping only our actual costs. Fate is funny; because we were honest, I was eating and had a place to stay the night.

"You know you're putting yourself in jeopardy by helping me," I said. "Why are you doing this?"

"You were always fair and honest with me. Also, I hate the Germans. There is a bathtub on the second floor, and you can sleep in my bed later if you wish."

I showed her some of my sores. "I don't know if you want to sleep with this, Cherie."

In the bathroom I undressed and soaked in the wonderfully hot water. Cherie then applied petroleum jelly and bandaged my arms and legs. Back in her room, we had a cigarette and I put on the pajamas she had laid out. When I was in bed, she undressed. She was tall and trim.

I drifted to sleep with the perfume of her body and warmth around me.

* * * * *

Cherie left for a few hours after fixing us some breakfast and telling me I could stay another night.

While she was gone, I tried to think, but I couldn't concentrate. How long could I go on like this? One day I'd be caught. Suddenly I wondered where Papa was now. I didn't know what made me think of him at that moment.

In the early afternoon, Cherie returned with a newspaper, a magazine, some cigarettes and food. Jokingly, she told me to read the paper to find out if the Germans would lose the war by the next morning.

Cherie had tried to locate someone who would shelter me, but everyone was afraid to become involved. In the newspaper was an article concerning a German Reich drive to round up deserters, saboteurs, and underground fighters, as well as Jews who were hiding or being hidden. I decided to stay the night and then leave because I didn't want to get Cherie into trouble.

In the morning we were quiet as we ate breakfast, then I got ready to leave. When I tried to thank her, she said, "Don't say anything. I was glad to help. I just wish I could do more. If things get bad and you have no other way, look for me on the boulevard."

* * * * *

The next day, Karl's mother was at the café when I arrived and invited me to return there for dinner with her that evening. When I arrived at five o'clock, she was already waiting at a table. While we ate she told me that the Germans had denied her any visits to Karl, and the Belgians were unable to do anything about it. It seemed she would have to wait for the war to end to see him. As I escorted her to the streetcar, we agreed to keep in touch.

I needed to find a place to stay for the night. At the café that the prostitutes frequented, a small placard on the door stated that the establishment was closed for the time being by order of the German High Command. I spent the night behind a shed in a courtyard.

The next day on Boulevard Adolphe Max I recognized a pimp I knew. He motioned me into a small house on a side street. It was dark inside and when he grabbed me, I was startled. He assured me I had nothing to fear from him. He figured I was looking for Cherie Coco. She had been picked up along with the other girls when the Germans raided the café, while the Belgians cheered them on. It seemed the Germans knew that Cherie was involved in an underground group.

One more possible place to stay was lost. It was too late to find another, so it was an alley for me again.

When I left the mansard where I used to live with Papa, I had given the couple downstairs some family papers and pictures to hold for me. I didn't think I should go directly there, so I decided to go by the butcher shop the next day to be sure it was safe to try to see them.

* * * * *

The butcher shop owner frowned a little, finally recognizing me. Hesitantly, he invited me in.

In the back, I quickly ate the food and drink he brought. The couple I wanted to find had moved, but he had their new address on the Rue de la Carpe. Before I left he asked about my father. The butcher hadn't heard anything from him in two years. As far as he knew, Papa was still in a camp in southern France.

When I rang the bell at the address on the Rue de la Carpe, Claudine answered the door and a wide grin spread across her face. "Maurice! Maurice! Lutz is back!"

They were pleased to see me and to hear what had happened since I left the mansard. I'd found them just in time; they had found work in Germany and would be leaving in two days. And after thirty-four years of living together, they had married!

Maurice brought me a small package, and after wishing them well in their new life, I left. On a bench in the park, I opened the package and looked at pictures of me as a scout, of Papa, of our friends Heinz and Jochem, and of Mama. Along with some papers of no importance, I found my school identification, a registration paper from Molenbeek city hall, three letters from my stepmother written from Berlin three years ago, a letter from Papa sent from Gurs, and some magazine and newspaper clippings. I folded the photos and official documents and put them in my wallet. Tearing the rest into pieces, I deposited them in a nearby trash can.

Today was the first of April—April Fool's Day! What a predicament I was in! All my friends and acquaintances either had been arrested or had somehow disappeared. It was harder to beg on the streets because the Germans picked up anyone who looked out of place. I was sleeping in gutters and alleys, scrounging in garbage cans for food. I hadn't taken my clothes off in about two weeks. My hair was long and scraggly and my beard was growing steadily. I didn't dare think about the condition of my sores. It might be a blessing if I were picked up, I thought. Maybe I should just turn myself in. Suddenly I realized what that would mean, and my resolve returned.

At Jean's café, a sign on the front door indicated it had been closed by the German High Command. Angrily I thought, he was my last friend. As I walked away from the café, someone called my name, startling me.

"I'm a friend of Jean's," he said. "I saw you looking at the sign on the café door. Jean gave me your description. Lord, you're a mess. Are you all right?"

"Oh, yes," I said sarcastically. "I'm filthy, weak, and hungry and probably look like I've come from the sewers. I'm just fine!"

"Sorry, sorry! I wanted to tell you that Jean was arrested by the Gestapo when they raided his place two days ago. He gave me this envelope, which a friend of yours had left with him to give you." With that, he turned and walked away.

I was so surprised I didn't think to thank him. In a nearby toilet, making sure no one was there, I opened the envelope. I removed a 100-franc note, and a piece of paper fell out:

> Lutz, you know who is writing this. Meet me Sunday
> afternoon at five o'clock at the first door at Sarma.
> We'll have dinner and go to a concert.

It wasn't signed, but I knew it was from Karl's mother. She was the
only person I knew who would give me money and write a note in
German. I tore the note into pieces and flushed it down the toilet.
Appalled at my appearance when I looked in the mirror, I knew I must
have a bath and shave before I saw her. Conserving as much of the 100
francs as possible for as long as I could, I waited until Friday to enter
the public bath.

When the attendant saw my condition, he agreed to let me have
double the time and lots of soap for thirty francs. He even scrounged
up an old pair of pants nearly my small size, a shirt, socks, and a
sweater. Again I had to soak my old clothes off, but by the second tub
of soap and water, I looked and felt much better. Upstairs, the little old
barber shaved me twice and cut my hair, which had grown into a
bush. The change was pleasantly surprising. And best of all, the barber said it was all a present from him.

At the automat I had three sandwiches and a cup of soup. Feeling
much better, I went to a hotel I had noticed before and asked for a
room. For sixty francs I received a key to a room on the top floor. The
room was not fancy, but the bed was large and clean. I stripped to my
underpants and fell into bed.

The next thing I heard was a lot of banging on doors and German
voices: "Open the doors, let's go, let's go. Military police. Furlough
passes or traveling papers ready for inspection."

There was no way out of this. In a moment, I heard loud banging
on my door. Two soldiers stood in the doorway with big, shining
police badges. A lieutenant walked in, looked at my legs and arms,
and stepped back. "What are you doing here? Do you have any papers
or an ID card?"

Answering in French, I told him my parents felt I should stay in a
hotel because I had contagious scabies. I showed him my city hall registration paper. He looked at it, then looked at my legs and arms

again. A disgusted looked crossed his face and he turned to leave. "Close that door. Let's get out of here fast." He motioned me back into the room and fading footsteps told me the men were leaving.

As I left the next morning, the desk clerk scowled at me. It didn't matter. I would be staying in the alley again that night; my money was about gone.

Chapter 25

Mrs. Kerslak and I met on Sunday at the Sarma restaurant. When I told her what had happened in the past few days, she smiled ruefully. "Lutz, Lutz, only you could have all this happen to you!"

We had a nice dinner and then went to a concert of modern music. The audience was enthusiastic, stamping their feet to keep time with the rhythm as the musicians played. The whole concert was delightful and I relaxed and enjoyed the selections. After much applause and six curtain calls, we got up and followed the crowd toward the exit.

After a snack and some coffee, I escorted Mrs. Kerslak to the street-car. She hugged me and stepped aboard.

Before I could cross the street, two Flemish SS men approached me. One addressed me in Flemish.

"Good evening. Nice to see you. You don't remember me, but I remember you quite well. Do you know Jean and the café Clef d'Or?"

I shook my head.

The smaller one said, "You mean you've forgotten so fast? Now, tell me, you are a Jew, right?"

"Me? No, I'm not a Jew."

"Did you hear that? He's not a Jew! I'll ask again. Are you a Jew? Why lie about it?"

Before I could answer, I felt a burning sensation on my nose, and a little blood came out. Then a fist hit me in the stomach. When I straightened up, my face was inches from the grinning face of the smaller man. He squinted at me. "So, are you a Jew?"

"Yes, yes. I'm a Jew."

"Well, you could have spared yourself a little pain."

They took me across the street to a beer hall where the German military spent their evenings. The doorman and some girls looked the other way as I was led to a stairway in the back of the place. As soon as we entered a room in the basement, the little one kneed me in the groin. I dropped to my knees in excruciating pain. In rapid order, my nose was punched again, my stomach was punched again, and my head was pounded into the wall several times. An officer entered.

"Couldn't you have found a taller victim? There is nothing to this peewee. He looks horrible. That's enough, take him out of here." Then he left.

The small one sneered at me. "See what happens to you Jews when you lie? You're nothing but scum, and lying doesn't help because with our superiority we find out everything anyway. Let's go." The SS men marched me up the stairs and outside.

We boarded a streetcar and they stood in front of me. One had a revolver in my ribs and the other had his gun out of its holster. I didn't know why they bothered—I couldn't have gone anywhere because the streetcar was jammed.

A heavy woman looked at us, grinned, and said in Flemish, "Oh, you caught a *big* fish. Better watch out or he'll jump through the roof." Everyone in the whole streetcar laughed.

Embarrassed, one of my guards yelled, "Shut up, all of you, or I'll start shooting." We finished the trip in silence.

At Gestapo headquarters, I was taken to a room on the second floor. The only light came from a table lamp. An officer in a Sicherheitsdienst uniform sat at a desk. My two guards saluted, barked "Heil Hitler," and left. The officer pulled a manila folder from a cabinet and looked at it, then he looked at me.

"Lutz Posener, yes. Are you this little bird? Well, it took a little while, but finally we picked you up—one of the last ones from the transport. You should have known that you couldn't slip by us."

He showed me what was in the folder: my registration papers from city hall, school cards, and some other papers. Most important, there was my identification card with a photograph and, written in big red letters, the words "Juif-Jood"—the word "Jew" in French and Flemish.

Grabbing me by the lapels, he pushed me against the wall. With a sarcastic grin on his face, he raised me off the floor and hissed, "I

Photograph of Lutz (age 16) from his identification card, 1942

should actually shoot your sex jewels off. Then you at least couldn't make any more little Jews. But that will all come in time anyway."

I felt myself go limp, and my pants were all wet. He opened the door and called for someone, and in walked a Flemish SS man.

"Take this little dirt bee down to the basement. We will interrogate him tomorrow."

I walked down the stairs in front of the soldier and into the street. As we crossed the street, he said, "I wonder what you'd do if events ever turned around. You'd kill us all if you had the chance, right?"

I looked at him in the dim light. "I'd do more than that," I said. "I'd cut you all up into small pieces and feed you to the dogs."

He reeled back but didn't reply.

In the basement he asked, "Are you hungry?" When I nodded, I was given some bread and jam, then led into a room where an elderly man sat on the floor. There was no furniture, only a fragment of carpet. It was quite cold.

"Good evening, sir," I said.

He responded without looking up.

Breaking the bread apart, I offered some to him. He shook his head. When I finished eating, I lit a cigarette.

He looked me over and spoke in French. "You look terrible. What did they do to you?"

"Well, they had a little boxing match with me. I'm worn out. If you don't mind, I'll just roll up in this carpet and sleep."

I slept through the night and awoke stiff but somewhat better. The old man was sitting against the wall, still hunched in the same position. I don't think he'd slept at all.

"How wonderful it is to be young," he said. "You young people recover so fast. What do you think they'll do with us? I haven't done anything to be put here."

"Don't you know where we are? Aren't you Jewish?"

"Actually, I've just become aware of being Jewish. I wasn't raised in the Jewish faith. My parents didn't observe the holidays or associate with the Jewish community, but my birth certificate says I am a Jew. My wife is not Jewish and my two children are Protestants. They go to church and their children have been baptized. I have no idea why I am here."

"You must've been living in a cocoon not to see what's going on with the Germans!"

"Well, yes, but my grandparents were born in Belgium; so were my parents and my sister and me. Being Jewish was never mentioned. I looked at the war and politics from a Belgian Protestant point of view. I have a small bookkeeping office outside of Brussels, and my seven employees and I discuss only everyday events. We read about the war in newspapers, but nothing happened to us until now.

"One morning at my home, two civilians in leather coats knocked at our door. They said they were German Gestapo and wanted me to go with them because they needed some information about our business. During the questioning, they showed me papers identifying me as Jewish and said they'd have to keep me. I hope they release me soon."

"Are you kidding?" I said. "They aren't going to do that."

Just then the door opened and I was taken upstairs to a room. Two men asked me a lot of questions: where I was born, who my parents were, all about my schooling, my whole life up to now. They were polite and businesslike but wrote down everything I said. Most of what I told them was the truth, but I didn't tell them true names and places. When they ran out of questions, I was taken back downstairs.

My cellmate wanted to know what happened, but before I could tell him we were interrupted by a guard who brought us bread, jam, and a brown drink that I suppose was intended to be coffee. As soon as I'd finished eating, a guard led me out into the courtyard.

The air was fresh, but I couldn't inhale deeply because my nose hurt so much. The rest of me was sore, too. After I'd swept the yard and dumped the dirt into a garbage can, the guard gave me three cigarettes and led me back to the cell.

The old man was still curious and very anxious about what would happen to him. When I told him we'd probably be sent to a camp, he became very upset.

Suddenly we heard children's voices and the sound of shuffling feet. A nearby door opened and shut. After the guard left, we talked with the new arrivals through the closed door. A man's voice told us that his wife, her sister, their two little girls, and he were picked up by the Gestapo two hours ago. They were from the southern part of Brussels.

I slept most of the day. The old man just sat or paced in the cell. In the evening we got the same rations and then both tried to sleep a little.

We were awakened during the night when the lights were turned on. Women were crying, doors opened and closed, and German voices shouted. After the lights were turned off again, we called out and an answering voice told us that there were ten of them, including two children. They had been placed in three rooms nearby. By now I was wide awake and just lay awake on the floor for the rest of the night.

When morning came, the lights went on and the doors were flung open.

"Out, out. Let's go, let's go. Everybody stand in front of the doors in one row so that you are all visible."

When we stepped out, I could see the others; there were three girls and one boy, all small. The adults were in their midthirties. By now we numbered nineteen. After an officer had arrived, taken our names, and left, we were returned to our cells.

* * * * *

Three days passed very slowly. I suddenly realized that we could be watched without our knowing it. I had found a small camouflaged opening in the door, through which the guard was able to see inside our cell. The guard had left it open by mistake, so now I had a way to see out!

Once more I was taken out to sweep and clean the courtyard. I'd lost track of time and asked the guard what day it was. It was April 9, 1943, my birthday. I was seventeen years old!

Back in my cell, I showed the old man the full package of cigarettes the guard gave me. We agreed it was a very nice birthday present. The old man seemed resigned to his situation by then.

A few days later another group of people was brought in, and ten of them were put in the small room with us—six men and four women. It was quite crowded, but we huddled together to try to keep warm. There were no sanitary facilities. We had to bang on the door to be taken outside to the toilet. The men had scraggly beards and we were all filthy.

On the 13th of April we heard German voices shouting and someone being dragged down the stairs. "You are a spy. Just tell us the
truth, that you are a spy." Peeking through the hole in the door I saw
three SS men throw a young man against the wall. They were all
shouting at him so it was difficult to understand everything they were
saying—I heard something about names, places, and information on
underground activities.

The three SS men all had bullwhips, which they used to flay the
man when he didn't speak. One whip caught him across the face, and
blood spurted everywhere. A water hose was turned on, washing
down the man and the walls. Then the shouting and whipping began
all over again. The sight made me nauseated, and I slumped back
down in a corner and gagged.

After more yelling and sounds of whips cracking and striking flesh,
our door opened. One of the SS men stepped inside our room and
looked around. Spotting me he said, "Let's go, you Jewish peewee.
Out." I left the room and pressed myself against the wall outside.
They must have put the poor wretch in one of the cells. Not wanting
to look at the blood on the floor, I stared at the ceiling.

"Why are you looking at the ceiling? You are supposed to clean down
here. You Jews are sure stupid. Take the water hose and the broom, and
I want to see everything sparkling clean. Don't take all day." With that,
the SS men marched out and up the stairs, leaving only the regular guard.
As I started to wash down the walls, I became nauseated and reached the
toilet just in time. Feeling a bit better, I cleaned the blood from the walls
and floors, then I was returned to my cell.

Late in the afternoon I was taken from the cell: it was my turn to
be questioned. A strong light shining in my eyes blinded me. Two SS
men wanted to know where I was from, where I'd lived, and what I'd
done with myself for my entire life. They accused my papa, me, and
all the Jews of stealing money from the German Reich and declared
the punishment should be death, that we were thieving, conniving Jew
criminals and the scum of the earth. They didn't like my answers. A
flat wooden board hit one side of my face, then the other, and then the
men poked me in the stomach. I was hit everywhere until I fell on my

knees. The pain was so bad I couldn't think. As they walked away one said, "This Jew pig is not going to last long anyway."

I cleaned myself up in the toilet as best I could. My face was swollen and my clothes were stained with blood. No bones were broken, but I was very sore and bruised. When the guard took me back to the cell, the old man put me in the corner on the rug and stroked my head. There were tears in his eyes. I fell asleep, not waking until the evening coffee arrived.

The old man looked at me. "I know why they beat you. It is because you are a German refugee, and they don't like that you left Germany."

I answered sarcastically, "That must be it because I don't know any other reason."

The door opened and the old man and I were called out, to be replaced by seven people, all women and children. We followed the guard upstairs to a very small room that smelled of disinfectant. We were ordered into the room—actually more of a closet. The light kept going on and off. Since my childhood, when I was punished by being shut in a closet, I had been very uncomfortable in the dark. The only time we could see anything was when the light came on briefly. We talked to keep our fear under control.

Suddenly the light was turned on and the guard motioned us out. We were told that we were leaving, to get our belongings ready, and to be in the courtyard in an hour. I had very few items—a little pouch, my wallet with some pictures, my cigarette case, pocket watch, Papa's Iron Cross ribbon from World War I, some cigarettes, and matches. Outside, the air was cold but fresh.

We were marched to trucks, which took us on a bumpy, wild ride. When the trucks slowed down, I saw a sign: "Malines-Mechelen." This was the place, I realized, where the train stopped last year on the way to Germany, where the wagons were attached, where I saw those faces and heard the crying. This was the camp everyone had been talking about. The trucks moved through the gate, past a plaque indicating that the installation had been an infantry garrison during World War I. The place was a fortress.

Assembly camp building in Malines, Belgium, where Jews were picked up for transport to Auschwitz

We jumped from the trucks in an area surrounded by huge four-story buildings. People were looking at us through windows. A voice shouted, "Bonjour, Lutz! Up here, on the third floor to your left." I looked up and saw David. Before I could respond, a voice over the loudspeaker shouted, "Quiet. Silence. Everybody away from the windows, right now."

Two men approached. After the smaller one spoke in German, a guard translated. We would be assigned to one of the buildings. Single men would be billeted with single men, and women in another building. Families would be placed with other families. We would be served three meals a day that could be supplemented twice a day by purchases at a canteen. We would be allowed outside only two hours a day to march around the court in an orderly fashion.

We were herded into one of the buildings and given room assignments. I had a bed in the middle of a room on the third floor.

As soon as I got settled, I asked to see David, and a guard agreed to escort me to his building. When we met, David and I embraced in a bear hug. He introduced me to his wife and small son. He told me that all the Jews in Antwerp had been picked up and everyone who had jumped from the transport had been rounded up except for two or three people. We agreed to try to stay together, but I had to return to my room in order to receive food.

Outside the room, we were issued a bowl, a cup, a spoon, and a fork. The food wasn't much different from that in the camp at Boulogne-sur-Mer or the basement where I was confined. It seemed that we didn't have much choice but to buy overpriced items at the canteen to augment the poor food distributed by the camp guards.

Out in the yard, I planted my back against a building and looked around. I wondered how long we would be here. Trying to escape seemed hopeless; I'd be picked up if I went back to Brussels, and anyplace else wouldn't be safe unless I could get help from the underground.

Obeying instructions broadcast over the loudspeaker, people streamed out of the buildings and began walking around the yard, the way prison inmates walk around a prison yard. I found David and his family and walked with him as he carried his son. A voice behind me called my name. "Lutz, is that you?" Turning around, I looked at a tall, young, thin man with a mop of straight black hair and horn-rimmed glasses. "Willie, Willie Levine. I cannot believe this! What are you doing here?"

"I've been here for a week. Eugen and my sister and parents are here, too. Come see us after the walking period. We are on the second floor to your right."

Back with David, I told him that Willie was my scout leader with the Hanoar Hatzioni, and he and his brother were at the jamboree in Dinant. The loudspeaker blared that our time outside was over. Once back inside the building, I found the Levines. Willie, Eugen, and I caught up on what had happened to us since we last met. They'd had as difficult a time surviving as I'd had.

As the day ended after a game of chess with David, I got into bed. It was not the Grand Hotel, but I was not on the street or under the noses of the Gestapo.

The next day was boring except for chess sessions with David, but it gave me time to recuperate from my beatings of the last few days. David relayed the rumor that in two days we would leave for Poland and be put in work camps. While we were walking around the yard in the afternoon, my old Gestapo enemy, Hans Frank, appeared and planted himself in the middle of the circle, looking us over. He spotted me and gestured for me to come to him.

"Well, we caught you after all, Posener. You should have known that we would catch you. Nobody can escape through our nets. The day after tomorrow it will be over anyway; it is off toward the east for you. It is time that we got you all under lock and key."

He dismissed me and when I resumed walking with David, people asked me all sorts of questions. I realized I was regarded with some suspicion by the others. In the hall when we were alone, I confirmed to David that the rumor was correct: we would leave for Poland the day after tomorrow. I said we'd have to wait until sometime in the future to try to escape.

David declined, reminding me that this time his family was with him. I told him I understood and then walked around, trying to find out more information. But to ask questions was to invite suspicion, so I quit.

* * * * *

After breakfast the next day we were ordered to stay inside. Soon two trucks drove up. I excitedly called David over to the window. We saw our old friend Jossel climbing down from the truck. We watched to see which building he was assigned to and after the trucks left, we surprised him. Jossel said that he and the others had been able to hide for a time but were finally picked up. Either they were betrayed or the Gestapo found them in one of their raids. Jossel's girlfriend was picked up, too, and was in the women's dorm.

When the lights went out, I tossed and turned, feeling jittery. Trying to think of something pleasant to dream about, I thought of Papa. Where was he? How was he? I reached for my bag and took out his ribbon. A lot had happened since he left. I whispered softly, "I haven't done too badly, Papa, but I am just holding on. Don't worry about me."

Chapter 26

The next morning the guards shouted, "Up, up, everybody. Let's get ready." Everyone dressed and packed, rapidly ate the meager breakfast, then assembled in the courtyard. I stayed close to David, his wife, and child.

We were led into a large room where four SS men sat at each of two long tables. The man in front of me was ordered to empty his pockets and I understood what was happening. Putting my pocket watch on the floor, I ground my heel into it and then broke the spring in my cigarette case. When it was my turn to empty my pockets, I put both broken items on the table. Cold eyes stared at me and I received a sharp boot in the backside. One of the SS men held up the ribbon from Papa's Iron Cross medal.

"It's my papa's from the First World War," I said.

He gave it back to me. The watch was thrown in the garbage pail and everything else was pushed across the table to me. "Pick up all this trash and get away from here. No papers for you to sign." On my way out I mentioned what was taking place inside to a man who quickly dropped two large diamonds into a sewer trench and smiled at me.

When everyone was processed and reassembled in the courtyard, we were marched out the gate and through the town in small groups. People stared at us; some smiled, some waved, and others just shook their heads or looked away. At the railway station, a long line of cattle cars was pulled up. Before we boarded, German shepherd dogs were led among us by SS men and some gendarmes; no one knew what they were looking for. After everyone was accounted for, we were herded into the boxcars. There was much pushing, shoving, and shouting, which amused the guards. Sticks and rubber hoses were used as prods to hasten the loading process. The dogs barked loudly, adding to the confusion and frightening everyone.

We were no sooner in the boxcar than we were ordered back out. The SS men moved among us, obviously searching for someone or something. Three men were pulled out and marched toward the front of the train. Shouting "Here is the fourth; I got him," one of the SS men grabbed me and I joined the first three men as well as others who had escaped from the transport the previous October. When all the former escapees were accounted for, their heads were shaved. On orders from Frank, who was accompanying the train, only one-half of my head was shaved. "You, Posener boy I wouldn't want you to get any ideas. With half a haircut you can't slip away too far. Also, we thought it would be nice for you to have a little company, so guards will be posted outside your car."

With that, I was hit in the back with a rifle butt and pushed into the boxcar with the other escapees.

* * * * *

All the cars were jammed with people. The door was closed, cutting off all air flow into the car, and we were locked in. Air holes in the walls of the boxcar had been boarded up. The only light came from the numerous cigarettes being smoked. Two buckets in a corner of the car were for sanitary purposes. Working my way to the middle of the car, I sat on the floor, not having any luggage to sit on. My backside was very cold. With whistles and hissing, the train moved out.

"Lutz, Lutz, where are you?" I heard. In a moment, Phillip, an old acquaintance, and another man were beside me.

"How about jumping the train again if we can get out through the air openings? Maybe we could hammer the boards off." Phillip handed me a board and told me to climb on his shoulders and try to push the nailed boards out. After several swats, the boards slowly gave way. I could just about fit through the opening, but the train was going too fast to jump safely. When it slowed down, I put my hands through the opening and tried to lift myself out. Suddenly, bullets whizzed by and I quickly pulled my head back in.

They were shooting at me! I decided not to try to leave but wished Phillip and his friend well if they wanted to go.

When the train came to a halt, boots crunched on the gravel outside our car. "Looks like one bird wanted to fly but didn't have any wings," said a voice, laughing. The boards were hammered back in place and we resigned ourselves to sitting in the dark as the train rolled on.

For several days the door remained closed. The stench of sweat, rust, rotten wood, and the contents of the two overflowing buckets was overpowering.

The train stopped briefly but continued again until finally we reached our destination. We heard dogs bark and loud German voices: "Let's go! Out, out! The luggage stays in the car. You will get that later. Down, down with all of you." There was a big scramble, which the guards seemed to enjoy. It gave them an excuse to hit those who weren't moving fast enough or simply crossed the guards' paths.

Even in the dark I could see some people holding their heads where they had been hit. We were formed into columns on a platform and marched past three SS officers. As we passed them, the one in the middle, who seemed to be the chief doctor, signaled women, children, and older men to the left and younger, stronger men to the right. I walked on tiptoe behind a large man, expanding my chest to look bigger, and I was sent to the right with the more able men.

A group of very thin men in suits and caps with blue and white stripes were trying to collect the suitcases. Trucks arrived and the younger men and some women were ordered aboard. When people tried to retrieve their luggage, the guards tore it from their hands and sometimes beat them. Everything was chaos. Men tried to hold on to children and women screamed and cried hysterically. Finally, the younger men were loaded and the trucks drove out of the station and into the deserted countryside; the women were sent in another direction. The area was very flat with a snow-capped mountain range rising in the distance. The weather was quite nippy.

A truck passed us going in the opposite direction. Standing in the truck were women in the same blue-and-white-striped clothing we had seen at the train station. They all had very short hair or none at all.

Their faces were hollow and gray, and their eyes stared, but they didn't seem to see us. We approached what looked like a camp. White smoke rose in the sky and there was a peculiar smell in the air. I couldn't identify the smell, but it was somehow familiar. Our trucks stopped at the gate and we took a look at what was going on.

Two SS men with rifles and two prisoners stood on each side of the gate. Long columns of inmates marched past the SS men, removing their hats as they passed. Some of the men were singing an old marching song. The guards counted the men, keeping a tally. Judging by the numbers of men who passed through the gates, this was a huge camp. When the marchers had all exited, the trucks entered and we were all ordered to jump out. Almost immediately I saw Jossel and David.

A prisoner walked past and whispered that we should eat now because there wouldn't be a chance later. Everyone ate whatever food they had and lit a smoke. Two of the prisoners who had stood beside the SS men at the entrance gates came up to our group. They both wore suits with vertical white and blue stripes. A green triangle and number were mounted on a white patch on the left breast pocket of the jacket and near the right pants pocket of each man's suit. One of them had the number one on his jacket.

The larger of the two spoke in accent-free German: "Silence, silence. It sounds like a Jewish school. Everybody silent and listen. All of you are now in Auschwitz Concentration Camp III, or Monowitz-Buna. The reason we wear vertical stripes is because we are not prisoners but inmates in protective custody. No one is addressed as 'sir.' It is 'you'—no formality—from the highest to the lowest rank. Those who understand German, translate this for those who do not understand."

He explained we would be assigned to a barracks and a working unit called a *Kommando*. We would go through a delousing process, have showers and haircuts, and then be issued inmate uniforms. We could keep our belts and shoes. We must keep clean and not drink the water to avoid cholera and dysentery. The barracks elder would explain everything in more detail.

"One more thing," he said. "A number will be tattooed on your left forearm for identification, so you won't be tempted to leave. You must

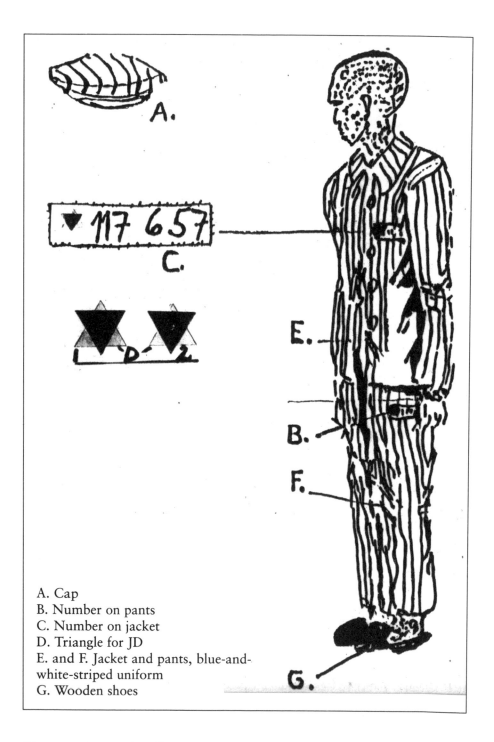

A. Cap
B. Number on pants
C. Number on jacket
D. Triangle for JD
E. and F. Jacket and pants, blue-and-white-striped uniform
G. Wooden shoes

The camp inmates' uniform

not go near the barbed wire surrounding the camp; it is electrically charged; if you get closer than three meters (about nine feet) you will be sucked into the wire and burned to charcoal. Outside this barbed wire, guards patrol with dogs. And beyond that is another charged barbed wire. Every fifty meters, there is a guard tower manned by two SS men with a machine gun. If you think you can escape, remember that this whole area consists of camps and SS men are everywhere.

"When you are ordered into formation, make rows of five and stand at strict attention when any member of the SS comes by. I am Bruno, the *Lageraelteste* (camp chief). The man next to me is Otto, the *Lagerkapo* (chief of the workforce).

"Let me welcome you to Auschwitz—hell on earth."

About forty of us were marched in rows of five into a small barracks. In a completely empty room with white walls, we were told to remove all our clothing and put it in a neat pile. Our clothes as well as everything in our pockets and all rings and watches were to be discarded. When I undressed, I could see how bad my sores were. The hair on our heads and body was clipped to the skin and our bodies swabbed with some kind of horrible smelling disinfectant. It burned my skin terribly.

Each pair of men was given one towel to share. We entered a large shower room with many pipes hanging from the ceiling. Spurting from the pipes was water so hot it burned. I tried to wash myself as best as I could with no soap, and as I started to catch some water in my hands it stopped. Some disinfectant had mixed with the water and stung my eyes before I could towel them dry. We were rushed from the shower room and stood naked outside in the cold air, shivering. My legs were burning from the disinfectant left on my sores. SS men stood at a window, grinning at our predicament.

When everyone had showered, we were marched into a nearby building and each issued a uniform of striped cotton cloth. The pants, jacket, and socks I received were way too large for me; I exchanged with David, who had received items much too small. He was quite depressed, but I assured him we would get out of this, just as we did from the camp in Boulogne-sur-Mer.

During the shower and uniform processing, I noticed two brothers I knew, nicknamed Bulli Schott Number One and Bulli Schott Number Two, who had convinced Papa to let me join the Maccabee-Hacoah boxing team. They had taken me under their wings then, and it surely couldn't hurt that they were near me now.

Under the direction of the camp elder and three of his men, four inmates set up tables and equipment. We were ordered to remove our jackets, and an SS man instructed the man at a tattoo machine: "Numbers go on the left forearm on top." One by one, we received a tattooed number; the process produced a funny sensation, rather than pain. My arm was imprinted with the number 117657. A voice behind me said, "That is your ID from now on. Names are used only by very good friends."

David looked at me in disbelief. "Lutz, we are slaves—marked and branded slaves!"

Outside, we were marched to a barracks near the far end of the camp. The sign identified it as Block 26. Two inmates emerged from the building and the taller one, in his midthirties and quite heavy, spoke in heavily accented German. "Hello, everybody. I am Moishe, your *Blockaelteste*. The man next to me, Siegfried, is your *Stubenaelteste* [room elder]. He will explain the rules to you. Today you will be assigned to bunks, assemble for a head count, and have a meal. You will stay inside the camp tomorrow and Siegfried will tell you what else you need to know."

Siegfried was a bit taller than me, thin and about fifty years of age. Two men at a time were led inside the barracks and assigned bunks and given soup bowls and spoons. David and I were to share a bunk near the middle of the barracks. We were dismissed and sat in the sand outside without speaking a word. I was waiting for a chance to talk to the Schott brothers.

Chapter 27

One of the Schott brothers motioned me to follow him to a small anteroom. He had been in the camp a year, since the spring of 1942. He began to give me advice that might help me survive in the camp.

He told me that I had arrived at the main camp of Auschwitz. Another camp—Birkenau, or Auschwitz II—was two kilometers away. This camp was Monowitz-Buna, or Auschwitz III. Adjoining camps, called *Nebenlager* (near camps), included salt mines, coal mines, and cement factories. There were 13,000–14,000 inmates in this camp, which was built by I. G. Farben Industry.

Auschwitz operated like the camps in Germany, Bulli Schott told me. The supreme head of the camp was the commandant. He had an adjutant, and all operations were under him: mail censoring, the administrative department, the political department, and the garrison that guarded the camp. The SS doctors and medical staff were a part of the SS garrison. An SS officer with the rank of captain had direct responsibility for the camp. Under him were SS privates designated as *Blockfuehrers* (block leaders). At first only one was assigned to each barracks, but now there were three or even four because the camp had grown so large.

The *Arbeitsdienstfuehrer* (work service leader), a captain, was charged with organization of the labor force and *Kommandos*. SS privates oversaw the work of the individual *Kommandos*.

The garrison commander oversaw the guarding of the inmates, watchtowers, and perimeters. Guards with well-trained dogs accompanied all *Kommando* work details so no prisoners could escape. Some guards, he told me, were more humane than some of the camp staff.

As in all camps, inmates were involved in administering camp affairs. The highest ranking was the camp elder. His authority was divided into two branches—the work force and the living quarters.

The work force was headed by the *Lagerkapo* who assigned a *Kapo* under him for each *Kommando* group; they all wore yellow armbands. Two or three men in each *Kommando* were designated foremen.

In the living quarters branch were the *Blockaelteste,* who wore red armbands. For each block there was also a room elder, who assigned inmates to clean the barracks each morning.

Inmates were divided by duties necessary to maintain the camp. Some worked in the records and registry room, the tailoring room, and the shoemaking room. The camp also had a kitchen *Kommando* and a latrine *Kommando*.

The hierarchy was mostly German Aryans—Germans from the Reich who came from overcrowded prisons and were either professional criminals or prisoners with life terms. They had absolute rule over the camp inmates and were arrogant and merciless. They were especially vicious to intellectual and political inmates.

"Avoid them," said Bulli Schott. "We have a few Reds in the hierarchy—Communists from Germany or Austria, who are increasing in numbers. They stick together and help each other. Reds are arriving from all over Europe every day. Make friends with them but don't trust anyone.

"There are some Berliners here you might know. Remember Fred Zeink? Your father knew him quite well. He arrived four months ago.

"A few more things to know. A *Kalfactor* is a little guy who caters to the *Kapo* or the block elder and gets a little more food. But be cautious; many times the upper boys are homosexuals who only want to use the younger boys. You might make some friends at the *Haeftlings Krankenbau* (inmates' sick bay)."

Next he explained the uniform patches. Green triangles pointing upward designated lifers or security risks; green triangles pointing downward were worn by professional criminals. A red triangle meant a political inmate. Purple triangles were worn by Jehovah's Witnesses. Black ones were for Gypsies, blue ones for immigrants, and pink ones for homosexuals. If a red triangle had a black *P* in it, the inmate was a Pole; with an *F*, a Frenchman. A red triangle with a dot below denoted a penal *Kommando*. If there was a large hyphen at the top, the wearer had

Insignia worn by Jews through the first half of 1944	 *(red and yellow)*
Insignia worn by Jews from the second half of 1944	 *(red and yellow)*

Political inmate	Jehovah's Witness	Immigrant	Gypsy	Common criminal	Homosexual
▼	▼	▼	▼	▼	▼
(red)	*(purple)*	*(blue)*	*(black)*	*(green)*	*(pink)*

Polish	French	Member of penal *Kommando*	Recommitted to camp	Inmate confined to camp, possible escapee *(im Lager)*	Criminal with life sentence, security risk
▼P	▼F	▼•	▼	iL	▲
(red)	*(red)*	*(red)*	*(red)*	*(red)*	*(green)*

Insignias worn by camp inmates

been recommitted to the camp. A red dot with the letters *IL* meant the wearer was confined inside the camp as a possible escapee.

And, of course, the Mogen David insignia on the patch denoted a Jew. A Jewish criminal wore a yellow triangle and a green triangle.

"You are a Jew, a number now," he said, "only worth the work you can produce. Dying is normal; nobody bats an eye. There is a weeding-out process. Those who can't work are sent to the gas chambers at Birkenau and then into the ovens. So, stand straight, walk with élan, always look good—keep clean and don't lose too much weight. During any selection process, tighten your rear—the Germans feel that those with padded backsides can work and take punishment.

"Don't drink water unless it has been boiled. It is okay to hold your bowl under the steam pipe at the side of the barracks to collect drinking water. And don't eat bad food—you'll get dysentery and die within hours. And don't steal from other inmates. That's punishable by immediate death."

My head was swimming with information as I returned to the barracks.

When it was time for the count, we assembled in the large square in rows of fives. Music started as five SS men approached. On command, we took our caps off and stood at attention. One of the SS men inspected the arm tattoos of each one in line. His look sent shivers through my body; I planned to avoid him as much as possible. The first *Kommandos* came into the square and regrouped according to their block assignments. Their faces were immobile and despairing with eyes set deep into their sockets. The men dragged themselves along; some carried others who couldn't walk. Moishe's head count was checked twice by an SS man who recounted everyone and then took his final count to the three SS men on the reviewing platform. When the count was considered accurate, we were dismissed.

Everyone in the barracks seemed to be quite young. I was eyed by one inmate who spoke fluent German in a Berlin dialect. "Where do you all come from?" he asked.

When I responded that we were all from Belgium he said we jabbered like Berliners and we admitted we were. He told us this was a youth block and we'd get along fine.

* * * * *

The first night, David, Jossel, and I sat on the ground when it was time to eat. It was my turn to eat first from the soup bowl David and I shared. The meal consisted of a sort of oatmeal soup, but at least it was food. Siegfried let me have a second bowlful. Before long I drew a lot of attention while I ate several bowls of soup other inmates gave me. I explained that I was in a camp in France and then, although free, very hungry on the streets for five months, and now I was hungry enough for two people.

David and I shared one bunk; we were very cramped but so tired we fell asleep almost instantly. In the morning, we straightened the bunk then stood in line to use the washroom. We brushed our teeth as best we could with our fingers, using the awful-tasting water. The latrine was similar to that in the camp at Boulogne-sur-Mer, except this one was closed in and roofed.

Breakfast was a quarter of a loaf of bread (250 grams), a small square of oleomargarine, a tablespoon of jam once a week, and half a liter of what passed for coffee. I turned to Jossel and commented, "You know, this would be a shocker if we hadn't already gone through this in the camp at Boulogne-sur-Mer."

After the count was completed we were taken to the records to be officially registered. In groups of five the inmates were led inside the room, where two inmates with red triangle patches and very low numbers sat at a huge desk. Nothing could be seen behind the big curtain at one end of the room. When I sat down in front of the desk, one inmate asked me a lot of questions while an SS man listened. The last question was, "What is your father's name and when did he come here?"

"My father's name is Kurt Posener, and I don't know if he ever came here; the last I heard he was in Gurs."

"Okay, show me your number."

I raised my arm. He nodded his head and I was dismissed. Outside, David and I wondered why they asked about my father. Siegfried was waiting back at the block to explain the do's and don'ts.

"Listen carefully. I am not going over this again. Five o'clock is the time to get up and make your bunks. Watch me; this is very important. Fluff the straw in the sack and smooth it out so it is even with the wooden sides of the bunk. Take the wedge bolster, fluff it, and straighten it so it looks like a new stairway. Then leave the block so the room cleaner can clean. Only when it is very, very cold can you come back inside to eat, but don't lean on the bunk or dirty the floor. Otherwise, don't enter the block until you return at night.

"There is oil outside to clean your shoes. Be sure to dust your clothes off—take care of them, you won't get any more. When your leather shoes are worn out, you will be issued wooden shoes. Wear your cap at all times. Take it off only when an SS man goes by or at the count. Once a week you will get a shave and haircut and delousing. It is important to keep clean; otherwise, you will die.

"You can go to the sick bay or infirmary in the evening. If you are sick in the morning, report your illness to me and I will make a note of it. Then, after the count, you can go to the infirmary.

"We have a seven-day work week. *Kommandos* that do important work for the war effort have to work each Sunday; the others work every other Sunday. If you are found not working or trying to con your way out of work, you will be reported and receive an unpleasant punishment. Today is yours to do as you please. Tonight after the soup, I will tell you which *Kommando* you will be assigned to tomorrow."

I went to the sick bay to see if I could get something for my sores. In the last block area I saw the sign for the infirmary: "Haeftlings Krankenbau." There, a man in a white lab coat looked at my arms and legs, asked me my name and number, and left the room. He came back with Dr. Wolfsohn, who looked at my number and asked for my father's name. When I told him, he said, "There is a Kurt Posener who has been here for quite a while. His number is in the sixty thousands and he's in Block 4. Could he be your father?"

My heart beat faster. "It's possible. I haven't heard from him since 1940 and don't know what happened to him. I'll try to find him tonight. Thank you very much for the information."

"That's all right. We don't have any sulphur, but here's some cream. If it doesn't help, come back."

When I left, I couldn't hold back the tears any longer. Papa, here. I couldn't believe it. I had heard the camps in the south of France had been dissolved. I decided not to say anything to anyone about this yet.

David and I wandered all around the camp. We even peeked into the kitchen, where many inmates were working. Some were standing on ladders to stir the contents of huge kettles with big wooden sticks. Others were cutting vegetables, and some were cleaning the floor. Everything was spotless.

On the other side of the camp, one block was designated as the tailor shop and shoemaker shop, and the inmates there were very busy. Farther on was the block for clothing, and, of course, the infirmary.

There was far more to see but we returned to our block and sat outside the barracks. We decided to do our best to survive until the war ended, hopefully won by the Allies. Eugen, who had been in the camp for a while, said we would soon learn how to tell from an inmate's number where he was from, when he arrived, and his status. *Kommando* assignments, he told us, depended on what an inmate could do and who he knew.

In the evening, I went to Block 4 and asked for Kurt Posener. I was directed inside to the last tier, where a man lay on an upper bunk. My heart was pounding and I could hardly speak. "Kurt Posener?" He climbed down from the bunk.

"Yes, that's me. Why?"

My heart sank. He wasn't Papa. "I'm Lutz Posener. For a moment, I thought you were my father," I said.

"We both came to Auschwitz in September 1942 and met as we were being registered. I don't know what happened to him because I left the next day and he wasn't with my group. Sorry I can't help you more."

I thanked him and left, very dejected. Eugen had indicated that only a few were still alive who had come to Block 4 that long ago. I didn't think Papa made it, but I was still going to try to find out more if I could.

David, Jossel, and I were assigned to the cable *Kommando* and would start work the next day.

During the night, inmates were not allowed to use the latrine. Instead, a bucket was provided in the block. When it was full, the next person to use it had to take it outside, accompanied by a guard. That night, David had to do this task and later complained about how heavy the bucket was.

* * * * *

In the morning, after the usual routine, we followed Eugen to the work area. Both *Kapos* in charge wore green triangle patches with points facing upward. One *Kapo* shouted, "All the new ones, come forward." He checked our arm numbers, staring at us with cold, sinister eyes and a sadistic look. Then the command came to move out. When we neared the gate, a voice yelled, *"Muetzen ab!"* (Caps off!) Inside the gate were influential inmates, and outside was the SS. If one of them thought a man's head was dirty, he got hit with a rubber hose with a steel rod inside. If he got hit too hard, he didn't get up anymore.

Outside, the voice again shouted *"Muetzen auf!"* (Caps up!) Surrounded by eight German army soldiers, we marched for a half hour and entered a huge complex of buildings. Eugen said in a low voice that this was the I. G. Farben Industry—many kinds of work took place there, with foreign-forced labor workers. Most were afraid to even look at us. If we were caught talking, it meant punishment. He said the French workers might be willing to talk, but not the Poles and Russians.

Eugen and I were shown to a bin by a site foreman. Many other workers were standing around. "Okay, you two, this is your section. Loosen the soil, smooth it out and plane it flat." A siren sounded, which meant we started work—mostly with our eyes!

I almost laughed at that familiar refrain. "Not too fast, right?"

"You bet. We are not going anywhere. Watch out for soldiers and *Kapos*. *Kapos* will get you if you cross them or they don't like your face."

Five hours passed. Two guards approached, escorting inmates who were carrying familiar-looking soup kettles. The siren tooted and we took our bowls to get soup. After we finished the same awful soup those kettles always contained, Eugen offered me a cigarette. I refused because he could trade it for some food or other necessity. I rolled a thin cigarette with a bit of paper and some tobacco I had scrounged the night before. The siren tooted again and Eugen urged me to get up and start work to avoid a beating. Everybody—*Kapos,* the foreman, the *Meister* (German work boss), and other guards—was shouting at us.

When the workday was finally over (5:30 P.M.), we cleaned our tools and stored them. When we were in formation, the count was taken six times before we could march back to the camp. Eugen said each *Kommando* assignment was for three weeks and the next assignment might be worse or better.

The march back was long and tiring. As we went through the gate, we took our caps off and then put them back on our heads. We finally arrived at our block area and were assembled with the smaller men in front. Moishe shouted at us to be quiet while he was counting. His count agreed with an SS man's count and Moishe announced, "Block 26, with 224 inmates at the count. Everybody is here, Mister Block Leader." We were dismissed, and everyone rushed into the block.

We ended the day with the same routine. The lineup for soup was as long and slow as at noonday. We cleaned ourselves up and visited the latrine—another long wait—and then fell on our bunks. Curfew was 8:30 P.M., and everybody had to be in his bunk. Lights went out and soon one could hear snoring, moaning, groaning, and at times, screaming following a nightmare.

Chapter 28

We went through the usual morning procedures, even though it was Sunday. Eugen walked me to another block to meet Eduard, a slim man from Berlin. About fifty or fifty-five years old, Eduard wore a patch with a red triangle. He pulled out a little wooden box with white cotton in it. Holding some cotton next to a stone, he struck a flint stick against a stone, creating small sparks that ignited the cotton enough to light his cigarette. I followed his example and leaned back to smoke, too.

"Eugen told me about your father," he said. "He must have been a sixty-thousander; there were a lot who were red ones, even Jews. I came here in the spring of 1942 from Dachau after being in two other camps. There aren't too many like me left."

He explained camp life to me, saying that Auschwitz was basically an extermination camp. Inmates were worked to exhaustion, and then it was the gas chamber and the oven. I should preserve my strength as much as I could. Many inmates went through "quarantine," which was designed to break a person physically and mentally—I was lucky to have avoided that. I should try to get into a *Kommando* with professionals as a helper or apprentice. Eduard mentioned that sleeping and living quarters were all the same except for the inmates with green triangles; a lot of them slept in a separate block.

He then told me the best way to survive there. I should get extra soup if I could. I should never eat anything dirty, no matter how hungry I was. I should always wash in the morning and evening. I could wash my clothing on Sunday, and I should sit beside it as it dried. It was an advantage to look clean, and we were issued a change of clothing only once a month, if at all. I should try to get leather shoes; the wooden ones didn't fit and were usually half broken. They created burns and sores. I should never walk barefoot, and I should keep my head clean to avoid getting hit.

Since I was registered when I arrived at camp, that meant I didn't have a police dossier or other papers with me. It also meant I was condemned to die. Eduard said there were three ways of dying. The first way was by not adapting to life and work at the camp. The second way was by overwork and *dreckfressen*—eating dirt, becoming sick, and then dying. The third way was to just run out of luck—to be in the wrong place at the wrong time, to constantly get in trouble, or to associate with the wrong people.

He warned me to avoid inmates with green triangle patches; they were B-Vauers and couldn't be trusted. The B-Vauers were professional criminals serving a sentence. They were very dangerous because they felt they were Reich Germans and thus superior; they stuck together with the SS. Even worse were the S-Vauers; they were lifers who didn't care. They killed just for pleasure and a pat on the shoulder from the SS.

The Polish non-Jews who were arrested in 1939–40 as POWs kept to themselves and hated everything around them. Eduard said the best inmates wore red triangles; they were German political prisoners who were arrested in the early 1930s. Most of the intellectuals in that group had been killed over the years, and the rest had became hardened through years of imprisonment. Other groups to avoid were the ones with black patches, Gypsies; pink patches, homosexuals; and purple patches, Jehovah's Witnesses.

He then told me about the Jews. Most of them couldn't help me. A few had earned positions of some control, but we all had to work harder to try to gain the upper hand. If we could oust the green patches from controlling positions, our lot would be a bit more tolerable. The green patches and the SS treated merchants, lawyers, teachers, and intellectuals the worst, doing whatever they pleased with them.

Inmates wearing civilian clothing with hair on their heads were inmates to be reformed. They were released after eight weeks of "re-education." They all talked too much and too loud.

Eduard then spoke of the SS and the power they had over all of us. The camp commander for Monowitz and its twenty-five to twenty-six annex camps was Captain Schwarz, a big brute who was to be feared at all times. Under him was the camp chief, a Bavarian named Schoettel with the rank of lieutenant. Then came Sergeant Goering, the chief of reports, and Sergeant Schoelte, the chief of the work force. Goering was a brute, so I should try to stay out of his sight. And then came those Eduard said he hoped would burn in hell very slowly—the corporals, the block chiefs, who were sadistic and brutal. Eduard said they were thieves who stole anything they could lay their hands on. The guards who were of different nationalities were supervised by German army men in SS uniforms.

He said Jews had some influence in the infirmary, where the red patches and SS doctors were. Not even the camp commander interfered. There were three SS doctors and one aide. The head doctor was Dr. Fischer, and under him was Dr. Entress; they were both captains. Dr. Koenig was only a second lieutenant. All of them were young, arrogant, and superficial. There was one staff sergeant, Neubert Wendt, who was a medic. He was also considered the camp doctor and was the only infirmary worker with a little human spirit.

Eugen and I thanked him and left. Back in our block, David was already in the bunk. I related to him everything I'd been told. He fell asleep, but I lay awake wondering what happened to Papa. Sadly, I conceded that he was probably dead; he just didn't have the stamina or the desire to live in such conditions. He must have been heartbroken, never knowing what happened to me. Blinking back tears, I resolved to live through this ordeal just to spite Hitler and his evil regime.

* * * * *

A week went by. The only noticeable difference was the changing of faces. There were always a lot of inmates who could hardly make it back to the camp at night. They would report to the infirmary in the morning and we would leave without them. At night, they were gone, but nobody seemed concerned about them. The depressing apathy was everywhere—the dull faces, the disinterest in everything.

My scabs had completely disappeared, but I had gotten in the middle of my left calf quite a deep gash and it became infected. A helper held me down on the examining table while Dr. Wolfsohn poured liquid in the wound. It burned horribly and I screamed. He poured the liquid on once more and the infection was burned out. "Be thankful it was no deeper," he said. "You might have lost your leg. Keep these paper bandages in place for a day, until the danger period is past. If the wound doesn't close, come back and see me."

David took care of our housekeeping chores so I could climb in the bunk and sleep.

*****

In the morning, David pronounced me back to my "old rotten self," and the wound was only a little bit tender as we marched off to work. Along the way, Eugen handed me a sugar beet, it was sickeningly sweet, but it was food!

When we arrived at work, the *Meister* pointed at Eugen and me. "You two little guys, come with me. I have special work for you." We were told to unload eight bricks at a time from a truck and neatly stack them near a sand pile. We didn't move fast enough, so one of the SS guards yelled, "Well, let's go! What are you waiting for? All of this has to be finished in two hours."

I picked up six bricks, carried them to the sand pile, and stacked them neatly. When I picked up six more, the *Meister* loaded two more on top.

"I said eight bricks!"

I lugged the load to the sand pile. On the way back, I suddenly felt a stick hit my back. "Let's go, man, you Jew dirtbag. Get a move on or it will be the end for you."

I moved faster, almost at a trot. I realized I shouldn't have done that because then the *Meister* expected me to keep up that pace. I continued, panting and cussing to myself.

"Better," he said. "Keep moving!"

Thank God he moved away after a while.

By the time we had finished and marched back to camp, we were completely exhausted. Later, Bulli looked for me. "Well, little one, looks like you had some day! Tomorrow night after the soup, come to the bathhouse. I'll take you and your buddies to the black market gathering. I'll introduce you to some guys who can help you in the future." As soon as he left, we lay down in the bunk and fell asleep immediately.

* * * * *

At work the next day, I noticed that David had lost some weight. I probably had, too, although I hadn't noticed it. We'd been in the camp only a few weeks. I wondered what we would look like later on, but there was really no time to think about it—we had to concentrate on work and remain constantly on guard.

In the evening, we walked with Bulli to the platform where the SS usually stood to review the inmates. The area was crowded with inmates all haggling with each other about everything. Bulli led us to an older man with an eighty thousand number and a Mogen David patch. "Kurt, these are friends of mine," he said. "Tell them the prices and deals here."

"Okay, fellows. One medium slice of bread will get you three cigarettes. Half of your morning ration will get you seven cigarettes. Two cigarettes for margarine and one for a spoonful of jam. For three potatoes, five smokes. For leather or good clothing, we'll talk. If you have any jewels or money, we'll barter. If you have alcohol, then we'll really talk and you are in green pastures. Come and see me anytime."

Bulli walked around with us, pointing out what we should notice. He introduced me to Guenther, the shoemaker foreman, also a Berliner. He told Guenther I had very small feet and asked him to help me when I needed new shoes.

When we walked away, Bulli said I was lucky to have small feet. I'd always get leather shoes instead of the awful wooden ones. Next, we met Leo, the all-around *Stubenaelteste* from Block 8. Bulli said Leo would always help us if he could.

Back at Bulli's place, he told us to remember the others we'd met that night. We might need them someday.

When the others had left, Bulli took me inside and sat on the edge of his bunk. He said he wanted me to meet some men at the infirmary who could help me; they might also ask me to do something in return. I would be transferred to Block 5 soon. The block chief was Gust'l, a B-Vauer who had five more years to serve. He was arrested for some sort of sex offense and could be extremely violent, but he treated youngsters well. Some suspected he was a homosexual, but he had never touched a boy yet. In fact, he tried to help them, especially if they were bright and quick. His room chief was from Austria and was also a B-Vauer. As long as I did as he said, he'd leave me alone.

I thanked Bulli and said I would never forget his kindness. He said that was good because he might need me one day.

Chapter 29

Quite a few new men had arrived—I felt like a veteran. It was about the middle of May and already pretty warm during the day. We were usually all too tired to talk much even about the war, although the Germans continued to brag about their successes. I'd stopped wondering what had happened to my friends from the camp at Boulogne-sur-Mer and those I left behind in Brussels.

On Saturday, we were told not to leave the block on Sunday until we were sheared and deloused. Right after the count, I rushed to get in line and save a place for David and Eugen. The clippers were dull, but after a lot of cutting and pulling, I was finished. At the front of the block, a man with a bucket was waiting, brush in hand. I removed my clothes and he dipped the brush in the disinfectant and smeared it all over my body. It burned terribly. The man smiled.

The smell was horrible! I put my clothes on and went outside to get some air. Jossel came out while I was waiting for David and Eugen, and I mentioned that I had not seen him for a while. He said he'd been busy just staying out of trouble and asked if I'd noticed that we were all keeping to ourselves and forgetting to be human.

The thought of losing our humanity made me angry. "That's what these creeps want. We're just numbers, not humans. A guard said to Eugen and me, 'Well, all of you will be in heaven soon anyway.'"

He asked if I'd heard about a *Block Sperre* (block detention) that was rumored to be scheduled for the following day. I hadn't heard anything about it.

Just then, Eugen came out and told us that it meant we couldn't leave the barracks; the SS would check everybody, and those who couldn't work anymore would be sent to the crematorium.

The day passed, and after the evening meal, as expected, Siegfried spoke to us. "Quiet, quiet. There will be a selection. Nobody may leave the barracks as of now. You will be counted in front of the barracks tomorrow morning. Do not go outside without our consent. There are guards stationed outside and you will be shot without warning. Now, all of you into the bunks."

After Siegfried left, I turned to David. "Do you suppose Eugen was right? Is this the end of the line? I wasn't too fat when I arrived here, and I've lost even more weight."

"Lutz, Lutz, wait until tomorrow and then you'll see. I bet we'll be all right. Where is your optimism?"

"I don't know, but I don't feel very good."

When the lights went out, I closed my eyes and took a deep breath. "Oh, dear God, let me live a little while yet; please stand by me."

*   *   *   *   *

In the morning, everyone woke up early and made their bunks, waiting for orders. The door opened and four inmates carried in the morning food and coffee. As soon as we finished eating, we were let outside for the count. Everyone was nervous. We stood and waited. Two men from the records room arrived, carrying papers. Next, the camp elder and the camp chief came with several B-Vauer *Kapos* and a number of men with red triangles who we concluded were block elders.

Bulli came near me, took my hat off—pretending he was inspecting my head—and whispered, "This is a selection. Five hundred youths from fourteen to nineteen from a number of barracks. Stand behind a strong inmate; look sharp—head high, chest out, eyes alert. When you are being looked at from the back, tighten your rear end and walk like a fighter."

Two SS doctors, the chief of reports, the chief of the work force, and two block chiefs entered. The chief doctor stood in front of us.

"Everyone under fourteen and above nineteen step forward." A third of the block, including David, stepped forward.

The numbers of those who stepped forward were checked by one recorder; the rest were checked by the second one. The older men were led to another spot to wait. Dr. Fischer gave an order to Moishe, who nodded his head at Siegfried.

Siegfried announced, "All of you, take your clothing off and put it in front of you, shoes included." I stood with Jossel on one side and a small Greek boy and Eugen on the other. Naked, we shivered in the cold. The first inmate was ordered to approach Fischer, who looked him over, front and back, and pointed to the right with his thumb. The next inmate, a large Polish man, was motioned to the left. I understood! The poor little guy who was directed to the right was condemned! I was so scared I didn't notice the cold air. After one more silent prayer it was Jossel's turn. He went to the left.

Siegfried came near me and hissed, "You've got good color. Remember, be a Prussian! Go." I marched toward Fischer and stood at attention, head high and looking straight at him. He regarded me with a quizzical eye. "Where do you come from?"

"From Berlin, Captain, sir."

"Turn around." He looked me over. "Well, yes, Berlin. Mmm, left. You will die in two weeks anyway."

On wobbly knees I went to the left and stood beside Jossel and began to shake. After a few deep breaths I calmed down.

The group sent to the right was growing and I realized how close I came to my end. One flick of the thumb meant life or death. I looked at Fischer and tried to guess what was in his mind. How could one human send another to his death just because he was too thin?

Pretty soon, it was all over. The group on the right—about three hundred—was marched off. We were ordered into rows of five and counted twice. We were dismissed but told not to wander away because we were being transferred to another barracks.

Jossel shook my hand. David and Eugen just stood quietly.

Inside, Siegfried read off numbers and names. David and Jossel were assigned to another barracks. Eugen and I reported to a barracks where the block elder was waiting for us flanked by his room elder and two other men. One by one, he looked us over. When it was my turn, I told him, "117657, Lutz Posener from Berlin via Brussels."

He nodded, "A Berliner—such a thing." He spoke with a Austrian accent. He continued, "I'm Gust'l and your room elder is Franz'l. Do as you are told and behave and we'll get along fine. No stealing, uncleanliness, or laziness. The two Berliners will share a top bunk at the end of the block and will be in *Kommando* 80. Your *Kapo* is also a Berliner named Heinz."

When we found our bunk, a man was sitting on the lower one. He introduced himself as Rolf from Cologne, the *Kapo* from *Kommando* 23. Most of his workers were Polish and good workers, but he would see if he could use us, too. Outside, Eugen and I agreed to be careful and not completely trust Rolf or anyone else.

Wandering around the camp I met David. He and Jossel were assigned to Block 8 and *Kommando* 41, a construction crew. I told David that I was worried Eugen didn't have the stamina or will power to hold out. David and I agreed to meet at night to keep in touch. It would take some time to find somebody to whom I could feel as close as I did to David.

After the count that night, I encountered Gust'l. "Well, my little man, did you get settled?" When I told him Eugen and I were doing all right, he continued, "He seems to be an awfully nice little fellow." Gust'l led me to my *Kapo* and said to him, "Hey, Heinz, here is one of the little guys from Berlin assigned to your *Kommando*. The other one is cute. I think I'll take him under my wing!" He left us.

Heinz quizzed me: where was I from, what part of Berlin, what was my name, what was my number? Others standing nearby gave me a sharp look but didn't say anything. Then I was dismissed.

Back at our bunk, I told Eugen about David's assignment and also that I suspected Gust'l was gay. He thanked me and said he would watch out.

* * * * *

The next morning we arrived at the work site, an electrical outfit with welding equipment. The building's steel structure was half completed. I was assigned to three big guys—Jaacov, Abraham (Abel), and Ladwick (Label), who spoke only Yiddish, which was no problem for me. We started work and I helped by handing them what they needed. When they climbed up to work on the structure, I sent up tools and other materials by tying them to a rope dangling nearby, which could then be hauled up. When I didn't have anything to send up, I sorted screws and other little items throughout the morning. The *Meister* passed by briefly only once, and no guards were on the site.

At lunch, the three inmates brought out good bread with some butter and shared it with me, explaining that it was "organized" (the camp term for the schemes we used to get extras). Jaacov said they talk to the Poles and Germans as they worked and bartered whatever they could. The afternoon passed rapidly and we started back to the camp. I told Eugen about my day but not about my fortunate gift of the bread and butter.

Back in camp after the count, Jaacov asked me to polish his shoes and those of Abel and Label. I did as he told me and returned the shoes to Jaacov. In return, he handed me a bowl of soup. It was thick, and I gorged myself, wondering how they managed to get good food like this. Before the soup was gone, Eugen came out and I gave him the rest. He needed advice. Gust'l had asked him to be his *Kalfactor* (houseboy) and Eugen wanted to know what he should do.

I reasoned if he said no, then he'd be in a bad spot. If he said yes, he'd get extra soup or other food, which would help him survive. If Gust'l was a homosexual, Eugen would have to talk his way out of doing anything he didn't want to do with Gust'l. I said if it were me, I would take my chances. If Gust'l didn't leave Eugen alone, he could transfer to another block.

* * * * *

The next morning on our way to work, Eugen told me he had accepted Gust'l's offer and would be given a bunk outside Gust'l's alcove. At work, I asked Jaacov if Eugen had made the right decision by becoming Gust'l's *Kalfactor*. He responded that Gust'l was not mean— he just wanted to be served and treated like someone important and wouldn't harm Eugen. In exchange for my good shoe polishing, Jaacov started to teach me welding—how to light the torch, melt the steel, and weld it with another piece of steel; how to cool it off and shave it down. The next day he would let me practice what I'd learned.

After supper, David reported that he and Jossel were suffering. Their *Kapo* was a sadist who didn't care who died in his *Kommando*, and each night they returned to camp with injured or dead inmates. I promised to try to get him and Jossel transferred to our *Kommando*.

Back at the barracks, Eugen showed me his new bunk. I slept very well alone in my bunk.

The next morning, Eugen told me his duties consisted of tidying the *Kapo*'s place, making his bunk, putting everything in its place, and sweeping the floor. In exchange he received an extra ration of bread and more margarine.

At the work site, after four tries I was able to complete a good weld. While cleaning up, I asked Jaacov if he could use David in our *Kommando*. He said he would look him over if I brought him to his barracks that evening.

But David had a really bad day. I found him lying on his bunk with his right eye puffy and bloody and his nose swollen. The *Kapo* thought David wasn't working hard enough and beat him, saying, "Back to work, you miserable Jew. Don't you dare look at a pure German that way or you'll wish you never looked at anything."

"Oh, David, I'm so sorry," I said. "I came over to tell you that one of the Jews in my *Kommando* wants to see you, and if he feels you are okay, he'll talk to the *Kapo* and try to get you reassigned to my *Kommando*. I think you should see him even if you are hurting. At least he'll see why you should change *Kommando s*."

David agreed and we went to see Jaacov, who liked David and said he would try to get him reassigned. I directed a prayer upward.

* * * * *

The next day the work was harder. Almost all day long, we loaded long, heavy pieces of steel on a pushcart, wheeled them to the other end of the building, and stacked them. Near the end of the day, Jaacov told me that Heinz agreed to David's reassignment. David looked worse that day but was ecstatic when I told him the good news. While he waited outside, I found his *Kapo* and gave him David's paperwork. After looking me over closely and then reading the paper, he said, "All right. Tell Heinz it is okay and that he's a good worker for a Jew."

I thanked him and reported back to David, receiving a big bear hug. I felt quite elated at having helped a friend.

Standing at the roll call in the morning, I told Eugen about David joining our *Kommando*. We agreed to try to help others as well. At the work site, David was introduced to the *Kapo* and then we received our assignments. David would be working with Abel and Label while I stayed with Jaacov. My first weld was a good one and Jaacov complimented me.

On the way back to camp in the evening, David smiled and said he had a very good day and he was sure the new assignment would work out just fine.

And I was learning more than welding. I was able to barter a piece of bread for three cigarettes—not just one—at the camp's black market. However, I didn't recognize any familiar faces there. Everything seemed to be changing. There were many new faces, and I'd lost another ten pounds.

*   *   *   *   *

The days went by and summer arrived. On June 24, I thought of Papa. It was his birthday, and I wondered what had happened to him. That day, I was assigned with a taller man to move large oxygen bottles from a truck into a building. After unloading ten of them, I walked back to get another with my head down, thinking about Papa. A motorcycle roared up and halted. The chief of reports signaled me to approach him.

I ran over and stood before him, tore off my hat, and recited my number.

"What do you think this is, a resort? You walk like you're taking a stroll. Well, we will blow life back into your legs. *Kapo, Kapo*, come here."

Heinz came running and the chief continued, "We have here a lad who thinks that this is a resort. I want the report tonight, understood?"

"Yes, sir, Sergeant."

As Heinz and I walked back, he said he wouldn't mention the incident and maybe the chief wouldn't remember. We started back to work but heard the motorcycle again. While the chief followed us on his cycle, we continued unloading bottles as fast as we could. When he finally roared away, I collapsed in exhaustion. Heinz realized that he would have to make a report, which meant I would have to stand in front of the camp and be punished. The usual punishment varied from five to fifty hits on the backside or some other punishment the chief of the work force thought up.

Chapter 30

A week went by and I'd almost forgotten the episode. One night after the count, the whole staff assembled in front of us, even the camp commandant. Two inmates placed a bench in front of the podium. Eugen said it was called the *Bock* and it was used for beatings. The roll call was over but we were still standing. Ten inmates were lined up in front. As each one stepped forward, the chief of the work force read something that I couldn't hear. Two inmates stretched the first man over the *Bock*, and two SS men took turns hitting him. I heard two yells and then nothing. I swallowed hard and my stomach was in knots.

When the last man was stretched over the *Bock*, Eugen whispered, "Man, he's going to get it. This is the third time he's been up there." He explained that the first time, the man—a red-triangle inmate from Hamburg—tried to escape and got fifty lashes and five days solitary in the bunker. The second time he was caught with underground papers and was questioned at Gestapo headquarters; then he received seventy-five lashes and ten days in solitary. He couldn't even walk after that.

Without a sound, the man received fifty hits and was carried off on a stretcher. We were dismissed and scrambled to our barracks.

Inside I asked Jaacov what would happen to the last man. Jaacov said he was in the infirmary and after his wounds were dressed, he'd probably be sent to solitary. He had a lot of friends inside the camp. He wasn't a Jew, he had a red triangle, and he was a Communist, and all the men with similar backgrounds stuck together. Jaacov had heard they'd formed an underground and were trying to remove the B-Vauers and S-Vauers from their positions and replace them with their own people. That would be good for us because maybe we could get a few Jews in good positions and improve our lot a bit.

The gong rang and I went to my bunk for the night.

* * * * *

One evening after roll call, I returned to the barracks to find a man standing next to my bunk. He said his name was Hans. He spoke German, but I didn't recognize his accent.

While I waited in the soup line, Heinz came to tell me that Bulli wanted to see me. As soon as I could, I went to the bathhouse, where Bulli was already waiting.

Bulli said that Dr. Wolfsohn had talked to him about me. The doctor felt that I could carry messages once in a while. Bulli asked me if I remembered Hans, the man in the bunk next to mine—he was the one who had gotten the beating the other evening.

Making sure we were alone and couldn't be overheard, he continued. He said that Hans was working with some important underground people and when Hans talked to me, I could be honest with him. I could also trust Heinz. I was to visit Bulli from time to time and see if the group had some small errands for me to do. He warned me not to tell anyone else what we talked about and to remain alert at all times.

Back in the barracks, Hans was asleep in his bunk, but Heinz was standing nearby. When he asked whether I had seen Bulli, I said that we'd had a good talk.

Heinz was pleased. He then told me I should be Hans's *Kalfactor*, to help him in any way I could. I agreed to do so and then went to bed.

When I awoke, it seemed as though I'd been asleep just a short time. I was right because it was only the night gong I'd heard. It had awakened Hans, too, so we carried on a whispered conversation.

Hans said he knew I had been told to be his *Kalfactor*, and he assured me that he wasn't gay. My duties would be to make his bed the way he liked it, keep his belongings in order, get his morning and evening rations, polish his shoes, and wash his clothing once a week. In exchange I would get an extra liter of soup, another half ration of bread, and three cigarettes a day. Sometimes he would have errands for me to run.

I promised to do the best I could. We shook hands and went back to sleep.

In the morning, I rushed to make my bunk and finish my morning hygiene, then I went back to the barracks to make Hans's bunk. Inspecting my handiwork, he said I would do just fine.

I looked at him as we ate together. Nearly six feet tall, he was very slim and was moving well considering his recent beating. I guessed that not many people knew his role there. At his direction, I cleaned his bowl and put it in a corner of his bunk. He assured me no one would take it. My new duties gave me a little more food, and I felt a bit better.

The news traveled fast; David and Eugen wanted to know how my new position was working out. I said that so far, everything was going well, but I'd let them know for sure after a week.

At work, David and I caught up on camp happenings. He was getting very thin despite my sharing my soup with him. I hardly saw Jossel, who I figured must be busy with his own life and just trying to get along.

* * * * *

It had been a week and a half, and Hans had been great to work for. One morning he said he wasn't going out with the *Kommando*. Later, Gust'l told Eugen and me that Hans and Bulli were picked up during the day, interrogated, and beaten. They hadn't returned. And there was more bad news: I was transferred to Block 12 and Eugen to Block 16. Block 12 had a red triangle Austrian as block chief, and the room chief also was a Berliner. I knew it! I said to myself. Just when things were going well.

When Gust'l handed me my papers in the early evening, I walked over to Block 12. I was met by a small man who looked like Papa— heavy brown-rimmed glasses, a sizable stomach, and an inviting, warm smile. He took me to meet block elder Sepp and then directed me to my bunk, which was the top one in the last tier.

* * * * *

At work the next morning, there was little talking because the *Kapo* of this *Kommando* was a nasty man with a miserable streak who seemed to be everywhere. He was an S-Vauer and walked around barking about our looks and the dirt and saying, "You Jews all look alike; that's why you'll all go into the chimney."

At the work site, the *Kapo* and *Meister* had a serious discussion and then approached us. David and some others were chosen for work the *Meister* wanted done and they were marched off. The *Kapo* showed the rest of us a large pile of rocks to be moved and stacked near a building. The smaller ones weren't too bad, but the larger ones cut our hands. Eugen moaned and groaned. By noon we were so exhausted we could hardly eat the soup. David had told us that our *Kapo* had a very bad reputation. He hated Jews and whenever an inmate was to be beaten, this *Kapo* was sent for. David said we'd have to somehow get out of this *Kommando* or the *Kapo* would kill us. We agreed. It was too bad the *Kapo* knew of my friendship with Heinz, Gust'l, and Hans.

The day passed and we managed to finish stacking the rocks. But when the *Kapo* inspected our work, he said it was neat but stacked in the wrong place; the next day we would have to relocate the pile!

Back at the barracks, I showed my hands to room elder Siegesmund—Siege for short. He sent me to the infirmary to try to get a paper stating that I couldn't work at the same job. Dr. Wolfsohn cleaned my hands and put ointment on them, then gave me a note. Over soup later, Siege asked a lot of questions, but I was very cautious in answering, especially about names. He arrived in Auschwitz in the fall of 1942 and had been in Monowitz since December of that year. By the end of our conversation, I was more at ease with him.

* * * * *

At the work site I handed my note to the *Kapo*. I could see he was fuming. He led me to a huge sand pile. "I want you to plane and even this into four hills. You'd better finish it today, or you'll wish you stayed on the rocks." Handing me a rake, he left but reappeared every 15 minutes to check on my work.

I finished by the end of the day. The *Kapo* didn't say anything; he just walked away. My hands were a little better, but my back and legs were aching. Eugen had spent the day shoveling gravel into sacks. I didn't know where David had been until we assembled for the march to the camp. He had a bloody nose and his right eye was blackened.

Eugen said he looked directly at the *Kapo* when being questioned by him and was beaten for that.

* * * * *

The next day brought more troubles. After I spent an hour planing sand with the rake, the *Kapo* returned me to the rock pile where Eugen was already waiting. Handing us cloth gloves he said, "This way you won't hurt your poor little artist's hands."

By afternoon we could hardly carry any more rocks. Eugen picked up a small one while the *Kapo* watched.

"Oh, are you tired? Well, let me help you." He took the rock out of Eugen's hands, picked up a big one, and dropped it into Eugen's arms. Eugen staggered backward but steadied himself and started walking.

The *Kapo* walked behind him and yelled, "Let's go, let's go. Faster, faster."

Eugen caught up with me and we tried to walked faster. But we apparently were not fast enough because the *Kapo* gave Eugen a big kick in the behind. Eugen lost his balance, stumbled forward, dropped the rock, and fell on top of it. I dropped my rock and bent over to help him get up. As I grabbed his shoulders, his body rolled slightly and I saw his bloody face. His head fell awkwardly to the side. When I let go of his shoulders, he fell lifeless on his back. I just stared in disbelief.

The *Kapo* looked at him. "He should have watched where he was walking. Now he broke his neck. Come on, you. Pick up your friend and put him aside until tonight. We'll have to take him back and I'll make an accident report."

I picked up my rock and was ready to hit the *Kapo* with it when he sneered at me, "Kill a German, would you? I'll tell you what I do with dirt like you."

Just then a guard came by. "What is happening here, *Kapo*? Are you crazy? Leave that inmate and go over to the other side. I'll call the foreman and he can give the orders. Helmut, keep watch on that *Kapo*. He isn't quite right."

The guard asked me if I saw what happened.

"Yes, sir, I saw everything." Another inmate and I picked up Eugen, his head bloody and dangling, and put him by the side of the building.

The foreman told me to relax for the remaining hour of the workday. As I sat, I wondered if I really would have hit the *Kapo*. Yes, I was sure I would have. "Oh, Eugen, I'm so sorry. Why, why, why?"

David had heard about the incident and got permission to stay with me. We sat together not saying anything.

On the march back to camp, Eugen's body was carried on a makeshift stretcher. He was laid near where his block assembled. At my barracks, Siege waited at my bunk. Shaking his head, he said I must have a guardian angel watching over me. The guard had already reported the incident and I would be questioned later.

Just as I finished my soup, a *Roter* (red triangle inmate) came by to take me to the records room and into the Gestapo's barracks. The chief of the work force was seated behind a desk. Next to him were two Gestapo men in civilian clothing. Standing at attention with my cap off, I recited, "117657 reporting, Sergeant Major, sir." I related everything about the incident and then was dismissed.

Back at the barracks Siege said I did the right thing, but it would be another week before he could get me into another *Kommando*. David told me more bad news—he was being transferred to a smaller *Kommando* that took care of arriving steel shipments. However, a new *Kapo* arrived at the work site who was much more fair and the guard was also replaced.

* * * * *

Days went by. One night as I was standing near my barracks, Siege said I was to go to the front after the count. At first, I couldn't recall any problems, then I remembered how the chief of records had caught me walking a little slow at work three weeks before and asked the *Kapo* to turn in a report on me. After the count in the evening, I went to the front of the assembly. The commandant, chief of records, chief of the work force, and four block chiefs were there. Four S-Vauers stood next to the *Bock*. I was fourth in a line of ten inmates.

When the first inmate stepped forward, the chief of the work force read the accusation and asked if it was correct or not. The inmate said it was correct. His punishment was twenty-five lashes and five days in the bunker, a square-meter room attached to the latrine in which an inmate stands all night. When the second inmate's accusation was read, he responded that it was correct but that he didn't do what was stated. His punishment was ten lashes and another ten lashes because he disagreed with the accusation. I realized it was to my advantage to agree with the accusation and hopefully limit the punishment. When my turn came, I was trembling.

"One hundred seventeen thousand, six hundred fifty-seven is guilty of being slow at work and not listening to repeated demands to move faster. Is that right?"

"Yes, sir, Sergeant Major," I said. I was to receive twenty-five lashes and five nights standing in the bunker.

When all the accusations had been read, the punishments started. The first inmate was laid over the *Bock* face down, his legs hanging and his arms held by two inmates. After the block chief's fourth lash, the inmate yelled with every blow. When the block chief was finished with him, two inmates dragged him away. The second and third inmates were lashed, and with every hit I felt sicker and my knees became more wobbly. The two walked away without help. Then it was my turn.

I was stretched over the *Bock* and my arms were jerked out from my sides and held firm. After a thousandth of a second I heard the swish of the stick and felt a huge pain and burning sensation on my backside. After the fifth lash I began to grunt loudly, and tears ran down my face. At the ninth lash, I went limp and my mind became a blank. My body jerked with each hit but I was so numb I didn't feel the pain any more. I felt myself being lifted up, carried a short distance, and dropped on my behind. Siege gave orders and I was lifted up and carried to my bunk. I heard his voice as if from a distance. "Come on, Lutz. On your elbows and take these aspirin." I swallowed them and a bowl of water and fell asleep.

It seemed like only a minute had passed when I was shaken awake to stand my first night in the bunker. The numbness had left and the pain was excruciating. I walked toward the latrine like an old man; with each step I felt skin tearing apart. We piled into the bunker, packed like sardines. I was able to get into a corner and bend my knees a bit. I pressed my buttocks against the wall, which relieved my pain somewhat. The smell was awful. The only thing to do was think or doze.

Sometime during the early morning hours, I realized what had happened to me. What pleasure did those animals get from beating a boy half to death just for walking slowly? Did this make them superior? I had seen men viciously and cruelly beaten. I had seen heads bashed in and eyes closed forever. Day in and day out, I saw men become weaker and thinner and finally carted off to the gas chambers and the ovens. I had often wondered why cruelty was inflicted on other inmates, but now that it had happened to me, I comprehended it even less. If there was a God, how could he let all this happen? What did all these people do to deserve such brutality? My brain nearly exploded, but I couldn't find any answers.

The chilly morning air seeped into the bunker, and shortly afterward the door opened and we were let out with orders to return in the evening. Tired and weak, it took a lot of effort to walk with any steadiness to my barracks. Siege had good news for me: he had been able to transfer me into Fred Zeink's *Kommando,* number 18. Fred told Siege that he knew me and my family—Bulli had mentioned that also—but I couldn't place him. And, thankfully, Siege had gotten some petroleum jelly for my behind.

I quickly ate my morning bread and coffee, stood for the count, and went to *Kommando* 18. The *Kapo's* back was to me. "Good morning, *Kapo.* Siege from Block 12 told me to report here."

He swung around and looked at me with soft brown eyes. "Well, little Lutz, I have been waiting for you. How are you?"

I smiled as I recognized him. "Fred, Fred Zeink! I can't believe it! Your name sounded familiar. It is so good to see you."

Everyone formed ranks and we marched out of the camp—cap off, stomach in, chest out, head high. Outside the gate we could ease up, and two inmates held me under my arms to help me keep up with the rest. At the work site, the inmates went to work and Fred took me to a small shack. The floor was cement, but it was warm. I lay down on my jacket with my shoes under my head and slept until a key rattled in the door. I sat against one wall while Fred and I ate some soup. He looked quite healthy; camp life apparently hadn't affected him at all.

I recalled a Sunday when I was ten and Papa took me to a soccer game. After the game in the locker room, Papa introduced me to Fred Zeink, a middle runner who won the game for his team. I had shaken his hand in awe. He was a nice-looking man and I remembered being told that he was a homosexual. But that was none of my concern. I hoped to have him as a friend. I slept through the afternoon and left the shack only when it was time to march back to the camp.

Shortly before the gong sounded I was led to the bunker. This time I couldn't make it into a corner; instead I was shoved into the middle of the group, but since my behind felt better, standing wasn't so bad. All sorts of thoughts ran through my mind during the night, and I dozed off and on until we were let out in the morning.

Chapter 31

At the work site, Fred assigned me to work with Erich, a middle-aged man who wore a red triangle patch. I helped him prepare his welding equipment and somewhat shakily started my first weld. Adjusting the torch to a fine flame, I heated the steel, picked up the welding rod, and began. Pronouncing my effort acceptable, Erich filed the rough edges. He was pleasant to work with and the day passed quite well.

* * * * *

Somehow, I got through the next three nights in the bunker, and when the door was opened to let us out, the chief of reports was waiting. As we stood at attention, he spoke. "I hope that this was a lesson. In this camp you will work for the German Reich. You are only paying back what you've stolen from the German people." He turned and marched away.

We put our caps on and walked off in different directions. From now on, I said to myself, no one would catch me doing anything that would warrant such punishment. I'd become a bit famous; people kept asking me how the bunker was and if I was still hurting. I was considered a veteran, which was not far from the truth, considering the death rate at Auschwitz.

One day at noon, Fred asked me to sit with him. While we ate, I told him about the camp at Boulogne-sur-Mer, my months on the streets in Brussels, and how I came to Auschwitz. He thought there would be more transports from Belgium because many Jews were still in hiding there.

He was right. When I arrived back at my barracks, Siege said a man from a Belgian transport that arrived that day would be looking for me in the evening. After supper, I was so deep in thought as I enjoyed a smoke that a voice with a heavy lisp surprised me. It was Walter Blau, who used to be an adagio dancer with his sister. He was considered very elegant then, but now he looked quite pitiful without hair. He was in Block 14. I gave him some helpful survival tips, sorry that I couldn't do more for him.

*****

A month passed. Jossel was doing better, but David had lost a lot of weight and moved like a zombie. I was afraid Walter wasn't going to survive either. He was exhausted and skeletal already—a marked man.

One morning in the washroom, Walter looked at me with glazed eyes. "Well, Lutz, I'll say goodbye. I am going to the infirmary with diarrhea. I am really weak and tired and can't stand the hunger and humiliation. Before I go, I wanted you to know I truly and honestly love you. Bye, Lutz." Without waiting for me to answer, he walked toward the infirmary. Seeing him go toward his death, I choked up. But there was no time to think about anything except trying to survive.

*****

The weather was colder. With fall coming, the rain and wind began. One night while we were lined up for the count, a strong voice called, "Hey, you, pipsqueak. You, peewee, the last one from *Kommando* 18. Turn around and come over here, but quickly." I trotted toward the chief of the work force and stood at attention. "117657, sir."

"The shoes are falling off your feet. You can't work this way. Off to the shoemaker *Kommando,* and tell him he should also give you a pair of socks, understand?"

The shoemaker found socks for me easily but my small feet were hard to fit. Finally, he handed me a pair of half boots of fine kid glove leather. They were a perfect fit and I strutted out feeling proud. And I would not have to hide the shoes at night; no one had feet as small as mine.

The next Sunday, while in the washroom trying to wash my shirt, a voice commanded, "Attention! Head high, chest out, in step, fall in!"

I couldn't believe it! That voice! It was Rudi Sonnenfeld, my physical education teacher when I was twelve in Berlin. He had arrived about two days before from the main camp to teach gymnastics to some SS officers. He had been in Auschwitz since the summer of 1943.

After we talked Rudi left for a while and I finished my chores and then looked for David. He was inside his barracks and didn't look too good. He said he felt weaker and very weary. My visit with him left me feeling very down. Back at my barracks I thought about David, Jossel, Eugen, Walter, Rudi, and all the others I knew in the camp. Depression could make every day feel so futile, but it had to come to an end sometime, and I knew I was going to survive.

* * * * *

I'd lost some more weight and was having a hard time breathing. I was wheezing a little and coughing a lot. At night, my face was quite warm. I decided I was probably just tired and hungry. The *Kommando* was not too bad, though. I got along fine with everyone, although I didn't have anyone to talk with. *Kapo* Fred was too busy, and I couldn't seem to get close to anybody.

On September 20, 1943, the first day of fall, the wind blew from the mountains and a drizzle fell. The chilly air went through my clothing and to my bones. By the time we headed back to camp, I was icy cold and miserable. While in the latrine I overheard two inmates talking at the other end. One voice seemed familiar, and I strained to see him in the poor light. As he walked by, I saw it was Noah! He was surprised to see a familiar face.

Outside I took a better look at him. He was taller than me and had a chunky build, a very strong square face, and gentle dark eyes. He was two years older than me. We had been in the scouts together, although we had been in different groups. He had also gone with his parents to Brussels as a refugee. I could have jumped for joy. Now that I had a true friend, everything would at least be tolerable for me.

He was in Block 26 and *Kommando* 54, but I told him I'd try to have him reassigned to my barracks and *Kommando*. Noah said he had a friend from Warsaw he wanted to bring with him; I asked to meet him so I could see if I could trust him. Back at the barracks, I found Siege sitting on his bunk, reading. While I told him about Noah, he just smiled as I talked a mile a minute.

I paused. Siege had the same mannerism Papa had. I used to talk my heart out while he just sat and smiled. I suddenly missed Papa so much. I shook off the feeling, trying to stay strong. I asked Siege if he could get Noah and his friend reassigned. He said of course he could. He wouldn't refuse anything I asked him for.

Again, thinking of Papa, I held back the tears. "Thanks, many thanks, Siege."

I was to tell Noah and his friend to get releases from their block elder and come over the following night. There was a bunk open toward the end of the barracks—the inmates who had it went into the infirmary that morning. Siege told me to talk to my *Kapo*, Fred, about the *Kommando* assignment.

I went outside to have a smoke, feeling great. Although I was losing one friend—I didn't think David would last much longer—fortune had found me another chance. Thinking unemotionally like this had its good points, but also its bad ones. I didn't understand how I could view living and dying so coolly, but in some way it helped me to survive in that horrible place.

Chapter 32

After my depressed thoughts of the day before, it was difficult to get going when the gong sounded. I managed to push my way to the washroom faucet and let the cold water pour over my head. I had finished my morning bread and coffee and sat smoking when Noah approached to ask me about a block detention in his block—number 26.

In the barracks, Siege didn't know anything about a block detention; he thought perhaps the rumor was a *Kapo*'s scare tactic. He took the opportunity to show Noah where he and his friend Janeck would bunk that night. Noah grinned broadly and left to tell Janeck the good news.

It was getting very cold and I really needed a winter outfit. I didn't know the clothing *Kapo*, but I decided to try to talk him into giving me some clothes. I was coughing badly and wondered if it was because of the cigarettes.

The clothing *Kapo* looked at me, my number, and then my boots. "Which *Kommando* ? Who's the *Kapo*? Where are you from?"

"*Kommando* 18, *Kapo* Fred Zeink, an old friend of the family. I am from Berlin, the north end, Alex and Rosenthaler."

This must have been the right response because he opened the door and I entered right behind him. I couldn't believe my eyes. There was more clothing than in a department store—inmate outfits and civilian garments, stacked in piles and hanging on racks, some stylish and tailor-made. This *Kommando* had the finest tailors in Europe—when clothing was made for the SS, it had to fit just so. The *Kapo* picked out a jacket and pants made for one of the higher ranking inmates. The pants were shortened for me while I waited and quite soon I was beautifully suited. When I thanked the *Kapo* profusely, he said, "Wear it in good health. With a suit and boots like those, they'll reject you at the crematorium." I left feeling magnificent, hoping that nothing bad would happen to me because of my good fortune. Siege admired my acquisitions but suggested I not tell anyone how I came by them.

Noah brought his friend Janeck to meet me. Janeck spoke only Polish and Yiddish. He was nice looking, quite skinny, a little round-shouldered, with a square face and high cheekbones.

I told Noah I had talked with my *Kapo*, and that he and his friend could belong to the *Kommando* I was in. All they had to do was get a paper signed by their *Kapo*. Nervous about it all, Noah left to talk with his *Kapo* before nightfall.

When it was bunk time, I folded my new clothes neatly, and put them under my straw wedge, and stretched out. Fate had brought Noah, Janeck, and me together. If we stuck together, we'd have a better chance of surviving.

As I finished my morning bread and coffee the next day, Noah rushed up to show me the paper from his *Kapo*. I handed it to Fred as we assembled for the march to the work site.

Fred instructed me to take care of the new boys, tell them about the procedures, show them what to do. I asked him if he thought we could have two hours for lunch so I could initiate them. He told me to go to the cabin I slept in. If we locked the door behind us, we should be pretty safe.

When the noon siren sounded, Noah and I went to the cabin (Janeck decided not to come with us), locked the door, set our soup bowls down, and laughed with pleasure. I related to him what had happened to me since leaving Berlin. He couldn't say much about his recent experiences because his family was still in hiding. He had lost contact with friends some time before. He was not sure whether someone betrayed him to the Gestapo or the Gestapo was just systematically finding all Jews.

That first day, in fact the first three weeks after Noah and Janeck arrived, passed rapidly. The three of us were always together. Janeck became a real pal, and I felt we could count on each other.

* * * * *

I developed a terrible toothache in a molar and went to the infirmary. When the Jewish "doctor" greeted me and looked in my mouth,

I felt he had never even seen a dentist's office! There was no anesthetic, but the tooth had to come out. He held my mouth open with one hand, clamped on the tooth with pliers, and started yanking. I was half out of the chair and ready to punch him. One more yank and he held the molar aloft. I bled all over the paper napkin until he gave me a cotton ball soaked in salt to bite on. The pain was bad, but it didn't keep me awake.

Two days later I woke up unable to speak. Siege sent me with a note to the infirmary even before the count. In fluent German, a man I hadn't seen before ordered me to open my mouth and depressed my tongue with a wooden stick. There was nothing wrong, he said, just tired vocal cords. Sure enough, three days later my voice began to come back. But I noticed I was short-winded, and I had been coughing a lot since last November.

January of 1944 seemed like an especially cold, snowy month. An icy wind blew from the mountains and right through our clothes. The harsh weather affected everyone's mood.

By the end of the month I could hardly walk without stopping to gasp for air. I had a peculiar pain in my lungs. The winter had taken its toll on a lot of inmates. David was just a shadow of his former self and his morale was very low. Jossel seemed thin, but he was in good spirits. Out of the many who arrived about the time I did, only a few had survived. I wondered how many of us would last until this misery was over.

One morning I could barely stand and asked Siege if I could stay behind and go to the infirmary. He touched my forehead. "My God, Lutz! You have a high fever. You'd better go. I'll give you old denims and shoes. Put your good things in a small bundle and leave them here so you'll have them when you come back. If they keep you in the infirmary, they'll throw away what you're wearing."

I protested. I didn't want to stay in there. I knew once I was in there, I wouldn't come out again.

Siege reassured me. "No, Dr. Wolfsohn knows you. He'll take care of you. Many guys came back from there. But with your fever, they'll keep you. Get a lot of rest and extra food there and everything will be all right."

At the infirmary, I sat and waited because many inmates were waiting to be seen. I was frozen stiff and numb by the time my turn came. I was given hot coffee and told to take my cloths off. Dr. Wolfsohn listened to my chest and made me cough, inhale, and exhale. My temperature was 104° Fahrenheit—I had double pneumonia. Dr. Wolfsohn said complications could set in, but since I was young and healthy otherwise, I'd probably be okay.

An orderly took me outside, still without clothes! We entered a door two blocks away, where I was greeted by an appalling sight. Sick inmates were lying in bunks half dead and the odor was overwhelming. I was issued a shirt and a blanket and assigned a bunk. The regulations were the same as in my barracks except I had to stay in the bunk all day, and I would be awakened for noonday and evening soup. At least I was warm. Surprisingly, in the morning my head was cool and I felt much better. I found out this was the tuberculosis block and some inmates had other contagious diseases, too. Most of the inmates who entered didn't come out again.

Dr. Wolfsohn and two other men in white coats entered, walked around, and circled everybody. When he came to me he checked my pulse and held his hand on my forehead. "I think your fever is gone and you look much better. We should know more in a few days."

All I could think of was how to get out of the infirmary as fast as possible. Each morning, the men who died during the night were carried out. One morning when I opened my eyes, I stared into the two blank eyes of a dead inmate next to me. His face stayed with me for a long time.

When Dr. Wolfsohn came by in the afternoon, I was sent up front to see him. I told him I was feeling better but still having a little trouble breathing.

The doctor leaned forward and lowered his voice. "The word has leaked out that there may be a selection soon, so we'd better get you out of here. Don't tell anyone or I'll have a panic on my hands."

An orderly woke me the next morning, put a finger to his lips, and motioned for me to follow him. Outside, Dr. Wolfsohn was waiting. "The rumor is true. The big wheels are staging a big selection this morning. It has been said that they want the whole infirmary emptied."

I thanked the doctor and received some old clothes to wear and was told to return to my barracks. It was still dark and the searchlights swept through the camp continuously. I was able to dodge them and arrive back at my barracks safely.

The night duty man told me to see the room elder, so with a soft touch I woke Siege up. "Siege, Dr. Wolfsohn told me to come back here because they're going to have a selection. He'll talk to you later."

"All right. Let me get your things. How do you feel?"

"Not bad. I think I've gotten rid of my illness."

"You'll stay in camp today and we'll decide what to do with you when I talk with Dr. Wolfsohn. I'll assign you to the *'Scheisshaus'* (latrine) *Kommando* for today." The latrine *Kommando* consisted of twelve men assigned to empty the camp toilets. Trucks were used to pump everything into a large barrel for later disposition.

I presented Siege's paper to the *Kapo* and looked over the others in the group. They were all physically depleted and looked like they didn't have long to live. I hoped this assignment was just for one day. It was nauseating work, and I was grateful when the workday was over.

After the count and evening meal, Siege and I met Dr. Wolfsohn at the infirmary. The doctor said all except four in the hospital were shipped to Birkenau. Although I still had a remnant of the double pneumonia, he couldn't put me back in the hospital. I would have to live with it and hope for the best. He told me to try to get in an easier *Kommando*.

Back in the barracks, I told Noah and Janeck this news. They said the potato-peeling *Kommando* was an easy one. The men sit around all day peeling potatoes for the German workers and could eat their fill.

Just then Siege came in, and before he could say anything, the three of us said in unison, "Lutz is going into the potato-peeling *Kommando*!"

Siege stood with his mouth open. "I don't even want to know how you found out about that."

Chapter 33

My new *Kapo* was Erwin, a red triangle inmate from a town near Stuttgart. There were fifteen of us, all under eighteen and looking bad enough to scare anyone. It took forty-five minutes to get to our work site, where we were seated three to a group. In front of us were a keg half full of water and a keg of raw potatoes. We were handed knives and told to start peeling the potatoes thinly. The other two in my group had done this before, but it took me ten potatoes and a small finger cut to get used to the process. We had to peel ten kegs in the morning and ten in the afternoon. At noon, lunch was a thick soup filled with potatoes. We could have seconds and thirds, so I stuffed myself until I could hardly move. At three o'clock, a Ukrainian woman kitchen worker brought us a bowl of boiled potatoes and we divided and ate them as we continued to peel.

When the whistle blew, we started the march back to camp. I felt odd; my stomach was not used to so much food. While we marched, Erwin made us sing. We passed many forced laborers from all over Europe.

Back in camp I told Noah and Janeck about the place. It was a *Kommando* for youngsters to recuperate in, limited to two-week stays. I didn't understand the system. Some children went immediately into the gas chambers and the ovens when the transports arrived, some were allowed to slowly die from overwork, and some were allowed to recuperate. I'd heard that the potato *Kommando* was initiated by a homosexual Jewish *Kapo*. He loved a little boy so much that when the boy became ill, he cared for him until he recovered. But the boy was still weak so the *Kapo* asked some German *Meister* at the work site if they couldn't use a few *Kalfactor* to serve them. They agreed, and eventually this *Kommando* and two others were reserved for youngsters.

After two weeks, when I had recuperated and even gained some weight, I was assigned to a *Kommando* sorting nuts and bolts all day. Even without potatoes, I continued to regain my strength. Then it was back to my old *Kommando* with Noah and Janeck. Noah made up a crazy game. When we marched out to work in the morning, he compiled a nice menu for breakfast and lunch; on the way back at night, he made up a dinner menu. His theory was that doing this would made us think we were full. Janeck and I thought he was crazy.

One night after the count, we were told to stay in place. A gallows had been erected. Siege came by and stood in front of us. In whispers he told us what had happened. "Moishe from Block 26 and two Red Poles escaped two days ago by digging a hole under the fence. Moishe had money; the other two had contacts. They reached the mountains safely, but one night before they made any contacts the two killed Moishe for his money and left his body lying there. Some dogs found it and followed the scent left by the other two. They were captured this morning twenty kilometers from here and were made to run all the way back in front of the chief of reports' motorcycle. The Gestapo put them through the wringer, and tonight is the end of the road for them."

I whispered back to him, "They deserve it. I always liked Moishe; everybody liked him. He was a decent human being, even in this awful place."

Just then the officers arrived and the chief SS man spoke. "Two days ago, three inmates escaped. Because of our superior abilities, our dogs found one murdered and then the two murderers. We will do these two the honor of waiting for them; they're due any minute from the main camp."

We waited and waited while it became colder and the wind blew. I began to get numb and my ear tips tingled. We were not allowed to move. It took all my strength to remain standing. Finally, I heard a motorcycle arrive and the gong started. When we were commanded to start walking, I fell flat on my nose. Someone picked me up and dragged me past others who had also fallen down. After a while I could walk a bit and we were marched past the hanging bodies and off toward our barracks. Partially thawed, I had some warm soup and fell asleep.

* * * * *

The escape incident triggered a big purge among the prominent inmates, and the SS and Gestapo were always watching and asking questions. The whole camp was on alert, and everyone was subdued.

Erwin Block was a new inmate—a thin little boy with an angelic look, large nose, and heavy lips. He was from the west part of Berlin. Siege asked me to teach him the rules.

We had a new foreman at the work *Kommando*. He was a red triangle from the north of Berlin, an older man with a slim build and medium height who was missing all his teeth. He had a very low number. When he heard Erwin and I were from Berlin, he began to talk about places I'd almost forgotten. Later, Fred said the new foreman liked me and I could learn a lot from him. So whenever I had a chance, the old man and I sat and talked.

* * * * *

My eighteenth birthday came, on April 9, 1944, but other than the old man, Noah, and Janeck wishing me a happy birthday, I had a terrible day. It was still cold and we were wheeling heavy equipment between buildings. Four of us struggled with a bulky cart over an icy road. When it slipped we jumped away, but it caught Erwin's right ankle. We wrapped the ankle in some cement paper and put him in the little shack to wait for the end of the workday. That night we took him to the infirmary, where Dr. Wolfsohn said it was only a sprain. He gave Erwin a note so he could stay in the barracks for a day.

Erwin was so thankful that he followed me everywhere. He had been a tailor's apprentice, so he made me a new cap. With his talent and my ability to obtain clients for him to sew for, we planned to get extra food to survive. Quite a few of the hierarchy would love to have tailor-made clothing and would pay a good price for them. Siege agreed to help us start our business.

* * * * *

The days passed and more people died. Even though it was the end of April, the weather was still pretty cold.

About twelve of our *Kommando* were placed with a new *Meister* in May—we would be making bricks. First, we had to empty a freight wagon with 800 sacks of cement. Two men inside the wagon put a sack on our shoulders that we carried to a nearby building. Two others piled the sacks in an orderly stack. Sometimes we had to carry two 100-pound sacks at once! SS men stood by to make sure we moved fast enough. In two hours, the sacks were all unloaded and stacked. Making the bricks came next: sand and cement were mixed together, then gravel was added. This mixture was poured into two steel forms, each form making five bricks. The forms were carefully lifted from the new bricks, which were left to dry. We switched duties every six forms; one man mixed the material, one poured it into the form, and the third one pounded it down firmly.

By noontime, we were barely able to swallow our soup and then fell asleep on the ground. At night we were so tired we finished our meal, cleaned up, and went directly to our bunks. Fred promised we would be changing assignments in another three weeks. Somehow we managed to last until we were replaced by others.

*****

On the second Sunday of the month, some of the people marched out on *Kommando* work. The rest of us had to stand for the count, then we got cleaned up and rested and underwent shaving and delousing. It gave me a chance to walk around and try to find old friends. In the black market area, I didn't recognize anyone at first. In a far corner, Jossel smiled. He looked pretty good. He said it was frightening how few of the "old-timers" were left.

We talked for a while and then I went toward David's barracks. I searched inside and outside, and then I spotted him coming from the washrooms. There was nothing left of him but bones! My eyes began to fill with tears, but I didn't want him to see that. I walked toward him with a big grin and gave him a hug. He stared at me, trembling.

Tears ran down his cheeks, and it took a moment for him to compose himself. "Well, Lutz, you don't look too wasted. I'm afraid I haven't got long. No use telling me differently. I have all the markings of a dead man. I am so tired and have no more strength to fight with. You told me in Boulogne-sur-Mer we'd make it. You were partly right; you will make it."

I had no words. What they had done and were doing to us was beyond description.

We sat in silence for a while, then shook hands. I returned to my barracks completely depressed.

The old foreman looked at me. "What happened, little fellow? You look like you buried your best friend."

I told him about David's awful condition and he looked silently at me with understanding eyes.

He had taught me much about life in general. I felt I'd learned more from him in the short time I'd known him than I had from anybody else, including Papa.

Morning came and as we formed the *Kommando* groups, I looked for the old man but didn't see him anywhere. When I had the opportunity, I asked Fred what had happened. Fred looked at me with sad eyes. He said the Political Section picked him up with many other red triangles. Nobody knew why or what had happened to them. He would let me know as soon as he learned any information.

I felt so bad. I thought I'd found a mentor, but I knew I'd never see him again. I didn't even know his name or if he had any family, and at the moment I couldn't even remember his number!

Noah and Janeck sensed something was wrong as they walked with me. When I finally told them I'd lost a friend, Noah put his arm around my shoulders and said we needed to go on. We had to get to work or we'd be in trouble.

We noticed one of the German guards looking our way, so we started to move.

All day as we worked, my mind returned to the old man. I couldn't shake the thought of his never returning.

It was August, and my health had not improved. I was coughing more and more, and I also got very winded easily.

At noontime, as we sat in a big building eating our soup, we suddenly heard a big explosion. Glass flew everywhere, and one piece hit me on the forehead. I felt blood oozing from the cut and someone screamed, "Air raid!"

Taking one huge jump from the top of the stairs where I was sitting, I landed on some people and fought my way outside. I threw myself to the ground and listened to further explosions. A small man tried to crawl under me for protection, and as I moved to one side, I had a chance to look up. I couldn't believe my eyes! All I could see were planes, like hundreds of birds flying south in formation.

A hundred yards away, a bomb hit a big cement pipe and the severed head of an inmate flew out. The man had apparently crawled into the pipe for protection. It took all the will power I had not to throw up. Suddenly, all was calm and we started to look for friends and tried to regroup. The word went around to form our *Kommando s* to march back to the camp.

As soon as we arrived there, I went to the infirmary, where one of the staff cleaned the dried blood from my forehead. Luckily, it was just a small cut. When I was dismissed, I headed toward the barracks and was greeted by Noah and Siege. Siege said that starting the next day Noah, Janeck, and I would be assigned to the coal *Kommando.*

"This is a terrific *Kommando ,*" Siege said. "You stand on top of a huge heap of coke and all you have to do is plane. You see, coke is burned coal, and as it comes from the trains it is unloaded on conveyor belts, forming big mounds. You need to smooth it out. Eventually, synthetic rubber will be made from it, as well as methanol and some kind of medication, I think. Should not be too hard on you. Besides, the coke is nice and warm. As the days get cooler, this will be great."

With that, he marched off, and Noah and I looked for Janeck to tell him the news.

* * * * *

When morning came, we joined the new *Kommando*. Both the new *Kapo* and the foreman wore red triangles and seemed to be okay. The *Kapo* checked and looked at my number.

When we arrived at the work site, instead of working with the coal, we were ordered to clean the mess from yesterday's raid. At noontime, there was another raid, and the alarm siren was sounded for a long time. Of course, the *Meister* and all the Germans and the foreign workers rushed into the air raid shelters, leaving the camp inmates outside. A big pole with a basket was lowered as soon as planes were sighted, and when the raid was over, the basket was raised again.

The next day we were finally assigned to the big pile of coke. With a shovel, we planed all the coke that came along the conveyor belt. The inmate who worked with me was a Frenchman from Tunisia and was about as short as I was. He was the boxing champion in the feather-weight division from Tunisia and Morocco in 1936 and 1937.

The work was easy and the days went by pretty fast. The raids continued and each noontime we watched for the basket to be lowered. As soon as we saw the planes, we lay on our backs and watched them fly by. The moment they had passed, we turned over because if bombs had been dropped, they would land about then.

With the beginning of October, we didn't see any more planes flying over. By that time, I couldn't have cared less. At the end of the month, I went to the infirmary to see Dr. Wolfsohn and get something to ease my coughing. He just looked at me, shook his head, and gave me four pills.

"That's all I can spare, little guy."

When he put me on the scale, it read fifty-two pounds and he shook his head again. With a sad face he said goodbye, but I didn't understand his expression.

Chapter 34

Christmas arrived, and from the scant news we received from the outside it appeared that the war was not going too well for the "Master Race." We heard some sort of rumbling, like thunder, coming from far away.

On the first of January 1945, Noah told me that the war couldn't last too much longer. I couldn't rejoice but just nodded my head and smiled faintly. I wondered where David was and hoped he was okay. Erwin, the little tailor's apprentice, finally broke down and was gone. Jossel was still around and, of course, Noah and Janeck, who always tried their best to keep me going.

By the 12th of the month we could hear what sounded like cannons. There was also talk that the camp might be evacuated so everybody walked around with glimmers of hope in their eyes. There was more speculation than knowledge, but it lifted our spirits. Unfortunately, I was having a tough time breathing and could hardly walk. I was always hacking. I knew I was near death and tried with all my might not to give in to hopelessness.

✳ ✳ ✳ ✳ ✳

It was very cold on the morning of January 15, 1945, and after I'd finished making my bunk, I left the barracks to wash up but fell flat in the snow. When I felt someone touch me, I opened my eyes and looked into Noah's face. He and Janeck picked me up and at Siege's direction took me to the infirmary to see Dr. Wolfsohn.

The doctor gave me a look, hurried me into one of the rooms, and dismissed my friends. My temperature was 103 degrees! He took my pulse and looked into the pupils of my eyes. When I coughed, he held a bowl under my mouth and left the room with it.

After what seemed like a very long time, Dr. Wolfsohn returned with the bad news. "You have tuberculosis, Lutz. We don't have an x-ray machine to confirm how bad it is, but one thing is for sure—you are going to stay here. Besides, this disease is highly contagious."

My clothing was taken away, and I was told to put on a funny-looking garment. An orderly took me to a barracks used for inmates with contagious diseases, and I was assigned to share a top bunk next to a window with another inmate. I was so exhausted that I didn't care if someone was in the bunk with me or who else was in the room. I fell asleep as soon as I lay down, waking only for soup at noon.

An orderly came by to take me to see the doctor. Wrapped in a blanket and wearing a pair of wooden clogs on my feet, I waited outside the doctor's office for a short time. When Dr. Wolfsohn came out of the door, a younger man, also a doctor, was with him.

"This is Dr. Semach. He will take good care of you."

"I am so busy, I don't know where to start first," Dr. Semach said, feeling the top of my head. "Just a little fever, I think, but let's check it."

Three minutes later, he took the thermometer from my mouth and looked at it. "Your fever is down. Let me give you something that will get rid of it completely." I swallowed the small white pill with a little water, thinking, what a bitter taste! The doctor just smiled.

"My cousin is in your room—the little Greek fellow. I sure hope he will make it! Let the orderly take you back. Do nothing but rest and sleep right now. That's the best medicine for you."

I was happy to be back in the room and in the bunk. Still shivering a little from the cold, I was soon asleep again.

In the evening, I was awakened by a big commotion. The evening soup was being given out and as soon as I got my quart I practically inhaled it, I ate so fast. My head seemed pretty clear and not so hot anymore. I wondered what the pill I took was. I could still taste some of the bitterness.

The night passed and another day went by. Toward evening on the 17th, we heard a rumor that this would be the last roll call. Everybody was to be evacuated toward Germany because the Russians were closing in. Another rumor was that we would all be shot. There were several other rumors, suggesting no one really knew what would happen.

On the morning of the 18th, Noah and Janek came to my bunk and said we were all being evacuated—the whole camp—and everybody who stayed behind was going to be killed. They wanted to carry me along with them and begged me not to stay.

While Noah was speaking, Dr. Semach came by and overheard Noah. "Don't go, little fellow. Nothing will happen to you or the others. In fact, I am even leaving my cousin here."

There was a knock on the nearby window—it was David! I had not seen him in a while. He was so thin and looked very tired. I could heard his voice begging me not to go anywhere. "You'll never make it, Lutz." I looked at him and nodded my head; I realized I was also saying goodbye.

Turning around, I shook Noah's and Janeck's hands and said farewell. I thanked the doctor, too, and shook his hand. As they all left, I felt a tear roll down my check and swallowed hard. I wiped my face and tried not to show any emotion.

I heard a lot of shouting but could see nothing. I felt change in the air—it was not even noon yet, but we got a bowl of soup. As the afternoon wore on, we felt the room becoming a little colder, and outside everything was silent. I managed to walk outside and feel the steam pipes attached to the barracks. They were cold, and the weather was beginning to get very chilly.

Back inside, I told everyone to keep warm because there would be no more heat. Of course, there was no more food either. While I was outside I had looked around but did not see anyone. The rest of the camp seemed to be empty. We were all afraid that soldiers would come and kill us all, but no one dared say anything.

About ten o'clock in the evening, we were abruptly awakened by big explosions. Through the windows we could see what looked like fires in the distance. Then a bomb suddenly hit the barracks next to us and it erupted into flames. Fortunately, that barracks was empty. Papa had always told me that when you hear a bomb, it is not for you. If you don't hear it, it has already gotten you. I heard this one only at the last second before it landed.

Half naked and barefooted, I went outside to find two men watching the fire. It seemed we were the only ones still standing at first, but as we looked around, other inmates came out of other barracks. It was ice cold and I rushed back into my bunk and tried to get warm.

In the morning, we found that two inmates had died. Another inmate and I took the bodies outside and dumped them in the snow. With my blanket wrapped around me and the clogs on my feet, I tried to talk to some men outside who were warming themselves on the ashes of the burned barracks. No one knew what was happening, so it was no use staying outside in the cold. During the day we heard isolated shots but no big explosions. I was feeling better; my cough had improved somewhat and I thought my fever was gone. Without food, the best thing to do was sleep.

*****

I awoke quite early the next morning and accidentally touched my bunkmate's foot; it was cold. I sat up with a jerk and looked into staring eyes. He must have died during the night. I called the inmate who helped me with the bodies the previous day, and we took my dead bunkmate and another inmate who had also died during the night outside and dumped them in the snow. That made four dead of the twenty-four inmates in our room. I was afraid there would be more.

I tied my clogs on my feet and tied my blanket around me. I decided to chance leaving the camp. The air was cold and hit me hard in the chest, but my coughing was not bad at all. The deep snow on the ground made walking difficult. As I walked toward the gate, I looked around me. Everything was quiet, as if nothing had ever happened. The barracks stood there like dead objects. I was so engrossed in looking around that I hardly noticed other men also walking outside. I was not thinking clearly. I trudged slowly through the gate and headed toward a POW camp about a half mile away. Maybe I could scrounge some items to make surviving a little easier.

I found no one at the camp, which I discovered was a former British POW camp. I entered the first barracks and found a treasure—some warm underwear, pants, a jacket, heavy leather laced boots, and a cap, all in sort of a khaki color. The uniform was somewhat big on me, but I didn't care. I also found a large number of cigarette butts, which I crumbled into loose tobacco. I began to feel very tired and started marching back to my camp. It was midafternoon by the time I returned, very hungry and tired, but feeling much warmer. I fell in the bunk and within seconds I was asleep.

* * * * *

Another inmate died during the night and was taken outside.

I felt pretty good with all the warm clothing. I was ready to explore to see if I could find any food anywhere. There was nothing. If there *had* been anything, the other inmates had already gotten it. On my way back to the barracks I met a man who stared at me. I looked at him, too, and knew I'd met him before. He felt the same because he started to speak to me in very broken German mixed with a little Yiddish. I asked him if he spoke French and he did. He talked and talked. He said I was the little boy he encountered the first day in the camp who did not want to talk. I didn't remember that, but accepted it since he said it was so.

"What is your name?" he asked.

"Lutz Posener." To speak my name rather than reciting my number sounded funny to me.

"I'm Primo Levi from Italy. And you are a Frenchman, yes?"

"No, I am a German, but I lived in Belgium."

We talked further about where I got the clothing and which barracks I was in and if I had found any food at all. I answered all his questions and told him I could find no food.

"Come on over to the typhoid barracks after a while and I'll get you something to eat."

I thanked him and said I would be there shortly.

What a nice feeling it was to be able to talk to a stranger and not be afraid and even be offered food. Maybe I would give him some of my tobacco.

I wandered through the barracks, not really knowing what I was looking for. They had all been ransacked by a lot of other men. I hadn't been aware that so many of the inmates remained behind. I felt as though I was walking in some sort of dreamland. As I walked, I encountered quite a few men carrying all sorts of items back to their bunks. I had no idea what they'd found, but they carried their bundles as though whatever was inside was important to them.

I was tired and hungry and started to shiver. Even through the warm clothing I felt the cold penetrating my body. Back at the barracks I lay on the bunk covered with the blanket and tried to warm up. After a while, I felt warmer, but I was still hungry. I looked around at some of the others. The doctor's cousin didn't look good at all. I had a feeling he wasn't going to survive. Two other inmates also didn't look so great.

When I warmed up enough, I made up a small package with the tobacco and went to the stranger's barracks. When I got there, I saw they had a potbelly stove and it was warm. He greeted me with a smile and introduced me to another inmate. Handing me a potato, he said, "That's about all we have."

In three seconds I'd eaten the potato and handed him the package of tobacco. "I don't even know if you smoke."

"Oh, yes, absolutely. Where did you get this?"

"From the English POW camp about a half mile from here."

I stayed for a while, enjoying the warmth. The men in this barracks looked even worse than the ones in mine. It was getting dark outside, so I left, trudging through the snow toward my barracks. It was not a good idea to be outside when it was dark. Not so much because it was freezing but there was no electricity and who knew if all of the SS men were completely gone. During the day we heard shots and far away there were sounds like cannons being fired.

Some of the inmates could see the road from their windows and commented that German military vehicles were rushing by and there were all sorts of armored cars with soldiers walking behind them and even some soldiers on horseback. A lot of civilians seemed to be hurrying through the snow, fleeing from the Russians. It was the 22nd of January. Four days had passed since Noah and my other friends had left. I sure hoped they were all right.

* * * * *

In the morning when I climbed down from my bunk, I looked into the expressionless eyes of the doctor's little cousin. He held my hand for a moment but didn't move. I could only faintly hear what he wanted to say. "I don't feel well at all. If, when you come back, I am not here, tell my cousin hello from me, if you ever see him again."

I had to get out. I couldn't stand the way he looked. The cold air hit me as I stepped outside and I started hacking for a moment. New snow had fallen during the night and there was not a sound in the air. I had a hard time walking through the snow but managed to reach the barracks where I stopped searching the day before. I continued through the barracks, looking for anything I could use but found nothing. About midday, when I'd just about finished searching, I entered the alcove of one of the block chief's sleeping quarters. I saw a chess set! It was an old German board made of washable cloth with numbers on two sides and alphabet letters on the remaining two sides. Pawns were strewn all around. I wondered why no one had discovered this before me. I rushed through the barracks to find some paper to wrap the set in, but all I saw was a piece of cloth. I wrapped the chess pieces, rolled the board separately, and then wrapped the whole set in cloth.

In the third barracks I discovered a prayer book in Hebrew. And looking more closely I found a prayer shawl and a pair of phylacteries still in their little pouch. They must had been left by someone who arrived in one of the last transports. Searching one of the remaining barracks for cloth to wrap these new finds in, I also found some string. When the items were wrapped and tied, I continued searching, hoping to find something to eat and drink. I had no luck. I tried with some success to melt some snow.

Back in my barracks, I saw the doctor's cousin's empty bunk. Two other bunks were also empty. Only sixteen of us were left. Nobody said anything, so I climbed into my bunk and hid my finds underneath the mattress.

* * * * *

I must have slept through the night without waking up at all. I ran outside a little way from the barracks to urinate in the snow. Standing there in the cold, I thought back to when I was a little boy in Berlin. We used to try to write our names in the snow. The thought made me smile. Oh, God, I was smiling.

Back inside the barracks I took my little package and marched over to see my new acquaintance. He was excited when I showed him what I'd found.

"Don't show them to anyone. Keep them wrapped good and tight. When you get home they will be something memorable for you."

I had not really thought about going home yet. For the time being, I decided to investigate the records room.

As I walked near the gate, I saw some uniformed men approaching the entrance to the camp. I hid behind the nearest barracks and kept my eye on them. They were three SS men. I had no idea what they wanted or what outfit they belonged to. Above, I heard the sound of an aircraft, and when I looked up I saw a one-propeller plane with a white star on the wing, flying very low. Apparently the SS men saw it, too, because they ran away as the plane circled.

I stepped out from behind the barracks and waved my hands at the plane. Whoever was flying it waggled the wings side to side, as if saying hello. I thought the white star meant it was an American plane, but that couldn't be—the Americans were too far away. But it sure felt good to see a plane that wasn't German.

Entering the records room I glanced around but didn't see anything of value. Everything had either been taken or destroyed. As I turned to walk away, out of the corner of my eye I saw something gray underneath a pile of dirt. I bent over to clear the rubble from around it and picked up a *cahier,* a sort of school notebook. Opening it, I realized it was a ledger from the infirmary listing incoming and outgoing inmates and an explanation for each entry. There was a total count of the sick and dead. Somebody would be interested in it. I wrapped it in some old paper and some string and tied it tightly so it would be difficult to open easily. I decided not to tell anyone about this find.

I had one more barracks to go—probably the affairs' barracks. I looked more closely at the eating space and found a medium-sized bag with no opening. I didn't have anything to open it with, so I poked a small hole in the bag. Out came three little grains of rice—food! I thought, my new friend will probably let me cook it on the stove in his room if I share it with the men. I hurried toward his barracks.

I ran up to Primo, who was sitting near the stove, and showed him the bag. His eyes lit up. Holding the bag over a bowl, he opened it with a makeshift knife and all the rice poured out.

Primo went to work, melting snow to make cooking water. We anxiously waited until it cooked on the stove. When it was done, Primo's friend brought out some salt and we started eating, sharing it with some of the others in the room—just a few were left. Everyone was smiling and my hand was shaken with heartfelt thanks. Full and content, I headed toward my barracks.

I didn't realize that, having had no real food for such a long time, the rice might not agree with me. All during the night, I was in and out of my bunk, fighting the pain of constipation.

The next day when I saw my friend, he realized immediately what my problem was. He gave me two tiny pills, which I swallowed.

"They should work in about six hours. Go back to the barracks and rest."

He was right. Toward evening, after three trips to the latrine, I felt much better. In addition, I had no more fever and my hacking had decreased considerably. That night I slept really peacefully.

Chapter 35

Another inmate in our barracks died. It hadn't snowed for several days; the existing snow was melting and we could see portions of some of the bodies outside. Fifteen of us remained in the room now.

I was cold, weak, and hungry. Slowly, daylight came and I searched the horizon. I saw something moving out there.

I kept looking and suddenly, not too far away, I saw men on horses. I hushed everyone, saying that I couldn't identify who was approaching.

I lay back in my bunk and waited. After an eternity, the door was pushed open and in the frame stood a huge man with a fur hat and wearing a long, khaki-colored topcoat. In his left hand was a bullwhip, which he moved constantly. We just stared at him. Finally, he spoke with a booming voice, "Greetings, comrades."

One man in a lower bunk replied with the same words and asked if he belonged to the Russian army. The man nodded and in Russian explained that he and the others with him belonged to a special group that scouts ahead before the rest of the army.

"You are free," he said. "Other soldiers will come and take care of you." With that, he marched out.

Everyone in the room was shouting and laughing, coughing and hacking at the same time. Two of the inmates ventured outside, but I lay back in my bunk.

It was all over just like that. For months we had been waiting for this moment, and now I didn't know what to do or say. I was numb. My mind was a blank.

When I finally got out of the bunk and went outside, the place was thronged with inmates, some of whom were wearing the same khaki POW uniform I had on. They were all jubilant. I just walked around listening to them but not really comprehending what they were saying.

I was free, but I was still cold and hungry and had no idea what to do. Near the entrance to the camp I saw the Russian army whizzing by with all sorts of military equipment. I sat down on a block of cement and watched it all, completely forgetting the time.

Suddenly, three uniformed men stood in front of me with machine guns slung over their shoulders. They all grinned and one shook my hand. "Comrade, hello," they repeated. When they asked how I was, I replied that now that they were here, I was not bad at all. I spoke a little Russian, which pleased them, and they asked all sorts of questions.

They were the first troops, they told me, who would make way for the infantry. The Russian army had practically encircled this whole area, and more military would come. A medical outfit would take care of us all. They said goodbye and left.

* * * * *

I had a good night's sleep and woke later than usual. When I ventured outside, many soldiers were talking to the inmates. We got some bread from them, but it was so hard we couldn't eat it. It was the dark bread they fed to their horses, and in order to eat it, it had to be softened. We put it into the snow and after a while it was soft enough to eat— it didn't taste bad at all.

For the next three days, Russian army units passed through the area. On the fourth day, a unit brought in equipment as well as several doctors and orderlies. They went from barracks to barracks inspecting the survivors. They sorted the ones who could walk and separated out those who were contagious.

I was assigned to a new barracks with ten other tuberculosis patients. We were all able to move around. I watch orderlies picking up all the dead from outside and putting them in one big pile. After they had recorded the numbers of the dead, they spread on the bodies a large amount of chloride of lime, which dissolves everything. They also spread it around all the empty barracks for disinfecting purposes. It smelled awful.

Another group of soldiers stayed to guard everyone so there would be no interference. In the morning, these soldiers ate kasha, which was some sort of grits. Half of the bowl contained grits and the other half

Top: Russian medical corps, Auschwitz, January 1945 *bottom:* Russian medical corps with liberated inmates, Auschwitz, April 1945

grease. Then they rolled a cigarette with Machorka tobacco in some heavy paper. Resting on the fenders of their big GMC trucks, they sometimes took big swallows of vodka.

* * * * *

For the next two weeks, we were told to just wait around until all the information on us had been recorded, and then we would be transported to the main camp. In the meantime, we got "real" food, which, of course, constipated many men. But having gone through that before, I was all right. I had time to wander aimlessly through the camp, and many times I sat down and dreamed. I was thinking of the past, the present; I could not even visualize the future.

During the last two days we were able to shower, which felt very good. We also were shaved and disinfected. We had to give up our clothing and were issued clean inmate outfits that fit properly. I was lucky and received a nice pair of leather shoes because of my small feet. And I didn't give up my treasures.

All this time gave me a chance to try to sort out my feelings, but I could feel nothing. I had no understanding of what had happened to me between April 1943 and January 1945. I could not grasp the enormity of it all. I was nearly nineteen years old, but I knew nothing of what was really going on. I promised myself I would learn more about this catastrophe—these unbelievable years of suffering, of being reduced to nothing. At that moment I was confused. I was happy to be free of all that oppressed me, but I was not only alone but very lonely and lost. Being lost was the worst.

Epilogue

When liberated from Auschwitz on January 27, 1945, I was in precarious health, weighing only fifty-two pounds. I was transferred to the main camp of Auschwitz and placed in a TB ward. (There were no more tiered bunks—someone had sawed off all the upper beds!) I was well treated by the Russian doctors and medical staff.

Slowly, over a period of several months, Red Cross representatives from various countries arrived at the camp and tried to repatriate their people. Many former inmates left on their own to return to their homes in their own countries or to search for other displaced family members. Unfortunately, no one was looking for me—I was stateless. I encountered a friend from before the war and we stayed together. Soon we were joined by two former inmates from Greece and Holland who also had no family.

We traveled on our own from Poland to Prague, Czechoslovakia, where we contacted the French Red Cross. It was there, in June 1945, that I changed my name from Lutz Posener to Louis Posner. Nobody at that time knew where I came from, and I was advised by a friend to change my name so I could stay safely during the French occupation and maybe pass as a Belgian. We were eventually sent to the German island of Reichenau, where the French occupation forces had established a small hospital. While there, we were treated royally. We met many high-ranking French military people, including General Charles de Gaulle, the leader of the Free French.

From there, I was sent to a sanitorium in the picturesque Black Forest of southern Germany, where I rested and recuperated. Once I regained my health, I lived by myself in the city of Muhlheim with the assistance of the International Refugee Organization (IRO) and the United Nations Relief and Rehabilitation Administration.

When the IRO ended its assistance program in the area where I was living, I moved to a rehabilitation camp in the district of Wuerttemberg, so I could learn a trade. In the fall of 1949 I met my future wife, who worked in the camp office, and we were married in October 1950.

After about a year of filling out paperwork, looking for a sponsor, and submitting requests, my wife and I were finally allowed to immigrate to the United States in September 1951, settling in Seattle, Washington. Ten years later, I relocated to Los Angeles, California, where I did various kinds of work but enjoyed a long career as a physical therapist until my retirement.

After the war, I began to investigate what had happened to my family. My father, I learned, was moved from the camp in Gurs at least twice and stayed for a time in a prison. At the end of summer in 1942, he was sent to Auschwitz and never returned. My favorite aunt, Felicitas, and her husband, Edmund Berger, also died in Auschwitz.

My stepmother, who stayed in Berlin, was deported to Riga, Latvia, near the Baltic Sea, in 1941. She did not survive the trip. All those on her transport were shot.

My friends Karl, Jossel, and Fred Zeink survived, and we had a happy reunion in December 1945. Manfred also survived, but I didn't see him again until much later. As far as I know, the others all perished. The evacuations from the camps were known as "death marches" because most of the people who were evacuated—among them most of my friends— did not reach their destination.

As for the "treasures" I found after Auschwitz was evacuated, I donated them to the Simon Wiesenthal Center in Los Angeles, California, in 1979. Visitors to the center can view the chess set, which is on display.

* * * * *

I needed to tell my story and to say that, although I have learned not to hate anybody, I can never forget what happened.

Glossary

aliyah	immigration of Jews to their homeland
Appellplatz	roll call place
block or barracks	housing for inmates of concentration camps
Blockaelteste	the senior inmate of a barracks
Blockfuehrer	SS chief for four barracks at roll call
Bock	bench where concentration camp inmates were publicly beaten
bunker	torture place in a concentration camp
B-Vauer	abbreviation designating a professional criminal
challah	braided egg bread
Chanukah	Festival of Lights
crematorium ovens	burning site for bodies of inmates
Dachau	the first concentration camp, opened March 22, 1933

Diaspora	the scattering of Jews to countries outside of Palestine
Gestapo, Geheime Staatspolizei	Secret State Police, founded by Herman Goering
Gluehwein	hot wine
Haeftlings Krankenbau	inmates' infirmary
Hitler Jugend	Hitler Youth (a Nazi organization)
J	an abbreviation designating a Jew
Jude	Jew
Jungvolk	People's Boys (a Nazi organization for preteens)
Kaddish	liturgical prayer recited at specific points in daily Jewish services and on certain other occasions; also the prayer for the dead
Kalfactor	young boy(s) in service of the camp hierarchy
Kapo	chief of a work unit
kheyder	Talmud Torah school
kibbutz	cooperative community settlement in Israel, usually agricultural in nature
Kommando	work unit
Kueken Gruppe	Small Boys' Group (a Nazi organization)

Lager	camp
Lageraelteste	senior chief inmate of a camp; the highest rank for an inmate
Lagerkapo	senior chief inmate of a workforce
Maquis	member of the French Resistance
Meister	work boss(es)
Organization Todt	semimilitary outfit created in 1933 for construction of the Autobahn and military installations
Platz	place
rebbe	teacher in a Jewish school
SA	abbreviation designating Sturmabteilung, a storm detachment or storm troop
Schupo	police officer(s)
SD	abbreviation designating Sicherheitsdienst, security service
shul	temple
Sicherheitsdienst	security service
SS	abbreviation designating Schutzstaffel, protection squad
Strasse	street
Stubenaelteste	senior inmate of an inside block (room)

S-Vauer	abbreviation designating protective security, a professional criminal with a life sentence
tallis	prayer shawl
tefillin	phylactery: either of two small, black leather cubes containing a piece of parchment inscribed with verses 4–9 of Deut. 6, 13–21 of Deut. 11, and 1–16 of Ex. 13: one is attached with straps to the left arm and the other to the forehead during weekday morning prayers by Orthodox and Conservative Jewish men.
Wachtmeister	inspector(s) of the police

Bibliography

Eschwege, Helmut. *Kennzeichen J.* Frankfurt was Main: Röderberg-Verlag, 1979.

Holzer, Willi. *Judische Schulen in Berlin.* Berlin: Edition Hentrich, 1992.

Schoenberner, Gerhard. *The Yellow Star.* New York: Bantam Books, Inc., 1979.

Smolen, Kazimierz, ed. *Ausgewählte Probleme aus der Geschichte des KL Auschwitz.* Auschwitz, Poland: State Museum, Auschwitz, 1978.

Smolen, Kazimierz, ed. *Hefte von Auschwitz, No. 17.* Auschwitz, Poland: State Museum, Poland, 1985.

Steinberg, Maxime. *Extermination Sauvetage et Résistance des Juifs de Belgique.* Edited by S. Schneebalg. Brussels: Comite D'Hommage des Juifs de Belgique a Leurs Heros et Sauveteurs, 1979.

Thalmann, Rita, and Emmanuel Feinermann. *Crystal Night.* Translated by Giles Cremonesi from the French "La Nuit de Cristal: 9–10 November 1938." New York: Holocaust Library, 1974.

Time-Life Books, ed. *Storming to Power.* The Third Reich Series. New York: Time-Life Books Inc., 1989.

Van Eck, Ludo. *Het Book der Kampen.* Leuven, Belgium: Kritak, 1979.

Recommended Reading

For those interested in reading more about the Holocaust, the following books are recommended:

Delbo, Charlotte. *Auschwitz and After*. Translated by Rosette C. Lamont. New Haven: Yale University Press, 1995.

Eibeshitz, Jehosha, and Anna Eibeshitz, comp. and trans. *Women in the Holocaust: A Collection of Testimonies*. 2 vols. New York: Remember, 1993 and 1994.

Fogelman, Eva. *Conscience and Courage: Rescuers of Jews during the Holocaust*. New York: Doubleday, 1994.

Grobman, Alex, and Daniel Landes, eds. *Genocide: Critical Issues of the Holocaust*. Los Angeles: Simon Wiesenthal Center, 1983.

Keneally, Thomas. *Schindler's List*. New York: Simon & Schuster, 1982.

Levi, Primo. *Survival in Auschwitz*. New York: Collier Books, 1993.

Richmond, Theo. *Konin: A Quest*. New York: Pantheon Books, 1995.

Wiesel, Elie. *Night*. New York: Avon, 1969.